# STEEPLE
# CHASING

# STEEPLE CHASING

*Around Britain by Church*

## PETER ROSS

HEADLINE

First published in 2023 by
HEADLINE PUBLISHING GROUP

2

Cataloguing in Publication Data is available from the British Library

Hardback ISBN 978 1 4722 8192 0

Designed and typeset by EM&EN
Printed and bound in Great Britain by Clays Ltd, Elcograf S.p.A.

HEADLINE PUBLISHING GROUP
An Hachette UK Company
Carmelite House
50 Victoria Embankment
London EC4Y 0DZ

www.headline.co.uk
www.hachette.co.uk

*'For Strangers'*

The words 'For Strangers Only' can be read, in chipped and fading gold letters, on the doors to certain box pews in St Mary's, the church at the top of the Whitby's famous 199 steps. The words indicate that these seats were for the use of visitors to the Yorkshire port town, most likely sailors come by ship. I have known St Mary's for many years, but visited it most recently during the summer of 2021 in a week when there had been concern that new legislation might criminalise those, including the Royal National Lifeboat Institution, who rescue migrants found crossing the English Channel in flimsy overloaded vessels. 'For Strangers Only' – those three words painted long ago in a church overlooking the sea speak of a better Britishness: a desire to welcome and give comfort to those who journey in need and in hope. This book, likewise, is for anyone, native or newcomer, believer or sceptic, wearying for a place to rest. Welcome, seeker. Welcome, stranger. Take a pew. Have a brew.

I am tired, I am afraid.
My heart is full of dread.

– Richard Dawson


The anchor is cast and all shall be well.
I'm resting here a while in the sun.

– Virginia Astley


How England consoles & warms one, in these deep hollows,
where the past stands almost stagnant. And the little spire
across the fields . . .

– Virginia Woolf


I am tired, I am afraid.
But my heart is full of hope.

– Richard Dawson

# Contents

# DARKNESS

IT WAS THE HOUR OF THE OWL, the hour of the men who wear the cowl, and the church was in deep winter dark.

A monk ghosted in, a white shape in the blackness; a shape that took on greater definition as he lit the tall candles on the altar. His hood was up, his face shadowed, but his quick precise movements suggested that this was the young novice Brother Edmund. Bells rang out with an urgent clang, which meant that two other monks – out of sight in the north transept – were pulling long ropes that disappeared up into the tower, calling their brethren to praise.

It was six in the morning on 8 December 2020, the Feast of the Immaculate Conception, the day of the first Covid vaccination – a moment, it seemed, of answered prayers.

Pluscarden Abbey in the north-east of Scotland is a rare survivor: one of very few medieval monasteries in Britain still used for their original purpose. It is home to eighteen monks. The youngest are in their early twenties, but most are a good bit older, the eldest being in his eighties. They are Benedictines. They wear white robes. They are obedient, chaste and poor.

It is likely that most will see out their lives here and be buried in the abbey cemetery. The grave markers – simple wooden crosses – wear so thick a pelt of lichen that the intrigued visitor must trace with a finger the furred letters in order to make out this carved epitaph: 'After life's fit fever he slept well.'

If life is a fever, Pluscarden is immune, its natural resistance built up over centuries of isolation. There is a rare stillness here, a sense of physical separation and temporal slippage. The nearest town, Elgin, is six miles and several centuries away. The abbey is at the foot of steep fields with a palisade of firs at the top. Hill and woods are a looming wall, keeping the monks in, the world out. Lockdown has long been a way of life here.

I had arrived the day before, driving for four hours from my home in Glasgow. Freezing fog, ice on the moors, snow on the peaks, a last bend in the road and there, suddenly, was the great ancient building.

'Welcome,' Father Giles had said on answering the door, 'to this distant and uncivilised place.'

That was a very Father Giles thing to say. The guest-master – the monk responsible for visitors – has a sense of humour for which the word 'dry' is insufficient. It is arid, desiccated, parched as a desert hermit. *The Rule of St Benedict*, the sixth-century code by which the monks live, is not keen on laughter and entirely opposed to 'jokes and idle gossip and anything said to make others laugh'. Yet the Benedictines of Pluscarden, sticklers in so many ways, allow themselves some laxity in this regard. They do laugh and are fond of a funny story, and this is part of their warmth as a community. It is one way in which they put callers at ease, hospitality being an important part of monastic culture. 'All guests who arrive should be received as if they were Christ,' Benedict writes. *The Rule* states that the abbot and monks should wash the feet of guests. That, to be honest, might be a bit much. I would have settled for a kettle in my room.

Why had I come? I was at the start of a pilgrimage of sorts. I meant to go steeple-chasing, to wander from county to county, story to story, church to church. The UK had lately sickened and been much shaken. It seemed possible that it might come apart; that we all might. In William Golding's 1964 novel *The Spire*, a vertigo-inducing account of the construction of a cathedral on shallow foundations, one character observes that, 'Life itself is a rickety building.' The book is set in medieval England, but those words seemed, when I encountered them, to speak to our present sense of fragility. Rickety old Britain, one hard wind from the fall.

I had grown tired of the present with its anger and fear and lies. I was losing faith in the future. I wanted to delve into our deep past, to be buttressed and braced by history. A close examination of churches and the customs associated with them offered, it seemed, a chance to reconnect with who we were, rediscover who we are, and reconsider who we might yet be. The world, I thought, would look better through stained-glass eyes.

Churches are all around us. They remain landmarks in our towns, villages and cities, even as their influence and authority has waned. A map of churches is a treasure map. They contain art and architectural wonders, and might be regarded as one great hoard scattered, like a handful of jewels, across these isles.

People once loved and feared churches as they loved and feared God. Now, often, they fear for them. Fear that they will fall down. Fear that they will be converted into offices and flats. Do they still love them? They should. Even if you only attend church for marriages, baptisms and funerals, isn't that enough? These are among the most important times of our lives, moments when we speak most deeply of ourselves: our love, our hope, our sadness. Churches hold within them Britain's history, national and personal. That smell they have is not just damp and dust, but faith and time.

My own steeple-chasing began with my baptism at Viewfield Parish Church in Stirling, where my parents had married the year before. It was the start of a long connection with that Victorian building on its vertiginous hill. I attended

Sunday school there, in an implausible kilt, and learned to recite the titles of the Old Testament. The commuter-train rhythm of Genesis, Exodus, Leviticus made me understand that words could be music. In memories of those long childhood Sundays, The Bible is mixed up with The Beatles and the couthy comic-strip adventures of The Broons: marmalade skies; jeely pieces; darkness on the face of the deep.

As the years passed, as life scythed its scars, I left the Church. But churches never quite left me. For those of us who were brought up with them, as worshipper or visitor, those grey walls and hard pews are in our souls. For those born homesick for the past, old churches offer the consolation of homecoming. And so, as I grew older, I found myself drawn back – not to pray or praise necessarily, but to sit for a bit, to poke around, to get in out of the rain. I began to appreciate the wisdom of John Betjeman's words: 'Church crawling is the richest of pleasures, it leads you to the remotest and quietest country, it introduces you to the history of England in stone and wood and glass which is always truer than what you read in books.'

It became my habit, from time to time, to visit Govan Old Church on the south bank of the Clyde, where I would spend a while with the hogback gravestones and the stone sarcophagus thought to have held the body of a Pictish king. Whenever I was in Whitby, I would visit the cliff-top church of St Mary the Virgin which, lately, has grown so popular with tourists that a sign has been placed on the door advising visitors to please stop asking for directions to Dracula's grave.

Then, a few years ago, a month after my father's death, I travelled for the first time to Pluscarden Abbey.

I had gone there on assignment for a newspaper, but found that it brought me a peace that I hadn't felt for many weeks. I left far lighter than I had come. Was this a religious experience? I don't know. Perhaps it was just being forced to spend long hours sitting quiet. 'It kinda gets inside you / The silences I mean,' sings Linda Perhacs in her beautiful song 'Chimacum Rain', and old churches are like that. You are entering a building but really it is entering you.

\*

After his welcome, Father Giles showed me to my room. I was staying in the retreat house, adjoining the church. There was a crucifix on the wall, and on the headboard a silver plaque noting that the bed, which looked like an IKEA job, had been donated by the Knights Templar.

Laid out on a small desk by the window were a selection of books including *The Rule*, a book of Psalms in a slightly groovy 1963 edition, and, I was delighted to notice, a copy of Herman Melville's *Bartleby, the Scrivener*. This last must have been left by a previous guest, the monks not going in much for fiction, but the anti-hero's famous assertion – 'I would prefer not to' – seemed perfect for Pluscarden and renunciation of the world.

Father Giles is seventy-one and has been at the abbey longer than any of the other monks, coming up on fifty years. He has a shaved head, a piratical beard, a wry air. Today, as ever, he acknowledged, was a 'no-hair day'. He arrived here as a drop-out from Edinburgh University. The turning point in his life had come when he went, as a young man, to Lourdes to help the sick – 'And I realised that religion wasn't just for Sundays.'

Many of the monks have stories like this. There will have been a moment, or series of moments, when they felt the call. 'Every person in our community has kind of fallen out of the sky,' one would later tell me. 'We're all oddballs really.'

Father Giles pointed out the schedule on the back of the door. Here, he said, I would find the times for communal prayer. These prayers take the form of Gregorian chant in Latin; together, they are known as the Divine Office, and the names of the services have a chiming cadence of their own. The day opens with Vigils at 4.30 a.m. and closes with Compline at 7.50 p.m. In between are Lauds, Prime, Terce, Sext, None and Vespers, and the daily Mass.

The monks are woken at 4.15 a.m. by one of their brethren banging on the door of their cell and calling out, '*Benedicamus Domino!*' – Let us bless the Lord. They respond, '*Deo gratis!*' – Thanks be to God – and so it begins. They spend five hours in church each day, almost three hours on *lecto divinia* – prayerful reading – and up to five hours on chores and other manual labour, which can be anything from sowing chives to tending hives. The abbey bees, kept for honey, are ferociously aggressive, as is the abbey cat, Baxter, named for the soup, who, during my visit, was recovering from fighting 'a monster feral cat' with whom he had developed a particular enmity. The theology of these fierce creatures, apian and feline, seems rather more Old Testament than New. They are all for an eye for an eye, not turning the other cheek.

To an outsider, the monastic life can appear narrow and relentless. Certainly, it is hard work. This is a prayer factory, a light salvific mill, the workers grafting night and day on behalf of all mankind.

One evening, not long before travelling to Pluscarden, I had watched a distressing news report about a pastor and priest in Burnley who were giving out food to the needy, whose already difficult situation had become desperate as a result of the pandemic. Those people were hungry and lonely and in despair, and it was clear how the church was helping them. The social contribution of the Pluscarden monks is less obvious, but they, too, would see themselves as activists of a sort, I think. By withdrawing from the world, they participate in it.

'I'm fond of the analogy of the hydro-electric dam,' Father Giles suggested. 'Up in the middle of nowhere is a great puddle of water doing nothing, but if it wasn't there then down in central Scotland, when they turned on the switch, there would be no heat or light. Well, this is a spiritual hydro-electric scheme, if you like, providing energy and support.'

Whether or not one has a Christian belief, this is a pleasant and reassuring idea, or at least I find it so. While we work and eat and sleep, the monks are busy in their valley, in their abbey, singing through sunrise and sunset, singing God to our side, making a dead language live.

*

The Latin chant drifted through the dim church in a soft lapping murmur; tidal, it flowed and ebbed, flowed and ebbed, the white-robed men bowing, now rising, now bowing once more, caught in the sublime surf of their song:

*Deus misereatur nostri et benedicat nobis . . .*

This was Psalm 66, always sung as part of Lauds, morning praise. Lauds begins at 6.15 a.m. In summer, the sky might be pink through the great arched windows, but now, so late in the year, it was still dark. An owl had called a neighbourly greeting as I walked from the retreat house to the church. Later, the sun risen, I would see pheasants swaggering through the cemetery, ducal plumage bright in the weak winter light. The third of Pluscarden's characteristic birds is the jackdaw. These have lived around the abbey for centuries, their bones appearing in the archaeological record. With dark hoods and harsh jabber, the jackdaws seem shadow versions of the monks, their opposite in many ways, although some of the brethren have, when they sing, the same bright eyes.

The jackdaws have been witnesses to the long history of this place: its first magnificence, its long period of desolation, its ongoing restoration. Where once they claimed the abbey as their own, nesting in its ruins, now they cram twigs into cracks and gaps in the masonry, making a home where they can. Still, they are patient. The future is not certain. Their day of supremacy may come again.

Pluscarden Abbey was founded in 1230 by King Alexander II for monks of the Valliscaulian order. Between 1454 and 1560 it was a Benedictine monastery, but fell into disuse with the Reformation. Years, decades, centuries passed. Glass fell, roofs collapsed, ivy choked the church. Much stone was scavenged for construction elsewhere. The revival began in 1948 when five monks from Prinknash Abbey, near Gloucester, came north to settle and rebuild.

Fuzzy colour film exists of the Mass, held on 8 September 1948, to mark the new era: the sky blazes blue through unglazed arches; the monks sing in the roofless sanctuary; in a field next to the abbey, with a practised swoop of his pitchfork, a farm worker gathers stooks of hay. By 1955, the central tower had been roofed and the valley, after a pause of almost four hundred years, echoed with bells once more.

With song, too. The singing one hears at Pluscarden is much the same as would have been heard at the time of its foundation; indeed, the music was already centuries old by then. There may only be eighteen monks in the church now, but there are hundreds in a line stretching back through the generations, and they are somehow in the music, too. It's not an echo, it's the same song. Just how far back in time this music goes is unknown. The chant tradition is like a bell rope hanging in a darkened tower. You know that it connects to the source of the sound, but you cannot see that far.

Gregorian chant is named for St Gregory, pope from 590–604. It is sometimes said that he composed the melodies of the repertoire, but there is no proof of this, and certainly none for the legend that they were sung to him by the Holy Spirit in the form of a dove perched on his shoulder – an event depicted in a window at Pluscarden. 'Gregorian chant, Romanesque architecture, the *Iliad*, the invention of geometry were not, for the people through whom they were brought into being and made available to us, occasions for the manifestation of personality,' Simone Weil has written. 'Truth and beauty dwell on this level of the impersonal and the anonymous. This is the realm of the sacred . . .'

The first written document of chant with musical nota-tion comes from manuscripts dating from the ninth century. It is likely to have had a long period of development as an oral culture, spreading across Europe from voice to ear, choir to choir, and although it was functional, a vehicle for the praise of God, it must surely have been thrilling – in a world without recorded music – to sing and to hear.

Listening to it remains a remarkable experience. I sat for hours in one of the small chapels kept open for public use. The monks took their places in choir stalls below the east window, facing one another; first one side would sing a verse and then the other would take the next. There is no sense in which their singing is a performance. It's not especially loud and in no way flash. It's about as showy as waves lapping the shore, or the breath of a body in sleep. It has that sort of rhythm: inhalation not elation, exhalation not exultation. It is gentle, patient, insistent, human. One monk, I noticed, had a cold and kept having to blow his nose. Another yawned widely. A third seemed troubled by his back. None of this detracted from the music. The opposite. Here were songs of human frailty being sung by frail humans. The text was hard to follow. My schoolboy Latin picked up only a phrase or two. But that didn't matter; the intent was clear. These were songs for and from the dark times; tunes to sing to, words to cling to. They were a thousand years old and ever new.

At 6.31 a.m., just around the time the monks were singing *Laetentur et exsultent gentes* – Let the nations be glad and exult – ninety-year-old Margaret Keenan from Coventry became the first person in the world to receive the Pfizer Covid-19 injection as part of the mass vaccination programme. A little later, Brother Michael, the abbey organist, stood at the lectern and spoke in English: 'We pray for an end of the pandemic,' he said. 'We especially pray that the poorest nations may receive the assistance they require to vaccinate and protect their most vulnerable citizens.'

It was jarring, if welcome, to hear the affairs of the contemporary world referenced in the midst of the ancient rite. A reminder, though, that these Benedictines are present in three zones at once: the deep past, the here and now, and eternity.

The air smelled of incense as the monks processed out. The sun was up. A military jet passed overhead with a sound of rolling thunder.

\*

It was time for lunch. Meals are taken in the refectory at long wooden tables. Grace is sung. A monk ascends a pulpit and reads aloud from some dry volume. He also reads out a necrology – a list of all the Benedictines around the world who died on that particular date, and all those who have recently died. The monks do not fear death. It's on their to-do list. If you are going to die tomorrow, Father Giles had once said, 'then why are you worrying about the fact that the mince has burned today?'

The monks eat liturgically. Dishes tend toward the austere – simple bread and cheese – but important days in the religious calendar are marked by what was described to me as 'mega-food'. On the Feast of the Immaculate Conception they ate pork steak, had pears in mulled wine for pudding and enjoyed a glass of red. 'We read that monks should not drink wine at all,' Benedict writes in *The Rule*, 'but since the monks of our day cannot be convinced of this, let us at least agree to drink moderately, and not to the point of excess, for wine makes even wise men go astray.' Benedict himself, the story goes, once came close to being murdered by monks who poisoned his wine, but the glass shattered – miraculously – before he could drink.

When they have finished eating, the brethren wipe their cutlery and bowls with a cloth and return them to a shelf beneath the table. Each monk brushes the crumbs from his place and then passes the dustpan to his neighbour. All of this without a word. Other than the reading from the pulpit, meals are taken in silence. Chat is reserved for the twenty minutes to half an hour set aside each day for recreation.

Silence is important here. The hours between Compline and Lauds, broken only by Vigils, are known as The Great Silence, but at all times conversation is kept to a minimum. External stimuli are largely absent. The point is to pay attention to God. There is no television or radio. Phone calls are rare. News reaches Pluscarden by way of the *Telegraph* app on a communal tablet. Family visits are infrequent. One monk told me that he sees his sister twice a year, but that he hadn't been home to England since a funeral twenty years before. On Sundays and the important feast days known as Solemnities, monks are allowed to go for a walk between lunch and Vespers; once a month, outside Lent and Advent, they have a free day. 'The rule is that you don't visit people's houses and you don't go into town,' is how it was explained to me. 'You don't have any money, but you can go for a walk and take a packed lunch.'

Poverty and celibacy are, of course, challenges. 'I sometimes think it would be quite nice to have a wife,' one monk mused. 'Or even a pair of socks.'

There are opportunities for fun. They watch, communally, around three films each year. When a monk is celebrating a significant anniversary he is allowed to choose some form of entertainment. Brother Finbar, to mark twenty-five years at Pluscarden, opted to screen *The Blues Brothers* for his brethren. At Epiphany, the monks perform songs and funny sketches. A couple of the brothers have comic talent, so some of these skits are completely original – 'There was one about two wasps next to a cake shop,' Brother Michael chortled – while others are adaptations of things they dimly recall seeing on telly before they entered the monastery. *The Two Ronnies* and *Monty Python* are strong influences.

I was curious about personal relationships between the brothers. They get to know one another very well, but these aren't friendships. It's more like the comradeship that develops in the army or navy when a group with a common task are forced, in challenging circumstances, into each other's company. Those bonds can be very strong, but they can also stress-test one's patience. In this cloistered world, small irritations become magnified. The way someone sings in choir, for instance, can be infuriating – so that at the very moment when a monk is supposed to be focused on God, he is instead tutting away inside. Confrontation, though, is out of the question. The modern concept of resolving conflict by airing one's grievances and talking them through has no place here.

Benedict writes that monks must 'bear with great patience one another's weaknesses of body and character' – in other words, put up with them. A former novice master at Pluscarden, well regarded for his phrase-making, once summed up the single available strategy. 'Ultimately,' he said, 'the only cure is more crosses in the cemetery.' That ain't Latin, but here's a translation: all you can do, if a brother annoys you, is wait for him to die.

Some of those who say they wish to become monks feel that the world has been unkind to them and therefore want to leave it behind. If I feel broken, this thinking goes, the monastic life might help me get fixed. 'But if you're psychologically weak you can't stay here,' one of them explained. 'Anybody on medication, forget it. You need a certain mental toughness. We get plenty of applications from people who want to get off the bus and live in a secure sweet environment, but this isn't the place for them. We can't take them.'

I am in danger of making this sound like a life with no pleasure in it. The truth is that every monk, as far as I could tell, felt they had gained far more than they had given up. There was no feeling of being in the company of hair-shirted martyrs. They were, it seemed, enjoying themselves.

'Overwhelmingly and daily,' Father Benedict told me, 'there's just such an astonishing sense of privilege to be here, to be allowed to live this blessed life. Just to be allowed to go to choir so often and sing this stuff – well, you'd be an idiot to throw that away.'

\*

Father Benedict is sixty-one years old and has lived at Pluscarden since 1984. He is the prior of the abbey, the second-in-command. He is a former head chorister at Exeter Cathedral School and platoon commander in the Light

Infantry. He left the army to become a monk. Music was one of the things that drew him: 'I could not hear any odd snatches of Gregorian chant without a terrible yearning to make this my life.'

He is tall and slender. He speaks with that clipped politeness officers deploy in conversation with civilians, a tone that often hints at emotion boiling away beneath. He wears, like all his brethren, a white habit, white socks and sandals, but it is easy to imagine him in khaki or tweed, occupying some senior rank of the military or academia. He is clearly very clever, but you never forget that you are talking to a person who believes deeply in something beyond rational thought. My strong impression was that intellectual ice and spiritual fire had reached a truce in his psyche.

We talked about the effect of singing in Latin. First, he feels, it is more beautiful than English, and being set apart from the language of everyday speech gives it a sacred quality. 'It immediately puts you into a different world. It's euphonious. I love the sound of it, and well-known prayers have this muscular strength. But also, singing the Psalms in Latin reaches us back into the centuries, back to the early Church. The Holy Spirit has got into this music big time. It's not only of supreme artistic value, it's of supreme spiritual value.'

Father Benedict likes his chant steeped in time. Anything after the year 1000 he considers rather new-fangled and suspect. Does he have a favourite piece?

'There's quite a few that bring tears to my eyes still, even after all these years. Some of the most simple.'

He sang a little, by way of example: '*Sanctus, Sanctus, Sanctus, Dominus Deus Sabaoth.* That's pre-modal. It's one of what they call the mother modes. This is speculative, but scholars say it could go back to very early days, even fourth century. And I find that fresh and new every time. With some of the more ornate chants, I daren't think about the words I'm singing or else I'll start crying.'

'Why?' I asked.

His voice broke as he answered. 'Because somehow, through the music, the words get through your skin.'

Novice monks are given weekly instruction in chant. They are taught Latin pronunciation and grammar, and also the musical technicalities: how the different modes are structured; how the music is written on the stave; how the notes are fitted to the words; how to sing complex melodies from sight.

It is one of the quirks of chant that the singing does not reflect the content or mood of the text. Quiet supplication of God and angry calling down of divine vengeance upon your enemies will both sound rather lovely. This, together with the obscurity of the language, explains why chant has come to be associated with relaxation and soft-focus spirituality. It is the music of bubble baths and scented candles. I had wondered what the brothers make of this, whether they feel that their deep religious art is being lost in the shallows. But no. As long as people are hearing it, they are content.

'You pray as you can, not as you can't,' Father Giles had said. 'It's not up to us to dictate: This Is How You Shall Consume This Product. You can eat your Mars Bar straight or deep-fried.'

The Book of Psalms, which forms the bulk of what the monks sing, is part of the Old Testament, and in a week they get through all one hundred and fifty. There is a tradition that King David was the author of many of the Psalms, although there is now consensus among scholars that the Psalter as a whole is the work of a number of writers over at least five centuries. 'The Psalms are a series of shouts,' wrote the French priest and composer Joseph Gelineau. 'Shouts of love and hatred; shouts of suffering and rejoicing; shouts of faith or hope.'

These are songs from before Christ, songs that would have been sung by Christ – a mind-blowing thought – and they have little of that New Testament reasonableness and relatability. 'In some of the Psalms,' thought C. S. Lewis, 'the spirit of hatred which strikes us in the face is like the heat from a furnace mouth.'

Catholic Church reform of the 1960s led to the omission and editing of the Psalms to remove violent content and curses. The Psalm, for example, which begins – 'By the rivers of Babylon, there we sat and wept, remembering Zion' – concludes in its unedited version with a call for Babylonian babies to have their heads bashed in against the rocks. You won't hear that in most Catholic churches, or indeed in the Boney M version, but the monks of Pluscarden are completists and sing even the most horrible parts.

'What?' I said. 'Even those Psalms asking God for an enemy's children to be left fatherless, for their eyes to be darkened and their backs bent?'

'All that!' Father Benedict replied, cheerfully. 'Yeah, it's brilliant.'

A lot of the curses are now read as allegories. The Babylonian babies are sinful thoughts, newly formed, and Christ is the rock against which they should be bashed – that sort of thing. When Father Benedict calls the cursing brilliant he does not, of course, mean that he is in favour of infanticide, but he does feel that Psalms which convey anger and anguish are both cathartic to sing and expressive of important aspects of the human condition. They are, I suppose, something like Christianity's version of the blues.

'We're at war,' he said. 'It's warfare. It's a serious business, life. So, yeah, we use strong language. We are beset by demons and we are beset by our own sinfulness and we confront that face on. If this was a matter of bland sentimentality, Christ wouldn't have bothered to pour out his blood on the cross. To me anyway, Gregorian chant is never not beautiful, but it's not always sweet beauty. This is in-your-face stuff.'

In some ways it is a simple life – the bells ring and you turn up to sing – but it is also intense, and there must be times when one's bones weary and throat aches. Every now and again there is a community discussion in which there is talk of reducing the length of the services, but Father Benedict would be unhappy if that ever happened. 'I came here for this,' he said.

How does one become a Pluscarden monk? The usual thing is for a young man to stay for a month and try it out. He can then spend six months as a postulant, wearing a black robe. This is followed by two years as a novice at the beginning of which his hair is shaved into the tonsure and he is given his new name by the abbot. At the end of the noviciate, he takes simple vows, living for three years as a junior monk, before the solemn vows in which he commits to spend the rest of his life in the monastery. There is a high drop-out rate during the long period from first steps to final commitment. Only one in four return after the initial month.

Even those monks who do last the distance can find what is being asked of them overwhelming. 'I remember I burst out crying when I first put on the habit,' one recalled. 'I thought, "Of all the stupid things you've ever done, this takes the cookie."'

It is better to realise you have made a mistake as soon as possible. However, it does happen that monks quit even after taking solemn vows. Pluscarden has had brothers leave because they lost their faith, because they decided to stop being Catholics and join other churches, or because they wanted to marry. Quite often such things are akin to a mid-life crisis. There's a romance in the idea of celibacy and poverty and sacrificing one's life that appeals to the young. But then you reach your forties and begin to think, 'It's not too late. I could still meet a woman, have children, a career.' And so they go.

'What,' I asked Father Benedict, 'does that feel like for the rest of you?'

'Horrible,' he said. 'Like a knife thrust through the guts. You feel a sense of betrayal, failure, grief, loss. Death? No problem. We don't mind death. Death is fine. It's natural. A monk who dies in harness, well, that's what he came here for. But a monk who walks out or goes bad . . .' He shook his head.

Monastic life is not for everyone; in fact, it's for hardly anyone. 'In some ways the Church is dying on its feet,' Benedict said. 'Go to a Sunday Mass and how many young people do you see? And of those, how many are willing to give their whole life to God?'

Pluscarden has been having problems attracting new brethren in sufficient numbers. Quite a few in recent times have come to the abbey, believing they have a vocation, but have left after six months or sometimes after three years.

'Why do they leave?' I asked.

He shrugged. 'Everybody's different. I suppose you have to put it the other way about: if anybody stays, it's just a miracle.'

\*

There was one other guest staying in the retreat house. I had noticed him sitting in the chapel on the other side of the choir, half-hidden in the dark. Between Lauds and Prime, we caught up over a cup of tea.

Martin Dunn was eighty-two, he told me, but I'd have taken him for twenty years younger. He was a Glaswegian who had become a Dubliner and seemed to have united the most garrulous qualities of both those cultures. 'I'm an adventurer,' he said. 'I am a wandering cloud. I go where the wind blows.' He had been a sailor and mountaineer in younger days. He was not long back from Cyprus, where he had slept for twenty-three nights on the beach at Paphos and swum naked around Aphrodite's Rock. Now he was making his annual visit to the abbey for what he called a spiritual MOT.

The wind had first blown him to Pluscarden in 1961. Burned out from studying for his final exams, he was hiking in the area and got lost. 'For some reason I walked up this valley. I think I was guided here.' He spent a month at the abbey. 'I thought I wanted to spend my life here, but things happen and God had another plan for me . . .'

A monk, Brother Andrew, sent him away and told him to return in a year. He should see a bit of life before deciding whether the monastery was still for him. What he saw, instead, was death.

In the summer of 1962, Dunn and two mountaineering pals – 'Beautiful guys who should be my best friends now' – travelled to Zermatt in Switzerland and climbed the Matterhorn. 'We started at two in the morning by moonlight, we hit the summit by twelve, and we were back down by seven that evening. It was an enormous output of energy, and the boys wanted to go and do the Weisshorn the next day, which was crazy. I tried to stop them. I told them they weren't able, that their whole body was still in shock.'

Pause. 'I didn't go with them.'

A longer pause. 'They didn't come back that night.'

He went to look for them, climbing 3,916 metres to the Frühstücksplatz, where he spotted their tracks. 'They had walked off the edge, roped together. Just walked straight off. When you get really exhausted, your head's down and you're just going. One guy went off and pulled the other behind him. I could see them four, five thousand feet below me, down on the glacier. So I had to get them out of there, get their remains home, and I had to meet one of their parents. The whole thing changed my life.'

He was blown off course. 'I got spaced out for a while. Without my mountains, there wasn't much left.' He didn't climb for more than thirty years, until Everest in 1993. Perhaps more significantly, he did not return to live at Pluscarden. He met an Irish girl – Brigid – and fell in love. They married in 1965, had four children and were together until her death in 2017. 'So my vocation was not to become a monk. My vocation was to marry and raise a family.'

Brigid was diagnosed with Alzheimer's in 2009. They travelled to Pluscarden together to pray, and he has been back many times since. His sense of the spiritual has intensified since losing his wife: 'Out of grief came gratitude.' He comes to the monastery to spend time with God, and with his guardian angel – whom he credits with keeping him safe during many days of danger and wonder. Here, he said, he feels as close to the divine as may be possible on this side of the grave.

Dunn talks as if giving his own eulogy. 'Looking back,' he said, 'I have loved my maker, and all the beautiful things he has made, since I was a child. I loved his mountains, I loved the sea, I loved high altitude, I loved the sunrises and the sunsets, each of which is a unique masterpiece of art. The most beautiful woman I ever met in my life, I married. So I'm very conscious of how much he has given me. I consider myself to be the luckiest man that God ever put breath in.'

Later, on the way to Compline, Dunn drew my notice to the stars and asked a question. 'Did He do that just to get our attention?'

\*

Compline is the final service before sleep. Its name comes from the Latin for 'completion'. Its power comes from darkness.

The whole church was lit by just four candles and the small red glow of the sanctuary lamp. The monks could not be seen. I could hear them, though, singing in the shadows.

Their voices, white horses on the wave of the organ, rose and dipped and rose again, within sight of sorrow and joy, but making landfall on neither.

It had been a good day. In a bad year.

The bells rang. It was time to go back out into the world. We were thirteen days from the solstice and the dark was still rising.

But a brighter tomorrow was no longer beyond imagining.

# STEEL

THERE WAS AN ANGEL in the sky. There was an angel rooted deep in the earth. It was the Angel of the North: facing south, the direction in which I was headed.

It was 8 a.m. on 6 January 2021. My intention was to begin a new day and new year with a new sense of faith in its widest sense; to try to feel a bit of hope for the future. The Angel seemed a good place to start looking ahead to the light.

Antony Gormley, the artist, has said that he wanted his Angel to be a focus for people's hopes and fears, and that too made it a suitable beginning; fear, perhaps, had the upper hand in the country for now. The occasion seemed to call for a few words. As it was Epiphany – the day on which, by tradition, the three wise men visited the infant Jesus – I spoke aloud the opening lines of T. S. Eliot's 'Journey of the Magi': *A cold coming we had of it* . . .

The Angel of the North has been on this spot, at the side of the A1 on the outskirts of Gateshead, since 1998. It is the height of four double-decker buses, has a wingspan greater than that of a Boeing 747, and weighs 208 tonnes. Its foundations are twenty metres deep, anchoring it to solid rock. I knew all this before visiting, but nothing could have prepared me for the impact of its presence.

That was especially powerful because I had come alone and in darkness. The Angel, as I first walked towards it, had been a black silhouette against a dark sky. The ground was frozen hard, the moon a shard of ice, the north star a shard of a shard. The sculpture was intensely cold to the touch, like the prow of a ship in some midnight sea.

Standing there, one hand pressed to the steel, I could see something glittering at the bottom of the slope below. It was silver tinsel strung in the trees that partly screen this place from the motorway. Moving closer as dawn broke, I began to understand that this was a shrine. Festive decorations had been hung by ribbon from the branches: stars, angels, unicorns and photographs of the dead. Laminated expressions of love were addressed to mother, brother, sister, dad. *In loving memory of my son Billy. I miss you and think about you every day. Love, Mam xx.* Folk had come here to keep Christmas, to cradle within the aura of the Angel memories of those they had lost. The lower parts of the sculpture, too, had messages scrawled upon them, as high as a sorrowful hand could reach. Within a hollow between two of the girder-like ribs, someone had left a small bouquet of flowers and, hidden behind them, an unopened can of lager – an offering to the thirsty departed.

Seeing this made me think of flowers and football colours laid at the site of sudden deaths: car accidents and the like; for years, not far from my home, a Rangers top has been nailed to a tree at the spot where a teenager was murdered. I was reminded, too, of a historical phenomenon I had been told about in Ireland: so-called 'eaves-drip burials' in which infants who had died before they could be baptised were buried close to the walls of old churches so that water running off the roof would become sanctified by contact and bless the unhallowed souls where it fell.

The shrine by the Angel seemed motivated by a similar loving impulse: that those remembered in the shadow of those wings should be protected. Around one in three people in the UK, according to consistent polling, believe that a guardian angel is watching over them. Martin Dunn, at Pluscarden, believed that. Whether or not we have a religious faith, many of us have a desire – a need, even – for the care and protection of something bigger than and beyond human. So, if it comforts and strengthens us to hang a Christmas bauble on a branch at the side of a motorway, or nail a football shirt to a trunk, or to bow our heads for a moment as we pass, by car or train, a giant steel angel on a hill, then why not? In dark days we find the light where we can.

It was time to go. The sun was up and I had an appointment with a saint.

*

What we know about the life and afterlives of St Cuthbert comes from two eighth-century accounts. The earliest, by an anonymous monk of Lindisfarne, was written around AD 700 – which is about the time Cuthbert's coffin was first opened and his body discovered not to have decayed. He had died in 687. This wondrous preservation was regarded as the work of God.

The later and far better known telling of the saint's life is by the monk and historian Bede. Writing in 721, he drew upon the anonymous work and added new details gleaned from correspondence with monks who had known Cuthbert personally; his *Vita Sancti Cuthberti* is full of Herefrith said this and Ingwald said that, a device intended to give his writing eyewitness authority, but which also conjures the charming picture of Bede travelling the north-east, talking to elderly brethren before their memories grew as dim as their sight.

Cuthbert was in his late thirties when Bede was born. While it is unlikely that they ever met, the two became intimates in death. Bede's bones, for a time, were kept in a linen bag in Cuthbert's coffin. Their shrines are at the eastern and western ends of Durham Cathedral, biographer and subject, who once shared a grave, separated by the great nave and the footsteps of a million joyful pilgrims. Thanks to the presence of Cuthbert's body – and the medieval belief that he was present in his remains – the cathedral became the most popular pilgrimage destination in England until the martyrdom of Thomas Becket in 1170 caused Canterbury to take that crown.

Like many people, I had often admired Durham Cathedral through a carriage window on journeys between Scotland and England on the east coast line. It had, I thought, a kind of magnificent aggression – a mailed fist shaken at passing trains, aggrieved at their modernity.

This, though, would be my first visit and it didn't feel right to go by rail or road. Given that long history of pilgrimage, I felt I should arrive on foot, so decided to follow the route known as Cuddy's Corse – 'Cuddy' being Cuthbert, an affectionate local nickname that has also attached itself to the eider ducks with which he is associated.

The eight-mile trail winds through the countryside between Chester-le-Street and Durham. It is an approximation of the route that may have been taken in 995 by monks travelling with Cuthbert's remains from the church at Chester-le-Street, where he had rested for 112 years, in order to prevent them falling into the hands of Viking raiders. They also carried with them the skull of Oswald, Christian ruler of Northumbria, and the Lindisfarne Gospels. The body of a saint, the head of a king, the word of God – with these treasures they set out.

A life-size bronze sculpture of six monks bearing the coffin on their shoulders can be found in Durham city centre. The casket is open, Cuthbert's face raised to the sun and rain, and the monks are distracted by neither the cinema to their left, nor the library to their right. They keep their faces

turned in the direction of the cathedral, and who can blame them? 'To step for the first time into Durham Cathedral,' wrote the architectural historian Alec Clifton-Taylor, 'must always be . . . one of life's most thrilling experiences.'

But this is to get ahead of ourselves. We are not there yet. There is the matter of the walk.

I set off from outside the church of St Mary and St Cuthbert, Chester-le-Street, at around half past eight. The wooden Saxon building which held Cuthbert's shrine was replaced by the present structure. The spire, at 158 feet, dominates the town, but sleety snow meant I had to squint up at it. Still, after long weeks and months of confinement, of stale rooms and bright screens, and the promise of much more of that ahead, it was good to be outside and on the move. The sting of cold air was a pleasure.

The first part of the route follows the Wear south. The river was fast, the going slow along the mud-slick bank. A few glum apples looked ready to drop into the high brown water. What with the weather and lockdown there was no one else around. Waymarked fence-posts offered reassurance: little white discs marked with the logos of Cuddy's Corse and the Northern Saints Trails. Climbing to higher ground along the edges of fields, I reached a stile and looked back at the way I had come. There was the Angel of the North, a jet cross set in a pearl sky.

It was strange to think of the monks carrying Cuthbert's body across this ground. What a precious burden. He had been regarded as a holy man, his life full of marvels. One Epiphany, while travelling by sea to speak with a Pictish tribe, he and two other monks found themselves cut off by a storm and in danger of starving to death; God, hearing their prayers, sent three portions of dolphin meat and, in time, a fair wind home.

Cuthbert died in his hermit's cell on Inner Farne, in his early fifties. His body was brought back across the water to Lindisfarne for burial. Eleven years later, in the year 698, it was decided to move his remains into an oak coffin carved with angels and apostles – to be revered above the ground. Remarkably, this ornate casket has survived, in fragmentary form, and can be seen in the Durham Cathedral museum; it is regarded as the most important wooden object surviving in England from before the Norman conquest. Even more remarkably, Cuthbert himself had seemed little worse for his time in the grave. 'On opening the coffin they found the body completely intact, looking as though still alive, and the joints of the limbs still flexible,' Bede wrote. 'It seemed not dead but sleeping.'

The miracle of the incorruptible corpse caused the monastery to grow rich and renowned. The Lindisfarne Gospels, perhaps the greatest book now in the care of the British Library, was created around this time, in honour of Cuthbert. But a wealthy island monastery was a soft target vulnerable to attack from the sea, and in 793 came the raid that is often regarded as the beginning of the Viking Age in Europe. It was seen as a desecration of a sacred place. Alcuin of York, a monk and scholar, wrote to the bishop of Lindisfarne that 'heathens desecrated God's sanctuaries and poured the blood of saints within the compass of the altar, destroyed the house of our hope, trampled the bodies of saints in God's temple like animal dung in the street'. How, he wondered, could churches elsewhere hope to remain safe from Viking predation 'if St Cuthbert with so great a throng of saints will not defend his own?'

Perhaps this faith in the protective power of the relics explains why it was not until 875 that the decision was taken to leave the monastery, a search for safer ground that took them to Chester-le-Street and, eventually, to Durham.

Following the Cuddy's Corse route, I came to the town of Great Lumley, passed along the edge of a housing development where all the streets were named after cathedrals – Canterbury, Salisbury, Gloucester, Exeter – and turned back toward the countryside. Two young lads were playing football on a snowy pitch, taking turns between the rusting posts. They were the only people I had seen all day and, glimpsed through a white veil of flakes, seemed emblematic of all the kids stuck indoors, their present becalmed, their future uncertain. A choir of starlings, clumped on bare branches, sang in praise of such resilience.

The whole day was blessed by birds. Pheasants strutted in frozen ruts. A heron rose by the ruins of Finchdale Priory. As

I passed Frankland Prison, a blackbird gave a solo performance from the razor-wire.

Birds and other animals were important in the life of Cuthbert. Bede tells us of an occasion when ravens on Inner Farne were tearing straw for their nests from the roof of a house built for visitors. Seeing this, Cuthbert admonished them; the birds took it to heart, expressed sorrow for their actions, and brought him a lump of lard as an act of contrition. On another occasion, an eagle caught a fish for him to eat. The best known and most beautiful of all those stories is that of the two otters: spying Cuthbert kneeling on the beach at Coldingham, the monk having prayed in the sea through the night, they used their fur to dry him and their breath to warm his feet. 'They finished,' writes Bede, 'received his blessing, and slipped back to their watery home.' These otters have a place of honour in Durham Cathedral on a banner hung by Cuthbert's shrine.

I first caught sight of the cathedral just before eleven. Across fields cratered with ice, there it was – the sky-punch of that great central tower. The sun came out and frost gleamed in the fields. The moment had the beauty of a clarinet glissando: the here-we-go prelude to some joyful overture. It was so exciting to approach on foot, that dark silhouette growing larger until, as I came once again to the Wear, I could hear its bells across the river – and a kingfisher flashed by, a rhapsody in blue.

The cathedral sits on a steep peninsula in a loop of the river. Construction began in 1093 and the core structure was complete within forty years. The western towers, however, date from the early thirteenth century. The central tower was rebuilt from 1429 after its earlier incarnation was struck by lightning. Although the cathedral, in its solemn massiveness, gives the impression of having been around for ever, indeed of somehow having grown out of the rock, it is not the original church on the site. That was a timber building built by the monks around the grave of Cuthbert. The first stone church, known as the White Church, was dedicated in 999. Nothing of that remains. Following the Conquest, the Saxon monastic community was dissolved and replaced by an order of Benedictines. There arose then a desire for a new church that would act both as an enormous shrine to Cuthbert and as an expression of Norman authority. It would beckon pilgrims and daunt rebels. Durham Cathedral says: we're here to stay, get used to it. On Prebends Bridge, approaching the cathedral, I read the inscribed words of Sir Walter Scott: 'Half church of God, half castle 'gainst the Scot.' I am Scottish myself, but fancied that it would be okay to have a wee look around.

I entered through the Galilee Chapel, where Bede is buried. The cathedral was open for public worship, private prayer, and for the lighting of candles. Visiting in its wider sense wasn't possible. Covid restrictions meant it had reverted to its central function: a religious building, not a tourist attraction. Churches in England were allowed to remain open, but a great many were making the difficult decision to close; with so many elderly worshippers and clergy, there were concerns about the safety of services.

There were only a few other people inside. They sat in the nave wearing masks and awaiting Holy Communion. A nativity scene was set out. The oak figures, carved in the mid 1970s by a retired pitman called Michael Doyle, honour the area's mining heritage and community. The donkey is a pit pony. The baby Jesus lies not in a crib but a 'choppie box' – from which the ponies were fed underground. The innkeeper, down on one knee, is dressed as a miner and has, as his companion, a whippet. Later, during evening prayer for

Epiphany, gold, frankincense and myrrh would be offered by the priests at this tableau.

I walked to the east end and the shrine of St Cuthbert. This is one of England's extraordinary places, and it was extraordinary, if for sad reasons, to be alone within it for as long as I wished. The shrine is a raised and enclosed area behind the high altar; you climb a few steps to get into it. Overlooking the grave is a fifteenth-century statue of Cuthbert holding the head of King Oswald, whose skull is believed to still be buried with him. Hanging above is a beautiful golden canopy, by Ninian Comper, depicting Christ in heaven. Comper felt that church architecture should have the power to bring you to your knees, and would no doubt have approved of the countless worshippers who have knelt beneath his canopy and prayed to the saint whose long journey from Inner Farne ended here.

Cuthbert's shrine, until the Reformation, was large and lavish, made of marble and alabaster and bright with gold and jewels. It was covered by an embroidered cloth; six silver bells chimed whenever this was raised. The shrine was destroyed by commissioners of Henry VIII. In stripping the structure for its wealth, however, they found rather more than they had expected. Cuthbert was discovered to still be in good condition some 852 years after his death. The only damage to the body, it is said, came from the hammer of the goldsmith who, in smashing open the coffin, broke one of the saint's legs.

Whatever the truth of that, when the coffin was opened again in 1827, time had finally done its work: Cuthbert was bones. It was during this exhumation that the famous gold and garnet pectoral cross – now in the cathedral museum – was discovered among his robes. Henry's men must have missed it. This cross had lain with the body for more than a thousand years; a treasure sunk in the hull of his ribs, a jewelled heart in the dark. The body was examined for a final time in 1899, one afternoon in March while the cathedral choir chanted psalms. There is no one now alive who has seen St Cuthbert dead.

The grave, since 1542, has been marked by a simple marble slab set into the floor, much worn and faded, and bearing one word in gold: CUTHBERTUS. It seems more becoming of an ascetic hermit than all that gaudy opulence. Royal and noble pilgrims once came to this place laden with curiosities and relics: the hair of Mary Magdalene, the milk of Mary the Virgin; a tooth from the jaw of St Margaret, bristle from the beard of St Godric; three griffin eggs (probably ostrich); two griffin claws (probably ibex); narwhal tusks thought at the time to be unicorn horns. These and much else, equally strange, were hung upon the shrine or displayed around it.

There was nothing like that when I visited, of course, but I did notice one simple offering. The conical shell of a limpet had been placed upon the slab. It made me think of Lindisfarne Castle rising steeply from the sea. Indeed, it is likely that it had come from the island. It is a regular thing for pilgrims to bring shells, carrying the sound of the waves to this great ship of a church, or so I had been told by Lilian Groves. The ninety-two-year-old guide is one of the cathedral's treasures, wiser than most books, brighter than any jewel, and I was sorry to miss her. We were supposed to have met, but she was staying safe at home, awaiting vaccination.

Why don't you come back in a few weeks, she had suggested. Around St Cuthbert's Day, 20 March, would be ideal. 'Normally it is a day of great celebration, but who knows what will be possible this year?'

Everything was uncertain, but it felt good to have made an appointment. I wrote 'Lilian Groves, Durham' in my diary and underlined the words. I had made my small pilgrimage to the cathedral. Now I wanted to see it again, this time through the eyes of someone who loves it.

I wrote to Lilian when I got back to Glasgow, telling her about the shrine at the Angel of the North, about Cuthbert's shrine, and about that wonderful moment when I had first spied the cathedral in the distance. The rush of it; the heart leap; the way those towers looked so strong, strong as a steel angel, at a moment when we all could use a little borrowed strength.

She knew exactly what I meant.

'Whenever I return home,' she replied, 'I feel a great thrill at the first sight of the Cathedral. Even after seventy-five years in the city, that joy never leaves me.'

*

BACH'S 'AIR ON A G STRING' drifted through the church. A nurse in a pale blue mask swayed a little to the music, never taking her eyes from the vial she held in front of her and from which she withdrew 0.5ml of clear fluid into a syringe.

'This is the Oxford vaccine,' she told an old lady in a plaid skirt who was sitting patiently on a chair, holding up the left sleeve of her top. 'The sooner we get this into you, the sooner you can get back to some kind of normal.'

The lady nodded. 'I've not seen anyone since Christmas.'

'There,' said the nurse, injecting her upper arm. 'You go and get a nice cup of tea now.'

Morningside Parish Church in Edinburgh was one of a number of churches around the UK being used as vaccination centres. Chairs were spaced two metres apart beneath the wooden barrel-vault of the nave. In the course of this after-noon toward the end of January, around 180 men and women aged eighty and over would be given the first of two jabs. The UK government target was that 15 million of the most

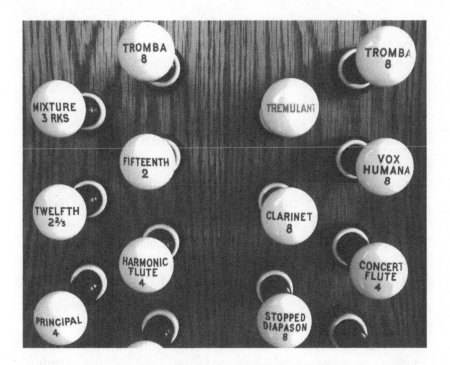

vulnerable people should receive their first vaccination by the middle of February.

It had been a year ago this week that the first cases of Covid-19 were confirmed in Britain. Now, as I arrived in Edinburgh, sombre front pages reported a statistic that was hard to comprehend: we had passed 100,000 deaths. The Archbishops of Canterbury and York, acknowledging that grim milestone, had issued a joint statement. 'In God's kingdom,' they wrote, 'every tear will be wiped away.'

You might find comfort in that pretty phrase, or consider it trite, depending on your life experiences and beliefs. Either way, there was something cheering about places of worship being used for vaccination. I admired the sleeves-rolled-up pragmatism of these big empty spaces being put to use. Salisbury Cathedral, with the tallest spire in the UK, was a great hypodermic pointed at heaven. Westminster Abbey gave over Poet's Corner for use as a clinic. It was extraordinary, said Stephen Fry, to receive his first dose of the vaccine 'in the nation's great seat of coronations, and in the sight of Oscar Wilde and John Dryden and Robert Browning'.

Morningside Parish Church may not be in the same league, but it is a pleasant church – douce, I suppose, would be the proper Edinburgh word – built from red sandstone in the last years of the nineteenth century. Those arriving for appointments entered through the south door, passing a stained-glass representation of St Benedict, and went out through the north, past a window dedicated to St Cuthbert, the focal point of which is a depiction of the saint's gold and garnet cross. Both windows had been made by Crear McCartney, an artist who, for a time in the 1950s, had lived with the monks at Pluscarden and had run the abbey's stained-glass studio. McCartney had synaesthesia, experiencing colour as sound – red for G and F, purple for D minor, and so on. Looking at his windows, at the butterflies around St Benedict, I could believe it. They seemed, as they shone, to sing.

The Very Reverend Dr Derek Browning had, a little earlier, given me the tour. A Church of Scotland minister in his fifties with a likeably irreverent manner, he had on his dog collar but not the replica St Cuthbert cross he often wears. He'd had a morning of meetings and felt the cross was perhaps a bit much for Zoom.

'You've got your first customer of the day,' he told the nurses, gesturing towards an elderly woman who had arrived on the arm of her son. 'Just don't let me see any needles or I'll faint.'

He wasn't kidding. Browning is syringe-phobic. A needle broke in his arm when he was a child and he has had a horror of them since. As we spoke in the chancel, he kept his back to the makeshift clinic and tried not to think about what was going on behind him. In any case, it was an opportunity to show me the church's chief point of interest: the east window, designed by the Pre-Raphaelite Edward Burne-Jones. The window depicts the four evangelists. 'Two or three of them look decidedly female, and that's because Burne-Jones used his mistress as a model,' Browning said. 'Luke, particularly, is a bit fey. Matthew's a bit more butch.'

Normally on a Sunday the church welcomes around 150 people. But all of Scotland's places of worship had been closed to the public since Boxing Day. 'It's a bitter thing when a congregation isn't allowed to congregate,' he said. 'Folk are missing the music, the singing, the meeting up with others. It's not just about the worship, it's also about the community that is created.'

He considered himself privileged to be able to come here on Sundays and live-stream services. But walking between his manse and the church, he would often see parishioners out for an aimless stroll, not knowing quite what to do with themselves. Their internal compasses pointed to the sabbath; without the anchor of church, they were lost, adrift. It was easy to understand why, in the face of such purposelessness, allowing one's building to be used by the NHS would appeal. 'You could over-spiritualise this,' Browning nodded, 'but there is a sense of ministering to people's mind, body and soul.'

Amelia Maclagan, who is eighty-five and a long-time worshipper, told me that she found it strange to be given the vaccine in a space where she is used to praying and singing hymns. Still, she was relieved and grateful, not least because her sister Moira had died of Covid-19. 'She went into hospital one day and was dead the next.' Amelia had been unable to attend the funeral and, nine months later, still can't get used to being unable to speak to Moira on the phone every night. Her name and photograph had been entered into an online book of remembrance, kept by St Paul's Cathedral in London, for those who had died as a result of the pandemic. 'Any man's death diminishes me,' wrote the poet John Donne, a former dean of St Paul's, 'because I am involved in mankind.'

I sat in the chancel for a while. It was a pleasure to just sit and watch people care for one another. The atmosphere was cheery, patient and gentle. A daughter helped her father rise from his seat. A nurse knelt at the side of a frail old woman, holding a piece of cotton wool to the injection site, waiting for blood to clot.

To witness the act of vaccination was an epiphany. To think of all the money, research, creative intelligence, planning, hope and fear that went into that tiny moment when steel entered flesh. Seeing it done in a church emphasised its eucharistic quality: a thing taken into the body to strengthen and save.

'You can see their sheer delight,' said Dr Eilis McKechanie when I asked what was her experience of vaccinating patients in the church. 'It's a real gift to be able to give that to someone.'

Such an occasion required a sense of proper ceremony, and this was provided by the organ: 'Adagio For Glass Harmonica', 'Jesu, Joy Of Man's Desiring', 'The Lord's My Shepherd'. A very loud man in very loud tartan trews, ignoring the only-slightly-less-loud protestations of his wife, marched over to the organist Morley Whitehead.

'Thank you very much for the music!' he roared. 'Most enjoyable!'

'A pleasure,' said Morley, and played on.

*

THE COLOURS TOLD the season: it was spring. Lambs embroidered clifftop fields, gorse braided the coast. As the train sped between Berwick and Newcastle, Holy Island came into view, the dark castle reflected in the silver sea. I longed to be there. The magnetic pull of Lindisfarne is strong. It makes iron filings of the soul.

Durham, though, was my destination – and there it was at last, rising above an Escher maze of red-brick terraced streets.

The bells were chiming eleven as I arrived. It was a Sunday towards the end of March. Families picnicked among headstones and daffodils in front of the cathedral's north side. Placed against the small boundary wall that separates the churchyard from the rest of Palace Green were bunches of tulips, lilies, roses and a scattering of half-melted tealights: the remnants of a vigil for a young woman who had been abducted and killed earlier that month. Although living in London at the time of her death, she was a graduate of St Cuthbert's Society, a college of Durham University, and her loss was felt hard here. 'RIP Sarah,' read one cardboard sign. 'She was just walking home,' said another. 'It could have been me' – a third. More flowers were being laid as I passed. Durham Cathedral is one huge shrine, but here in its shadow was another: a focus for anger and grief.

'Cathedrals are perfectly apt for the complicated times we live in,' wrote Richard Holloway in his wise book about death and dying, *Waiting For The Last Bus.* This may explain why, while church attendance has been in decline for many years, cathedral visitor numbers have been booming. Cathedrals remain the superstars of Christianity; they draw the crowds, the cameras, the cash. This is especially true of those that are iconic – St Paul's, Canterbury, York Minster and Durham. When we close our eyes and think of England, these buildings may be among the gallery of images that come to mind. In an increasingly secular society, they remain giants; they're still big, it's the faith that got small.

What is a cathedral? Simply a church that contains the seat – or 'cathedra' – of a bishop. It is an expression of authority as well as faith. There are forty-two Church of England cathedrals. Around 10 million people visit each year, numbers having grown significantly since the turn of the millennium. The major festivals, Easter and Christmas, are the most popular occasions, but people also seem drawn to cathedrals at moments of national significance. There is something about the grandeur that makes them appropriate for communal praise and remembrance, but that scale also suits the individual who feels alone and prefers to be left that way. It is easier to slip into a cathedral and sit quietly for a while than it would be in a little parish church. A cathedral is huge and old and cold and brute and mute – masonry and glass care nothing for human worries – and yet it represents eternal compassion. This tension between the look and meaning of the building is what gives a cathedral its power: it makes us feel small but also loved; we become infants swaddled in stone.

Lilian Groves met me inside, by the tomb of Bede. She gave the dark marble a fond pat. 'Hello, Bede,' she said.

She is a small lady. The candlesticks at the corners of the tomb, flickering in the gloom, were a good deal taller. She has been visiting this shrine since 1946, when she came to Durham as an undergraduate. She can't quite explain what drew her that first time – 'You see this great place standing on the hill and you feel you have to go there' – or what has kept her coming back. Yet the cathedral is part of her heart and she part of its. For the last thirty years, since retiring as vice-principal of the College of St Hild and St Bede, she has volunteered as a guide and shown Bede's grave to visitors. But what she feels on this spot goes deeper than familiarity and expertise. The relationship between the people of the north of England and the northern saints is, she believes, rooted in companionship rather than reverence.

'The saints are like our friends,' she told me. 'They've always been there. When I was a very small child, before I had any sense of history, I thought Cuthbert and Bede had been to school with my mother. They lived where we live. They saw the countryside we see. They met the people we meet. They're us.'

Lilian is especially keen on Bede, feels he is always with her, and needs no encouragement to list his many achievements: that he is known as the Father of English History; that he has been called the first English astronomer; that he translated the Lord's Prayer into Old English and was denounced as a heretic for doing so. His *Ecclesiastical History of the English People* was the first work of history to use Anno Domini for dating and therefore the reason why we date from AD now.

Bede was born in 673. At the age of seven he entered the monastery of Wearmouth, and a few years later moved to the new monastic foundation at Jarrow, where he was taught by Abbot Ceolfrith. A plague in the year 686 killed all those Jarrow monks save Ceolfrith and a boy – believed to be Bede – who were able to sing the psalms properly. Bede lived out his life at the monastery, passing on Ascension Day, 735. He was singing as he died. His remains were moved to Durham in 1022. His tomb is in the Galilee Chapel. That is Lilian's favourite part of the cathedral, but really she loves it all. 'It's a centre of pilgrimage and the finest Romanesque building in northern Europe. The ordinary local people regard it as their Cathedral, even if they never come inside.' This sense of ownership extends to the mystery of Bede's precise origins. 'If you say to somebody in Jarrow that Bede was born in Sunderland they're absolutely furious,' she laughed. 'They'll say: "He was a Jarrow lad!"'

Lilian herself was born in 1928 and spent her childhood in Newcastle: 'I'm a real Geordie.' Her father, a retired naval officer, was a Victorian – born in 1871. She is one of those people who seem, through their life and interests, to collapse time. A conversation with Lilian leads you from the age of Beowulf to the rage of the Blitz and beyond.

'I grew up in the Second World War,' she recalled. 'My younger brother and I used to go around collecting dead incendiary bombs and bringing them home.' She told a story of Durham during the war: one moonlit night in the early summer of 1942, German bombers flew over the English coast intent on destroying Durham Cathedral, part of the so-called Baedeker raids on towns chosen for their cultural and historical importance. But just before they reached their target, a thick fog rose up from the River Wear and hid the cathedral from view. 'Everybody,' Lilian explained, 'called that St Cuthbert's Mist.'

We walked through the cathedral to Cuthbert's tomb. As we went, she pointed out the twelfth-century wall paintings, the massive piers carved with chevrons and spirals, and the astonishing Neville Screen, a stone reredos made in 1380 which resembles some Gothic starship awaiting blast-off.

Lilian is one of the most celebrated guides in the country. She has shown rock stars and royalty around this place. A few years ago, a slip of a girl at eighty-seven, she won a public vote and was named VisitEngland's Tourism Superstar. The truth is, though, that what she does at Durham doesn't feel much like part of the heritage industry. Her tours are expressions of faith. 'This isn't a museum,' she insisted. 'It's a living church.'

She led the way up the steps to the shrine. She lit a tealight and placed it on St Cuthbert's grave, above the letter E in his name. She bowed her head for a moment in silent prayer.

I asked how she felt about the prospect of the Cathedral reopening to visitors. After all, it had been more than a year since she had last been able to give a tour.

'I can't wait,' she laughed. 'I just hope it happens before I pop me clogs.'

There are people you meet from time to time who somehow embody the spirit of a place; more than that, whose love for it and loyalty to it make it even more special than it would be otherwise. Lilian Groves is one such. She is, I suppose, just a small part of Durham Cathedral's long story, but as both a narrator of that story and a character within it, she is significant.

No one who meets her beneath those towers and vaults can feel they have had a cold coming.

No one can leave, having met her, without feeling brightened by their encounter with this angel of the north.*

---

* Eight weeks after my visit, on 19 May, Lilian gave her first tour in fifteen months. The Cathedral had reopened to the public and her clogs remained unpopped. I called and asked how it had been.

'It felt,' she said, 'like life was beginning again.'

# FIRE

JUST A DOZEN VISITORS in all that space. Like being inside some lonely canyon. One expected to see a murmuration of starlings twisting the air of the dome.

A cleaner was at work, passing a mop over the Latin epitaph to Sir Christopher Wren inscribed in golden letters on the floor: LECTOR SI MONUMENTUM REQUIRIS CIRCUMSPICE – Reader, if you seek his monument, look around you.

A loudspeaker announcement echoed from the walls. 'Welcome to St Paul's Cathedral. Pause for a moment, be still and silent, as we pray for all those in need of God's love and mercy and healing grace. At this hour we pray for the sick . . .'

I went down to the crypt, where Wren is buried, passing beneath three carved skulls at the entrance.

The crypt of St Paul's is England's Valhalla. Here is Nelson's tomb. Here is Wellington's. The boastful ghosts of Trafalgar and Waterloo seem to crowd this place. The air, though still and quiet, carries an acrid echo of cannon. Nelson's coffin was made from the mast of a French ship, *L'Orient*, destroyed during the Battle of the Nile; his grave is topped by a sixteenth-century sarcophagus of black marble that had been intended, until his fall from royal favour, to hold the remains of Cardinal Wolsey. The Duke of Wellington lies nearby in a massive sarcophagus of Cornish granite, flecked with pink, held aloft by four sleeping lions. His state funeral in 1852 was attended by 13,000; a painting shows men in scarlet tunics, women in bonnets and veils – a great wave of humanity rolling over the nave.

Wellington and Nelson: it is these tombs that draw crowds to the crypt in the days when there are crowds to draw. Few, I suspect, spend long looking at the far older funeral effigies that one must pass on the way to worship heroes. These must make do with sidelong glances at best. Yet, for me, they are the most powerful – and powerfully strange – objects in St Paul's.

They are black, these effigies, an almost glossy black, as if carved from coal or jet. In fact, they are alabaster, more or less life-size, and would have lain or stood atop the tombs of the great men and women of the sixteenth and seventeenth centuries whose likenesses they bear. They are time travellers, refugees from the past, but have not made the journey intact. They have passed through flame. They bear wounds and scars. They have known hell and reek of it even now. These seven statues are almost all that remain of the medieval cathedral that was destroyed in the Great Fire of London, 1666. They are thought to have been protected from total destruction by the stone choir screen and crossing piers. They seem victims of some atrocity, blinded and limbless, as if the unfortunates of Goya's *Disasters of War* have risen from the page, a clotted mass of blood and ink.

Lady Elizabeth Wolley sits beside her husband John. She is the most intact of the people of the crypt, sitting peaceably with a book on her lap, staring through the centuries with a starless gaze. In life, she was a lady-in-waiting to Elizabeth I; on the evening of 15 September 1595, she accompanied the queen and Sir Robert Cecil as they went hawking, killing three partridges. Sir John Wolley was an MP and Latin secretary to the queen. His effigy is missing most of its head, the lips lie open below a nub of melted marble, and he is pulling his cloak about his body as if for comfort.

Engravings by the artist Wenceslaus Hollar show the tombs of St Paul's as they looked before the Great Fire. They

are huge and elaborate, magnificent expressions of power and wealth. The Wolley monument had an angel-topped pillar at each corner and cost £4,000 to build. Nothing remains but the two charred revenants, yet it is remarkable that anything remains at all. Though foolish to ascribe emotions to stone, it is difficult to stand in front of these and not regard them as traumatised victims. If Sir John's lips could move, if Lady Elizabeth could read to us from her book, they would surely speak of the malevolent intensity of the blaze.

'I find them a little creepy,' said a passing guide. 'If the Fire could do that to statues, what could it do to a human body?'

The burning of St Paul's must have been a frightening sight. That cathedral was bigger than the present building; physically and psychologically dominant – a sentinel tree in a forest of spires. 'It was London's own cathedral, at whose altar each Lord Mayor prayed for guidance on the day of his installation,' wrote Adrian Tinniswood in his history of the Fire, *By Permission of Heaven*. 'But it was more than this – a godly fortress, a divine bulwark against misfortune, of greater significance at an emotional level than the City churches, the Exchange or the Guildhall or any of the Company Halls. Its destruction was unthinkable.'

There has been a cathedral on the site since 604, the first being founded by Mellitus, Bishop of the East Saxons. That wooden building burned down in 675, was rebuilt ten years later, then destroyed by Vikings in 962. A church in stone followed, but this too burned. The Normans, in 1087, set out to build the largest church in the world: a symbol of their conquest. This St Paul's was consecrated in 1300, survived a lightning strike in 1561 that brought down its enormous spire, and was, more or less, the same church lost in 1666. Digging the foundations of his new cathedral, Christopher Wren discovered graves dating from Saxon London and, deeper still, items from the Roman occupation. A basin, found near the Cheapside corner of the church, was decorated with a picture of Charon, boatman of the Styx, ferrying the dead to Hades.

Upon these layers of ash and myth and bone grew the cathedral that became a national icon. Associated with English and British power, it came to be known as the parish church of the Empire. 'Motherly Queen Anne went there seven times to thank God for the deliverance of her country,' wrote the historian John Prebble in a 1951 article for *Illustrated*. 'George III went in thanks for the release of his unhappy mind from darkness.' Queen Victoria's diamond jubilee celebrations in 1897 were captured on film: flickering images of a silent city.

The writer Frances Partridge considered the cathedral nothing less than the nose on London's face, and noted in her 1940 diary that it was 'disgusting to think of that familiar face being destroyed'. Destruction, though, has been crucial to the life and meaning of St Paul's. No resurrection without crucifixion. No phoenix without fire.

At around eight o'clock on 4 September 1666, just after sunset, a fourteen-year-old schoolboy called William Taswell stood among a crowd upon the bridge at Westminster and watched as the cathedral roof caught fire. By nine, the flames were such that he could read the book he had carried with him. It was to be a bad night for books. The booksellers and stationers of Paternoster Row, thinking to save their stock, had moved it to St Faith's, the remnants of an old church down in the St Paul's crypt. But the roof fell in and the books went up. Samuel Pepys estimated the cost of that loss at £150,000. Burning paper fell on Eton, twenty miles west; indeed, the smoke is said to have stretched fifty miles, a dark train for a fiery bride.

The diarist John Evelyn, that same evening, rode as close to the scene as he was able: 'the stones of Paules flew like granados,' he wrote, 'the Lead mealting downe the streets in a streame, and the very pavements of them glowing with fiery rednesse, so as nor horse nor man was able to tread on them . . . the Easter[n] Wind still more impetuously driving the flames forewards: Nothing but the almighty power of God was able to stop them, for vaine was the help of man . . .'

Returning three days later, he found St Paul's 'a sad ruine', its stonework broken and calcined with heat, parts still on fire. 'Thus lay in ashes that most venerab[l]e Church, one of the [most ancient] Pieces of early Piety in the Christian World, beside near 100 more . . .'

The Great Fire destroyed 460 streets and 13,200 houses. Of the eighty-nine churches that burned, only fifty-one were rebuilt. London is a city of ghost churches, haunted not only by those lost in the Fire, but in the Blitz, and those demolished to make room for development. It is easy, even pleasant, to imagine spectral steeples looming in the twilight. A night walk can be made more melancholy, if that is your taste, by chanting the necrology of names: All Hallows The Great, All Hallows Bread Street, All Hallows Honey Lane. All gone, all gone.

When William Taswell visited the ruins of St Paul's, two days after he had seen it burn, the ground was still so hot that his shoes were scorched and the air so warm he felt faint. The walls had fallen, the bells had melted, and he discovered the body of an old woman whom he judged had fled to the cathedral for safety: 'Her clothes were burnt, and every limb reduced to a coal.' Samuel Pepys, almost a week later, examined the body of Robert Braybrooke, a Bishop of London who had died in 1404. He had been tumbled from his tomb in the destruction, 'and is here seen his Skeleton with the flesh on; but all tough and dry like a spongy dry leather . . . and now exposed to be handled and derided by some, though admired for its duration by others. Many flocking to see it.'

Eyewitness accounts of the aftermath at St Paul's describe the illustrious dead rising from their graves, somewhat early for the Last Judgement, and becoming objects of voyeurism. John Aubrey, in *Brief Lives*, records that the coffin of John Colet, the late dean of the cathedral, was opened and discovered to contain a 'Liquour' that had pickled the body against decomposition, so that it felt, when poked with a stick, like boiled brawn. This being an era of strong curiosity and stomachs, the preserving fluid was sampled: 'twas of a kind of insipid tast, something of an Ironish tast'.

The most notable survival of the Great Fire is the marble effigy of the poet and priest John Donne. Unlike the unchancy relics in the crypt, it has remained white, and has an elevated

position in the south quire aisle. It is remarkably life-like or, rather, death-like. Donne, who had become dean of St Paul's in 1621, is depicted in a burial shroud. His foxish, intelligent face is the only part of his body uncovered, and he appears to be rising, a genie of the lamp, from a funerary urn. The statue, by Nicholas Stone, is based upon a portrait Donne had made, knowing he was dying, in March 1631. Around a fortnight before his passing, he ordered charcoal fires to be lit in his study and there he posed for his likeness, standing on a platform, wrapped in a winding sheet, eyes shut, facing east as if awaiting the second coming of Christ. Trying death on for size, he found it a good fit. He kept the portrait by his bed and looked upon it until he looked no more. The statue is an unsettling mix of self-abasement and narcissism. Donne wanted to be seen as a corpse, but still he wanted to be seen.

It hadn't been the first time he readied himself for the grave. In 1623, England had groaned under an epidemic, the so-called 'spotted fever', and towards the end of November Donne caught it. He thought he was at the end of his life. But he was a writer so he wrote: composing in his sick bed a work that we would now recognise as being something akin to a cancer memoir. *Devotions Upon Emergent Occasions* is not, one imagines, much read these days, although two short phrases – 'No man is an island', 'and therefore never send to know for whom the bell tolls; It tolls for thee' – have proved immortal. Donne records his exhaustion and fear, and that he cannot taste food. The fever tears through his body like fire through a building; it pours out of him like molten lead; 'it doth not only melt him, but calcine him, reduce him to atoms, and to ashes; not to water, but to lime'. And how striking, in our own time of self-isolation and quarantine, to read these meditations upon loneliness: 'As sickness is the greatest misery, so the greatest misery of sickness is solitude; when the infectiousness of the disease deters them who should assist from coming; even the physician dares scarce come.'

Donne's tomb in the old St Paul's is thought to have been in more or less the same spot where the statue stands now. When the floor gave way, it fell into the crypt and there, somehow, survived the Great Fire with little more than light scorching and the loss of a handle from the carved urn. Toward the end of the nineteenth century, as his poetic reputation grew once more, Donne's statue was brought back up into the main body of the cathedral where he remained until the Luftwaffe threat saw him returned to the safety of the underworld. His bones were lost in the Great Fire, but perhaps not entirely so. In the mid 1950s, during the restoration of St Lawrence Jewry, which had been extensively damaged by bombing, a human jawbone was discovered sixty feet up, within a wall of the tower. Wren's builders had used broken gravestones and material from beneath the floor of the burned church as rubble to fill the walls. This construction method – recycling the remains of the old building as infilling – was employed at St Paul's, too. It could be that a fragment of the skull of Donne, even now, is high over London, somewhere within the stone walls, hearkening to each tolling bell.

\*

Ahead of the Blitz, care was taken to protect the treasures of St Paul's. The more portable items saw out the war in grand country houses in Hertfordshire and Lancashire. Wren's oak and lime model of the cathedral was among those objects evacuated; rare books and manuscripts were sent to the National Library of Wales at Aberystwyth.

'Monuments which could be moved only a short distance were taken down into the Crypt and encased in brick or buried beneath sandbags,' Walter Matthews, the then dean, wrote in *Saint Paul's Cathedral in Wartime*. 'It happened that I slept in the Crypt almost on the sandbags which covered the effigy of my great predecessor, Dr. John Donne, the poet and orator, who characteristically had himself represented in his life-time dressed in his shroud.' Matthews would sometimes dream that Donne was stirring; that he who had lived through moments of personal and national crisis might summon the words to express the anger and anxiety of the new dean, down there in the crypt as death was dealt out in the dark. 'I felt that only Donne could have done justice to my feelings.'

The statue is, therefore, the survivor of two infernos: the fire that tore through London's streets and the fire that fell from the sky. Donne is as much of a phoenix as the great bird sculpted on a pediment above the south portico, wings spread above smoke and flame and a single carved word: RESURGAM. The idea for this symbolism came to Wren, the story goes, as he was standing in the devastation of the old cathedral. Keen to mark the place on the ground that would correspond with the centre of his great dome, he asked a labourer to bring him a flat stone from among the rubble. The workman handed over a broken chunk of gravestone on which nothing remained of the inscription but that word, Resurgam. It means 'I shall rise again' and it is delicious to think that, in that moment, as Wren turned the stone in his hand, reading as he set it down amid the ruins, his vision for St Paul's was complete.

I shall rise again: the battle-cry of the cathedral, of London, and perhaps the nation. It speaks of deep resilience. That is why it is so meaningful that St Paul's is topped by a dome, a defensive shield, rather than a sword-like steeple. The cathedral prompts feelings of English exceptionalism even in those who know they should know better. 'It is hard not to sound like a bad Churchillian parody,' wrote the architectural critic Ian Nairn, 'but in fact this is why we fought the war.'

Nairn was nine years old when the Second World War began and in his mid teens when it ended. His Surrey childhood was spent in the shadow of conflict. He learned to fly at university, and following graduation joined the RAF. He flew Gloster Meteors, the first British jet fighter. At his wedding in 1952 he wore his uniform and a black armband to mark the death of George VI. It is understandable, therefore, that he saw St Paul's as he did – but it is a building that calls similar feelings out of those of us who do not have such a sympathetic background. St Paul's makes one feel both protective and protected.

Walking past on the night before my visit, I had heard its clock strike nine and was moved by its beauty and bulk, lit up in the London night. At our own moment of national adversity, there was something strengthening about that sound and sight.

The exterior of St Paul's has long meant more to London as a symbol than the interior has meant to Londoners as a church. Historically, it has been regarded as a rather cold building. 'Wren did a wonderful job, but he left one thing out,' a priest observed as the Second World War approached. 'He didn't give it a soul, and nobody knows how to remedy the omission.'

If, from within, the cathedral feels soulless, from without she is dauntless. As the architect Arthur Butler put it, the dome of St Paul's is 'a supreme and culminating summit guarding London with a fat maternal benignity'. When he wrote those words in 1926, Butler could not have known that, a few years hence, he himself would spend his nights guarding that summit as German bombers 'like silly screaming dragons' seemed to circle the dome. He had joined a group dedicated to saving the cathedral from destruction. 'Men from forty to sixty who can walk upstairs and not fear heights or fire are those we call for,' the advertisement ran. 'The emergency may not arise; on the other hand it may – and soon and ferociously.'

The St Paul's Watch was formed in September 1939, led by Godfrey Allen, the cathedral surveyor. This volunteer force of eighty or so became known as 'the best club in London' on account of its social make-up: academics and artists; poets and postmen; choristers and clergy; medical and musical and theology students; members of the Red Cross and the St John's Ambulance Brigade. Many were above conscription age, or exempt for other reasons. Here was Dad's Army with high explosive, high stakes, high ceilings. In a letter written many years after the war, Robin Boyd, a former member of

the Watch, remembered 'a motley collection of volunteers . . . a friendly, intergenerational and democratic lot, and we loved the cathedral. Armed only with tin hats, bicycle lamps, axes and fire hoses, we worked to preserve St Paul's for posterity, so that it could continue to be a place for worship and witness, and for the promotion of peace and justice.'

This band of brothers – and a few sisters – patrolled the cathedral between the hours of 9.30 p.m. and 6.30 a.m., in many cases after their own day's work. They made the journey from often distant parts of London, cycling through dark streets of broken buildings, sometimes throwing themselves down at the sound of falling bombs. Fire from outside made the stained glass glow with unearthly light. One member of the Watch made it a personal ritual to climb at midnight to the Golden Gallery – 280 feet above the city – and recite the Lord's Prayer while circling the great gold cross.

Such an appeal for deliverance from evil could only be made, one imagines, on quieter nights – of which there were few during 1940 and 1941. The noise of incendiaries hitting St Paul's was likened, by those who knew it too well, to coal falling from a giant scuttle. The thump of bombing and anti-aircraft guns outside was magnified by the dome; it was like being inside a drum. Night after night the Watch went out on to the roof to look out for incoming shells while, all around them, London burned.

'It is like the end of the world,' one said.

'It is the end of *a* world,' replied another.

Thirty thousand Londoners were killed by enemy action during the Second World War, the majority in the last four months of 1940. More than 100,000 houses were destroyed. 'Men at the look-out posts on the roof glanced occasionally towards their homes and offices wondering what they would find there on the morrow,' wrote Walter Matthews. 'Some saw their homes go up in flames, but they did not flinch.' Matthews himself was not one for flinching. His son Michael had been killed by a bomb that fell on the bridge of HMS *Greyhound* during the evacuation of Dunkirk. He later wrote that he sometimes lay at night on his pallet in the crypt – beside the sandbagged Donne – and felt such sickening hatred that he wished he could annihilate the whole German nation at once. The Blitz was a distraction from personal sorrow and consuming anger. He could not save his child. He could try to save his church.

Beginning on 'Black Saturday' – 7 September 1940 – bombs fell on the capital for fifty-seven consecutive days. Although industrial infrastructure was a priority, there was perceived value in hitting buildings of historical importance as it was known that these would be body blows to public morale. 'The Luftwaffe has an eye for good architecture,' is how the photographer Cecil Beaton put it, grimly waspish, in an article for *Vogue*. Among the churches bombed were St Mildred, Bread Street, where Mary and Percy Shelley married, and St Giles' Cripplegate, where Milton was buried. 'No one sees a church more clearly,' the painter Christopher Neve has written, 'than when it is burning.'

This clarity is apparent in Arthur Butler's *Recording Ruin*, a 1942 memoir of his war work – entering bombed homes and writing reports on their condition. Butler was a veteran of the First World War, no stranger to peril, but was now in his fifties, and the inspection of ruined houses seems to have been a dangerous business. He writes about surveying damaged roofs by holding on to wobbly chimneys, and climbing a glacial staircase down which water had poured and frozen. If he found this work dispiriting, perhaps this was because he spent his days alone. Nights with the St Paul's Watch offered comradeship, but also an opportunity to develop an intimate appreciation of the cathedral he was there to guard:

> If, however, you want the full vision of St Paul's you must stand under the dome at midnight, on the great empty marble floor with a single lantern in the middle. Then there is just a little light – amber below and blue and silver from the moon above. It is just enough light to show the main lines of the design and to blot out complexities of detail and all the added frippery. The aisles and dark caverns of the transepts fade into black velvet depths. The vaults and arches seem really to swing above you in great semibreves of rhythm. All the lines are soft and take on the quality of a big sketch in sepia, such as Wren might have done when he was conceiving it. This seems to me to be an instance when

architecture reaches the level of great music – and even higher, playing in perpetual splendour.

Those silvery nights offered their pleasures at a price. The last and worst major raid on London was 10 May 1941, an evening of treacherous moonlight during which around 1,500 were killed and 2,000 seriously injured. Gutted in that attack was St Clement Danes, home to an annual service in which school children were given oranges and lemons as the bells played the old song. A photograph shows the tower on fire, like a black candle on some hellish altar; found in its ruins, covered in dust, were five farthings.

'Here was the great collapse of civilisation going on all around us, loathsomely visible,' Butler wrote. 'London being heavily bombed. My streets and roads and trees, my shops and churches, my pavements, my buses and offices, my friends, being smashed up by beastly German toughs flying about unopposed above us – or so it seemed. And that felt frightful.'

Germany also suffered huge destruction from the air; around 600,000 civilians were killed during the Second World War, three and a half million homes destroyed. Operation Gomorrah, the name given to Allied bombing raids on Hamburg in the summer of 1943, was intended to visit the wrath of God upon the second largest German city.

On 28 August in that year, a young woman called Rosa Sebald found her train journey home from Bamberg interrupted by an air raid. She was travelling with her three-year-old daughter, Gertrud; her son, unborn, grew in her belly. They disembarked at Fürth and watched Nuremberg burn. The boy, Max, would grow up to be fascinated by fire, as if it had been seared into him in the womb. 'It was not bright, it was a gruesome, evil, bloody flame . . .' he would later write – inspired by reading Pepys – of the events of 1666. 'The churchyard yews ignited, each one a lighted torch, a shower of sparks now tumbling to the ground.'

In Cologne, the famous cathedral was damaged, but came through the war, its twin spires rising from the ruined city, 'erect like a majestic symbol of the perpetuity of faith,' in the words of the American military chaplain, Philip Hannan. However, many of the city's ancient churches were ruined. The *New Yorker* journalist Janet Flanner crawled through rubble in the Basilica of the Holy Apostles as mortar shells fell. 'The air shook,' she reported, 'and from the church's injured choir great drops of red mosaics bled down onto the altar.'

In London, likewise. St Paul's Cathedral survived where a great many other churches did not. But it could easily have been different. Although the dome looks solid and formidable, it is in fact a skin of lead stretched over a timber frame, and was therefore vulnerable to being pierced by incendiaries. These nine-inch bombs contained thermite, a compound which burned hot enough to melt steel. They could be extinguished by water or smothered with sandbags, but you had to be quick or fire could take hold. Had it done so then the heat would shatter the internal supporting structure and the dome and lantern would collapse into the rest of the cathedral, just as the roof of St Paul's had in 1666. It was essential, therefore, to spot incendiaries as they landed, and to try to reach them even in high and difficult areas. The job of patrolling the dome was given to those members of the Watch 'with heads for heights and a leaning towards acrobatics,' wrote the dean, 'for they were expected, if necessary, to walk along the slender beams . . . to reach their bombs or to thrust the nozzles of their stirrup pumps into the heart of an incipient fire.'

# FIRE

The cathedral was such a prominent and valuable target that Dean Matthews felt he was living and working in a bullseye. And indeed he was. 'Have you ever seen a map of London?' Hitler asked during a dinner in Berlin in 1940. 'It is so densely built that one fire alone would be enough to destroy the whole city, just as it did over two hundred years ago.'

How then did St Paul's survive? To try to understand the underpinning of this miracle, I had arranged to meet Chris Allen, a wandsman and guide. As we spoke, an organist played Tallis's 'O Come in One to Praise the Lord' – music older than the church in which we were standing.

Allen showed me where 500lb high-explosive bombs had twice come through the roof – in October 1940 and again in April 1941 – causing significant damage, including blowing out all the windows and destroying the high altar. Arthur Butler had been on duty in the dome at the time of the April bomb. 'St Paul's rocked,' he later recalled. 'But only for an instant; then, quivering, settled down in its habitual majesty.' Shell fragments had driven holes into the stone interior, and these are still visible now. 'Honourable scars' is the phrase that comes to mind. That was how George VI had described the bomb damage to Buckingham Palace. It seems apt for St Paul's, too, and I was glad, seeing them, that not all traces of the ordeal had been lost.

Chris Allen next told the story of the eight-foot bomb, a ton in weight, that landed just outside the great west door. 'It buried itself twenty-seven feet down in the mud. Didn't explode but fractured a gas main on the way down. So the bomb disposal people were faced with a bomb that was at the bottom of a greasy crater, unexploded, in the midst of flaming gas pipes.' Had it gone off, it would probably have destroyed the cathedral. A team of Royal Engineers, unable to defuse it on site, dug it out of the ground over the course of three days and loaded it on to the back of a truck. Lieutenant Robert Davies, the leader of the squad, drove it at high speed across the cratered streets to Hackney Marshes, where it was detonated. He was given the George Cross, as was Lance Corporal George Wylie, known as Jock, who had extracted the bomb from the London earth.

The nightly work of the St Paul's Watch may not have been as cinematic as those particular acts of courage, but it was admirable in its tea-and-biscuits English way. These men and women were heroes. They saved history for the future, insisting – in the midst of evidence to the contrary – that we were going to have one. As Dean Matthews put it: 'let us hope that there will be a posterity to which these activities will be strange and for whom they will be interesting. It will not do them any harm to learn what things their elderly great-grandfathers endured for the love of St Paul's.'

With the cathedral so empty of visitors, it was much easier to imagine what the Watch endured, and how they went about their work. 'It is worth bearing in mind that the cathedral was not the bright, clean and airy place you see today,' Chris Allen reminded me. 'It was pitch dark in the blackout, and the roofs are accessed by a highly complex network of staircases, doors, ladders and acres and acres of rather precarious terraces.'

Members of the Watch had to memorise the maze-like layout from crypt to dome, so that they could find their way around in the dark and, if necessary, improvise alternative routes to get around blockages caused by fire or fallen stone. A red light and a green light were placed on the floor below the dome so that those on patrol, looking down from the Whispering Gallery, could get their bearings. These lights, though intended to act as a useful compass, added to the strange romance of the situation.

Many of those in the Watch had been drawn to the role by love of St Paul's. The woozy dream-state of sleep-deprivation intensified their feelings for Wren's creation, while also opening them up to an appreciation of the sublimity of destruction. Arthur Butler noted the 'hellish magnificence' of London – the shadows cast by falling flares, the flames reflected in the Thames – as he looked out over it at night. The dean, Walter Matthews, seemed to detect something almost divine in the bombing:

> If the reader has not seen an air raid opened by the dropping of flares he has missed one of the most beautiful and thrilling spectacles which can be imagined. The so-called 'chandelier flare' contains a constellation of brilliant lights which very slowly fall together, illuminating the whole sky and diffusing vivid and unearthly radiance on the buildings beneath. The shadows that they cast are quite different from any that were ever made by sun or moon. It is to be hoped that some intrepid artist has caught and preserved on canvas this weird and terrible loveliness. To get the full picture you must imagine that a number of chandelier flares are released together and that they are of different colours, orange and red, perhaps, and you must add the angry red glow of a fire on the horizon. It may be supposed that we had other emotions than those of pure aesthetic enjoyment, but I believe that few of us were quite unmoved by the beauty. I remember that on such a night the sight of the stars, placidly shining above the man-made glow, seemed to complete the vision with the suggestion of an eternal order behind the confusion and restless conflict.

The Stone Gallery that runs around the outside of St Paul's, encircling the dome, is 173 feet from the ground. It is high, but not so high you feel at a distant remove from the city around you. On the worst nights of the Blitz, the men of the Watch were lighthouse keepers in a sea of fire. What on earth must it have been like?

'I imagine it was a mixture of terror and exhilaration, and also determination,' Chris Allen suggested. 'They were very dogged, that generation. I was born in the war, in 1943, so remember nothing of it. But my father was serving in the Royal Artillery on the south coast, aiming his guns at the bombers coming in. My mother-in-law was a warden – we still have her tin hat – and she would patrol the streets of Ealing, telling people to get under cover. Her husband, my father-in-law, was a fireman, and the fire service was amongst the most dangerous things you could do. But they were very matter-of-fact. They coped, they got on with it. They were determined they were not going to be defeated and they were inspired by a man, Churchill, who caught the mood of the moment. So to be up on the parapet on a night such as that, it would be a question of getting your damn job done and probably not a lot of time to think.'

'Do you think your dad stopped a few bombers before they got to St Paul's?' I asked.

'Well, he might have done. I'd like to think he probably did.'

Propaganda films made much of St Paul's as a symbol of indomitability and stubborn grace. *Fire of London* focused upon the infamous evening of 29 December 1940 when, over the course of three hours, 22,000 incendiaries and 120 tons of high explosives were dropped on the City. An extraordinary panning shot filmed, most likely, from a walkway just above the north portico shows the area around St Paul's ablaze, the silhouetted statue of St Philip holding his cross as if in benediction of the ruins. Down there, in flames, were the publishing houses of Paternoster Row, a street destroyed just as it had been in the Great Fire, this time with the loss of around 5 million books. 'The ruins around St Paul's unfolded; the obliterated acres of Paternoster Row like a Pompeian landscape,' Graham Greene writes in *The Ministry of Fear*. A thick dark smoke rose and enshrouded the cathedral. William Taswell, the schoolboy who, in 1666, had seen St Paul's burn would have recognised it. 'A black darkness seemed to cover the whole hemisphere,' he had written, 'and the bewailings of people were great.'

That black darkness was evident in what is perhaps the most iconic photograph of the Blitz. Taken on 29 December, it ran on the front of the *Daily Mail* under the headline, 'WAR'S GREATEST PICTURE: St Paul's Stands Unharmed in the Midst of the Burning City'. It was the work of the photographer Herbert Mason, who took it from the roof of Northcliffe House, the newspaper building, on Carmelite Street. The same photograph was used in a very different context on the front page of the *Berliner Illustrierte Zeitung*, accompanied by the headline, 'The City of London Burns!' St Paul's, in Britain, was being used as a symbol of an almost sacred endurance; in Germany, it was presented as evidence that the Luftwaffe's lightning had struck at the enemy nation's heart.

'In half an hour fires were raging on every side,' recollected Walter Matthews, 'but we had no leisure to contemplate the magnificent though terrible spectacle, for many bombs had fallen simultaneously on different parts of the Cathedral roofs. Watchers on the roof of the *Daily Telegraph* building in Fleet Street, who had a full view of St Paul's from the west thought that the Cathedral was doomed and told us later that a veritable cascade of bombs was seen to hit and glance off the Dome.'

One incendiary pierced the lead shell and stuck halfway through. Here was the moment that the Watch had feared. The lead began to melt. It would not be long before the bomb set the internal timbers alight. There was a strong wind that night which would fan the flames. Wren's phoenix, his shield over London, would burn and fall.

The American broadcaster Edward R. Murrow, seeing the cathedral hit, thought that it had been destroyed. 'And the church that meant most to Londoners is gone,' he reported for CBS. 'St Paul's Cathedral, built by Sir Christopher Wren, her great dome towering over the capital of the Empire, is burning to the ground as I talk to you now.' Yet, as the wind cleared the smoke just for a moment, the happy truth became clear. 'No one who saw will ever forget their emotions on the night when London was burning,' *The Times* reported, 'and the dome seemed to ride a sea of fire like a great ship lifting above smoke and flame the inviolable ensign of the golden cross.'

Beneath that cross, beneath the dome, above the stricken streets, the Watch battled on. Dividing into small squads, they fought the various fires that had broken out. Incendiaries lodged in the roof timbers proved especially hard to put out, requiring men working stirrup pumps from above and below. It must have been desperate, but it helped that they knew they were not alone. Churchill sent a message: 'St Paul's must be saved at all costs.'

And it was. It is not clear how it happened; perhaps the watcher responsible preferred to remain anonymous, or perhaps it was simply a lucky chance of the wind, or the bomb shifting under its own weight, but the incendiary stuck in the dome fell backwards and out on to the Stone Gallery, where it was easily extinguished. The hand of man or a still greater hand? 'In either case,' wrote the dean, 'we thank God that our great church was spared at the moment when the situation looked almost hopeless.'

As the bombs fell that night, Virginia Woolf was at her country house in East Sussex, reading about the Great Fire. Blitz damage had forced her and husband Leonard to move out of their Bloomsbury home two months before. Now, on 29 December 1940, as she read about 1666, the parallels were not lost on her. She seemed to take the attack upon London personally. 'Eight of my city churches destroyed,' she noted in her diary.

She had written about London's cathedral eight years before for *Good Housekeeping* magazine. 'Something of the splendour of St Paul's lies simply in its vast size, in its colourless serenity,' she had observed. That serenity gave the cathedral, for all its centuries, a curious feeling of agelessness. 'Even the contorted and agonised figure of John Donne ... looks as if he had left the stonemason's yard but yesterday. Yet it has stood here in its agony for three hundred years and has passed through the flames of the Fire of London.'

It is strange to think of the mortal eyes which have rested a moment on that statue of Donne. Caroleans, Georgians, Victorians, Edwardians, the new Elizabethans; all have marvelled at this strange figure from the past. He endures, we do not. St Paul's endures, we do not. That is true of the human presence in all very old churches: a mingling of the transient, ancient and eternal. We are but mayflies alighting on marble.

The following morning, 30 December, Cecil Beaton visited the ruins of the City in the company of the writer James Pope-Hennessy, with whom he was collaborating on a book. Beaton, an aesthete, was disturbed by the aftermath, the charred churches still smouldering, yet there is in his account some of that same exhilaration felt by the watchers on the roof of the cathedral. 'We have trundled under perilous walls,' he wrote in his diary, 'over uncertain ground which, at any moment, might give way to the red-hot vaults below. We have known Ypres in the heart of London. We could not deny a certain ghoulish excitement stimulated us, and our anger and sorrow were mixed with a strange thrill at seeing such a lively destruction – for this desolation is full of vitality. The heavy walls crumble and fall in the most romantic Piranesi forms . . . We went to St Paul's to offer our prayers for its miraculous preservation.'

Also comforted by the cathedral that morning was Dorothy Barton, a typist on her way to the office. She had made her daily commute by train from the suburbs.

'As I turned on to London Bridge from the station I looked to the left and could see St Paul's Cathedral standing alone in an area of complete devastation,' she recalled. 'The air was full of smoke and the smell of burning, with dust from the debris over everything.'

So much of the old life, of the old city had gone – so much, but not all.

'As I looked at Wren's masterpiece I felt a lump in my throat because, like so many people, I felt that while St Paul's survived, so would we.'

# CATS

T. S. ELIOT, IN *Old Possum's Book of Practical Cats*, tells us that our feline companions have three different names. Nine lives, three names, one cat. The first is the everyday name used to refer to the pet in the home – Eliot suggests Augustus, Victor and George. The second is a 'name that's peculiar, and more dignified', allowing the creature to feel proud from tail to whiskers. The third is known only to the cat itself; its inscrutable expression is, the poet explains, the consequence of deep contemplation upon this secret.

This theory suits very well the small, half-Abyssinian, entirely awesome cat so closely associated with Southwark Cathedral. Before Doorkins Magnificat was Doorkins Magnificat, before she was even Doorkins, she was a feral predator in Borough Market, admired by the beadles and traders for her ferocity, tenacity and devotion to the swift dispatch and devouring of vermin. In those bellicose, belly-filling days, did she have a name? None of the witnesses to whom I spoke could quite recall how they referred to her then. Perhaps, one thought, it matched her reputation: Ratter.

Before that, though, it is believed that she had another life: a domestic cat who, lost or abandoned, found herself living on the streets of London and on her wits. What her name was back then – no doubt, something disgustingly homely and at odds with her hauteur – only she knows, and will never tell. It is the prerogative of a star to keep her origins quiet. Marilyn did not go by Norma Jean, nor Holly by Lula Mae, and so it was with Doorkins Magnificat, who would not come if you called for Tiddles. She answered, in all things, only to herself. And, at a push, to God.

I met Doorkins on a fine day towards the end of September. Sapphire skies, amber leaves. Summer was catnapping in London, but autumn put forth a marmalade paw and pressed a claim to the territory.

After many years of living in the cathedral, Doorkins had, for some months, been resident in the nearby home of Paul Timms, the dean's verger – a cosy Victorian cottage with religious art on the walls. Paul was in his early sixties; Doorkins was reckoned to be somewhere between sixteen and eighteen which made her, in cat years, by far the elder in their relationship. She was dozing when I arrived, beneath a medieval nativity scene, but soon woke, stretched and purred – this last action prompted not by my presence, but that of Paul and a helping of Sheba Fine Flakes. 'Someone's come to see you,' he told her. 'It's dinner time, isn't it? Yes, it is.' I was glad to hear her so happy. She never used to purr in the cathedral, maintaining instead a workplace demeanour that could easily be taken for froideur.

To meet her was an honour. I was being granted an audience: Doorkins, the most famous of Britain's church cats, with an active social media presence and a popular range of merchandise. Senior clergy elsewhere, seeing the fundraising and public relations possibilities, had been in touch with Southwark to ask whether they, too, should get a cat. She was part brand ambassador, part evangelist, part gateway drug. 'People come to the cathedral to see Doorkins,' Jon Dollin had told me. He was Southwark Cathedral's retail and visitor services manager and the cat's 'voice' on Twitter. 'For some people, crossing that threshold is really difficult. But Doorkins makes it more accessible. I don't want to say that the majority of visitors come here to see the cat, but she's certainly helped people get over their fear of coming into the church.'

# CATS

The first written reference to Southwark Cathedral is in the Domesday Book of 1086. It has been a cathedral since 1905, before which it was known as St Saviour's Church, and, before that, St Mary Overie. Its location at the southern end of London Bridge is dramatic, as is the juxtaposition of its great stone tower and the gleaming glass Shard. Charles Dickens knew that tower well; in 1869, he attended ringing practice there and wrote about it in *All The Year Round*: 'A very dark and cold evening in January found us crossing London-bridge, bellward bound.'

Those bells would have been familiar to Shakespeare, too – he paid for them to be rung at the funeral of his brother Edmund. The cathedral contains two beautiful painted tombs: that of the poet John Gower, a friend of Chaucer, and Bishop Lancelot Andrewes, who is said to have translated the first five books of the Old Testament for the King James Bible. The bishop's sermons were a profound influence upon T. S. Eliot's life and work; Eliot would, one suspects, have found in Doorkins Magnificat a likeness of his own Old Deuteronomy, who slept and dreamed on the vicarage wall.

*

There is a long association between cats and religious buildings. The short ninth-century poem known as 'Pangur Bán' is thought to have been composed by an Irish monk at Reichenau Abbey, a Benedictine monastery on an island in Lake Constance, southern Germany. It is a heartwarming reflection on companionship and concentration and the pleasure of work: the monk, bleary of eye and weary of mind, shares his scriptorium with his white cat, Pangur, sharp-eyed and clawed, seizing a mouse just as the scribe grasps a concept. Written in Old Irish, it has been translated by Seamus Heaney, Robin Flower, Paul Muldoon and W. H. Auden.

It was Auden's version that Samuel Barber set to music, very beautifully, in the early 1950s: 'How happy we are,' the monk sings. 'Alone together, scholar and cat.'

Auden's own cat was named Pangur. I wonder whether he knew the story of Faith? In 1936, a stray tabby found her way into St Augustine, Watling Street, which had been rebuilt by Wren after the Great Fire. The memoirist Molly Hughes had visited in the early 1930s and wrote about it in her charming book on London churches, *The City Saints*: 'Several young businessmen come in every day for private prayer. One worshipper is known to have come in every day for forty years. Their love of the place seems to pervade it, and you soon catch the infection.'

Taken in by Father Henry Ross, the tabby was named Faith. She became well known around the church, sitting in the front pew during sermons, or else in the pulpit while her master preached. Four years passed. Faith grew fat on mice and then fatter still on love. She was pregnant. The father was unknown, but what of it? Faith's kitten – Panda – would not be the first or last war baby of obscure parentage.

On 6 September 1940, Faith picked up her kitten out of its basket and took him down to the basement of the rectory, nesting between stacks of old sheet music. Father Ross, worried that Panda would find it cold, brought him back upstairs. This happened several times: down the stairs and back, down the stairs and back. Eventually, Faith was given her way and left alone to mother as she would.

The following night, the Blitz began. On 9 September, the church was destroyed. The priest had spent the night in an air-raid shelter. He returned to find only the tower left standing. The rectory, too, was gone. Four floors and the roof had fallen in, the whole building blazed. A fireman told him that his cats must certainly be dead.

But they were not. Hacking his way through smouldering timbers with an axe, Father Ross found the creatures unhurt, their survival thanks to Faith's instinct – or premonition – that the basement meant safety. 'She endured horrors and perils beyond the power of words to tell,' he later wrote. 'God be praised and thanked for his goodness and mercy to our dear little pet.'

Faith was given a silver medal in recognition of her bravery during the battle for London. She died in the autumn of 1948, a war veteran, on her favourite hearthrug, as Father Ross worked at his desk; alone together, priest and cat.

\*

Whenever you walk into Southwark Cathedral it feels serene. This despite it being in one of the buzziest, noisiest parts of the city, hard by Borough Market with its hungry crowds and traders' cries. This serenity is, of course, to do with the stoutness of the walls and deep layers of spiritual history thickened to a carapace by centuries of prayer. When listing the reasons for this air of peace, however, one should not neglect to mention the work of the vergers.

The vergers are worker bees in the holy hive. They are the laity who handle logistics. As dean's verger at Southwark, Paul Timms heads a busy team. 'We open and close the cathedral and prepare it for every function,' he told me. 'We make sure the right vestments are found, the right books, the right silver, the wafers and wine. We lead the clergy in, we lead the clergy out, and then we turn the building around for the next event. We are one of the busiest cathedrals in the country. Last Christmas, for instance, we had forty-six carol services on top of our five regular services a day. You can be open from seven in the morning to eleven at night. It's intense. If we run out of candles, if we run out of coffee cups, it's my fault. One day I could be on the roof taking a dead pigeon out of one of the downpipes and the next day I'm leading Her Majesty the Queen into the cathedral. I've had that privilege' – the Queen, he means, not the pigeon – 'five or six times in my career.'

It is his job, in other words, to keep all the potential chaos in his head, absorbing that pressure so that the clergy and congregation never have to feel it. What you don't want, therefore, on top of everything else, is a problem with mice – and that's where Doorkins came in.

It was December 2008. Timms was opening the main entrance when he spotted a cat sitting by the door. It was a wet morning, and she looked as if she was tempted to come in. The verger said hello, held out the back of his hand for her to sniff, but she was hesitant, suspicious, careful, and did not seek sanctuary on that first day. Still, she kept coming back. He began to leave food out, and, one morning, when the weather was especially bad, she wandered in and was discovered asleep in the Dean's Stall. 'Oh,' thought Timms, 'she's adopted us.' This was a pleasing notion; he had experience of feral cats from his previous job, at Coventry Cathedral, having made friends with a particularly objectionable example – a real hisser and spitter called Hoppy, who was missing a leg – that lived in the grounds. Also, Southwark, in possession of a substantial population of mice, was in want of a cat. Acquiring one had thus far proved difficult. The rescue centres were reluctant to rehome a cat in a cathedral. Here, though, was an animal that seemed to have no interest in being a pet and appeared drawn to the ancient building.

But could she catch mice? The market traders, who knew her of old, were able to answer that question. Barry Topp, a cider maker, used to drive to London from the New Forest in his truck, and park behind the Globe Theatre for a night's kip, before setting up his stall early the following morning. This was in the days before Doorkins found her way into the cathedral. He would always see the cat around 11 p.m. and, as a countryman, was fascinated to observe her hunting technique. 'They say in London you're never more than ten foot from a rat,' he recalled when we spoke. 'Well, late at night, when it got quiet, I'd see about fifty of them. And Doorkins would be sat there, just observing, her tail twitching.' Topp would watch from the comfort of his sleeping bag as, slinking alongside a pillar for cover, she would select her prey. 'All of a sudden you'd see her get down and build herself up, ready to pounce. She was so fast that every night she'd be off with one. She was a ruddy good ratter!'

It was a deal. The cat could stay. And, although she did keep the mice down, it was through fear not violence. 'She never killed them,' Timms said. She would play with them, bat them around a bit, but spare their lives. 'I don't know if that was the influence of being in church. *Thou shalt not kill*, you know . . .' In her personal theology, the commandment did not extend to spiders, which she ate with gusto. 'Since she's been away from the cathedral,' Timms sighed, 'we've had so many problems with cobwebs.'

A cat with a job needs a name. Timms gave her one: Doorkins. This was in reference to the south-west doorway where they had first met – and Catikins, the word used by him as a child to refer to all cats. That Doorkins is a pun on Richard Dawkins was a joke made by the late dean, Colin Slee. People want it to be true that she was named after a prominent atheist, but it isn't. As for Magnificat, that excellent pun was an addition made by the present dean, Andrew Nunn. The Magnificat, or Song of Mary, is part of the liturgy, taken from the Gospel of Luke, and can be heard sung or recited at the cathedral daily.

When Doorkins came to live at Southwark, it did not take long for a routine to be established. She spent most nights outside patrolling the area, but would be let in each morning and fed, before going off to find a place to sleep. This was always within the church itself, rather than any of the adjoining administrative spaces. 'The sacristy wasn't for her – all that gossiping in there probably put her off,' Andrew Nunn has written:

> She preferred the holy spaces and every so often she would move to another place which became her favourite spot. At one time it was the Harvard Chapel, secreting herself in a tight little space beneath George Pace's brutalist sedilia where there was a hot water pipe, then it was one of our stalls, then a seat in the retro-choir, or the north transept, or spread-eagled on one of the grates from which the hot air emerged into the Cathedral.

Visitors became used to seeing Doorkins around. She found human attention tolerable, but essentially tiresome, and would sometimes hiss or even strike out a paw if she felt her dignity was being infringed upon by uninvited attempts to stroke and pet. The clergy received no special treatment. She regarded them with disdain and enjoyed snoozing on their cushioned chairs.

'She has a well-developed sense of her importance,' Timms said. 'She knows she's a star. At Southwark, she had a sense of place and occasion. She knew she was somewhere special. You can imagine an ordinary cat – and she's extraordinary – would be jumping on altars, clawing at materials, in the wrong place at the wrong time, causing disruption and mayhem in what is a very dignified ministry. A cat jumping on the altar in the middle of a consecration of the elements would be a disaster. But of course she never did that.'

This is not to say she was unobtrusive. She knew how to inhabit the spotlight, to pull focus, to be ready for her close-up, Mr DeMille. She crashed weddings and memorial services and visits by bishops. 'She always seemed to know if there was somebody posh around,' Andrew Nunn said. 'Princess Alexandra was sat here once for some charity service where she was the patron. I was doing my stuff from the pulpit, and Doorkins just wandered straight down to her. Then, of course, everybody wanted to watch the princess stroking this cat, and I lost every bit of attention. I might as well have given up.'

There was a celebrated occasion when she met the Queen – 'This is Doorkins Magnificat, Ma'am' – who was visiting the cathedral to view a stained-glass window installed to mark her Diamond Jubilee. More notable, however, was her behaviour on the death of the dean, Colin Slee, with whom she had been on good terms. Doorkins had spent the night before his funeral sleeping beneath the coffin as it lay in state in the nave, and, during the service itself, returned to that spot. 'Colin was a great cat man, he loved cats,' Paul Timms recalled. 'She knew that he had gone, but that he was there.'

The idea of a cat in a cathedral is in and of itself pleasant. But there is something about Southwark in particular that suits the taking in of a stray. The cathedral has long had a reputation as a liberal citadel within Anglicanism. 'Our longstanding commitment to the full inclusion of all God's people in ministry, regardless of the definers of gender, ethnicity, sexuality, ability, age means that we have a clear stance that some others find very difficult,' states a document on the cathedral website:

Our championing of LGBT+ people, our solidarity with those living with or affected by HIV/AIDS, our presence over the last two years at Pride in London, makes us unacceptable to some. The presence amongst the clergy of openly gay and partnered priests, women and others has been the issue of public debate not least during the scandal surrounding the appointment to the episcopate of Dr Jeffrey John. We are 'Marmite' in the Church of England . . .

For Andrew Nunn, Doorkins was a small cat he loved, but also a narrative device. If people know the story of a lonely cat who wandered into a church and found herself at home, maybe they'd wander in and find themselves at home as well. She was, for him, a symbol of the 'radical hospitality' he wants the cathedral, and the faith, to embody.

Doorkins was a witness to history, not all of it good. Her encounters with royalty were only part of it. She was present during the Islamist terror attack of 3 June 2017, when eight people and the three perpetrators died on London Bridge and around Borough Market. Paul Timms had closed up the cathedral at 9.20 p.m., putting Doorkins out for the night. The killings began at just before 10 p.m. when a van was driven at high speed into pedestrians on the bridge; the terrorists then went about their work with knives. The cat is thought to have been in the middle of all this, the screaming and sirens, the blood and blue lights, and to have been traumatised by the experience. Counter-terrorism forces, concerned – incorrectly – that worshippers were being held hostage in the locked cathedral, blew open the doors in a controlled explosion. This meant that the cathedral became a crime scene and no member of the clergy or wider community was allowed access for a week. Doorkins had to go back on the streets for the duration, although, happily, the police fed her. When, at last, she was able to return to the cathedral, she never went outside again during her remaining time there, choosing to spend her nights within the familiar clutch of stone. As Andrew Nunn has written: 'After experiencing the kindness of humans, she saw the evil that they can do.'

That evening was, perhaps, the beginning of the end. Her health began to slide. Her eyesight was going, her hearing too. There came a time when she no longer responded to the dean's calls when he arrived for morning prayer. She slept the days away. Then, in October 2019, during a busy service, she was seen to bump into the altar and fall down some steps. Her safe space was no longer safe. A vet, examining her, explained that her body was failing and that there was a choice: she needed lots of love and rest and tender attention, or she could be put down. Paul Timms wasn't ready for the latter. As long as she wasn't in pain, he felt, she should be allowed to enjoy a retirement. 'I found her,' he said, 'and I always thought she'd end her life with me.'

He could never have known, on that wet December morning in 2008, that he would end up sharing his work and home with this creature of the streets.

'I do feel that she was God-sent,' he nodded. 'She has become part of what Southwark is.'

At that, I left them. Alone together, verger and cat.

*

A few days after I had the privilege of making her acquaintance, Doorkins Magnificat went into sharp decline. 'She died in my arms to the sound of a familiar voice peacefully at 8.20 p.m.,' Timms said. 'I miss her more than words can say, such was the impact she had on me and all who loved her so dearly.'

It was decided to hold a service of thanksgiving for her at Southwark Cathedral. This drew some fire. One northern bishop wrote online, 'Is this a joke? I do hope so. If not it's grossly insensitive to bereaved families and those ministering to them in the NW under the regional Coronavirus restrictions.' A priest in Stockton-on-Tees agreed: 'I love my cat. And I love Southwark. But this, coming at a time when so many people have been unable to hold loved ones' funerals in church, comes across as insensitive.'

The service took place on a sunny but cold afternoon. Thirty of us had gathered – the maximum number allowed for funerals under Covid restrictions – and were seated on plastic chairs in the nave. Candles were lit on the altar and there was a great stillness in that great space; in no sense was this occasion ironic or kitsch or lacking in dignity. It was a farewell to a friend. Sunlight shone through the Shakespeare window – through Titania's wings and Yorick's skull and Prospero's golden cloak – and cast dappled colours on the old stone. Andrew Nunn, in a black cassock, rose to speak. In its long history, he observed, Southwark Cathedral had hosted memorial services for the great and good, as well as funerals for ordinary people from the parish, but he rather doubted that they had ever before had a service for a cat: 'Some may think that cats don't deserve ceremonies and eulogies and prayers, that their death should pass without comment or occasion. But I can't agree.'

This, we understood, was a response to the criticism.

'And I'm not particularly a cat person,' he continued. 'Or at least I wasn't before I met her. But this little cat who arrived at our door, who chose us and stayed, changed our lives and enhanced our mission and ministry. She did more to bring people to this place than I will ever do.'

It was a beautiful ceremony. Readings and psalms. A

member of the choir sang of Pangur and the scribe. A poem in the order of service noted that Doorkins had not been 'domesticated but churched' – which sounded about right. The occasion was live-streamed for those who wanted to be there but couldn't, provoking an intense emotional reaction from huge numbers of people who had never met Doorkins. One vicar in Nottinghamshire commented that she hadn't been able to cry for her aunt, at whose funeral she had officiated, but had been in bits crying for the cat. 'It's ok if you don't get it,' she wrote online, 'it's ok if you think it's silly, but for me this helped, it really helped.' The air was swollen with grief and had been for months. The death of Doorkins was a purging.

The dean, in his homily, reflected on Adam naming the animals: 'As soon as you give them a name, you give them something fundamental: a character, a presence, almost a personality.' Part of the power of the Doorkins story, he said, was what it had to teach us about how to treat strangers in need of kindness and welcome. He remembered, in his closing prayer, four migrants – two children and their parents – who had died the day before when their boat sank while crossing the English Channel from France. They were thought to be Kurdish-Iranian but their names were not yet known.

At the close of the service, Paul Timms carried the remains of Doorkins in a small wooden casket, bowing to the altar as he passed. Following him, we walked out of the cathedral, into the train noise and market smells and the wind that whirled fallen leaves, and the verger laid her in the earth – that body which had once ratted and slunk and pounced and dozed, and delighted so many with its evident grace.

She lies by the churchyard wall, across from the door where she first came in; the door from which she took her final name.

# STONE

CLEMENTINE ELIZABETH Hartshorne, known as Clemmie, was sixteen months old on the occasion of her baptism, the ceremony having been twice deferred as a result of the global pandemic.

'She was a lockdown baby,' her mother, Catherine, had told me, born into a world stranger than she could know; a world of masks and gloves, of feared breath and touch, of security guards at hospital doors. Yet her heartbeat had been so strong during pregnancy that her parents had a sense of her, before birth, as a child of unfaltering determination, a child able to cope, and so it proved. They took her home to North Grimston, a village near Malton in Yorkshire, and spent the next weeks in isolation, which is to say in a bubble of intense emotion, falling in love.

Now, in the little church next to their home, the former vicarage, we sang 'All Things Bright and Beautiful' and we sang 'All You Need Is Love' and we meant it. Those hymns, Christian and secular, had a child-like optimism that everyone – the church was full of family and friends – seemed glad to feel. The air smelled of lavender; bunches were tied with ribbon at the ends of pews.

The priest drew our attention to the font: 'One of the oldest in England.' For perhaps a thousand years, he said, infants had been immersed in its waters. Clemmie, in a moment, would become part of that lineage. The precise age of the font is, in fact, uncertain. Some say it is Saxon, others that it dates from the early years of the Norman Conquest. It is limestone, cylindrical, a little under three feet high and a little more than that across. What makes it thrilling are the

carvings that cover every part. They show the Last Supper, Christ being brought down from the cross, and a depiction of St Nicholas (to whom the church is dedicated) as a bishop with a crozier.

This font is not elegant. Nikolaus Pevsner, the great chronicler of church architecture, called it a 'mighty and a barbaric piece' – a pejorative expression that can be read, if one chooses, as a compliment. The carving has raw power. Its figures thrum with unsettling energy, in particular the lolling corpse of Christ, gaunt of flank and shank. They make my heart beat harder when I look at them. If they are crude, even primitive, then this gives them a seriousness and purity. These, one feels sure, were not made by a skilled and expensive artist brought over from Normandy, but by a local, or locals, who did their best, with chisel and mallet, to express the force of belief. There is also a crackling tension between the familiarity of the subject and the alien style of the execution. The people who made this, and to whom it was important, are us, but at the same time they are so clearly not us – they saw the world differently, spoke a different language, baptised their children in a font that told stories of betrayal and death. Yet that very font, remarkably, is still used for the same purpose in the church for which it was made. That, most of all, is why it feels vital. This stone lives.

'Could the congregation turn towards the font, please, and remain standing?' asked the priest.

The family walked down the nave and gathered by the font. Clemmie was wearing a white flouncy dress and white shoes. She laughed and babbled, chewed the order of service. Her father, Edward, stroked her hair to keep her feeling safe and calm.

The priest made the sign of the cross on her forehead. 'May you fight valiantly as a disciple of Christ,' he said, 'against sin, the world and the devil.'

At this she looked solemn, as anyone might, but did not appear in any way troubled. It would be nice to think that this was thanks, in part, to the steadying presence of her particular friend – a yellow Labrador by the name of Finch who accompanies Clemmie everywhere and who had been given special dispensation to attend her big day.

Edward and Catherine have a strong faith, and so it was important to them that their child should be received into the church. Recent incomers to the area, they were moved by the idea that she would be joining a long local tradition; that through the ancient font, through that alchemy of water and stone and time and love, Clemmie would become part of the history – and future – of the village and its people. 'There is something amazing and humbling about the thought that children for hundreds of years have gone through the same thing in the same place and the same way, and their parents have had the same emotions we're having now,' Edward had said when we spoke before the service.

North Grimston is one of four country churches in this corner of Yorkshire with notable carved fonts, and it is instructive to spend a few hours seeking out these weathered vessels that carry not just water, but the wash of history itself. Langtoft, Kirkburn, Cowlam, we are lucky to have them. 'Fonts were desecrated and destroyed in religious wars, removed from churches to serve as Victorian flower pots and cattle troughs, sold at auction to overseas buyers . . . and rehoused in museums or modern churches when their original churches closed or fell into the sea.' So wrote Professor Carolyn Twomey in a journal article on Yorkshire's fonts. One approaches those that remain, therefore, with a certain amount of respect. The church of St Mary, Cowlam is a surreal presence in the stackyard of Church Farm, bellcote rising above a bow-roofed barn of wood and corrugated iron; its font shows, among other scenes, the Massacre of the Innocents, King Herod smiling, sword in hand, as he orders the death of the first-born. Even here, in this secret little church, which one might think altogether forgotten, there are fresh names in the visitor book and a couple of services a month. 'It's been kept alive all these years,' Diann Atkin, the farmer, told me. She had lived there all her life – she was now sixty-one – and felt determined the church should stay open and in use.

A few months previously, I had visited the church of St Michael and All Angels in Castle Frome, Herefordshire. Pevsner had no reservations about the twelfth-century font there, calling it 'one of the masterworks of Romanesque sculpture in England. It would arrest attention in any country.' Carved around the very large grey sandstone bowl are representations of the four evangelists – the angel of Matthew, the winged lion of Mark, the winged bull of Luke and the eagle of John. We also see Christ's baptism in the Jordan. The font rests on three grim figures carved from red sandstone that are sometimes said to represent sin crushed beneath the weight of this sacred object.

A local woman, Louise Manning, had opened up the church for me. Her husband had been baptised in the font, she explained, as had their children. She had a strong sense of occupying a brief moment in the history of the church and the longer history of the landscape. That yew tree in the churchyard was likely older than the building. Then there was the board listing rectors going back to 1299. She pointed out the plague years, 1349 and 1603; the times of civil war and world war; the church and its font had stood through all that, she said, and now here we were, struggling through our own age of sickness, and they were still standing. The font, for her, represented continuity and renewal, a meaning emphasised by its location in the countryside. She felt connected to previous generations not just by the church but by the land, which her family farms. The cycles of nature – life and birth and death – are felt strongly in a rural church, she thought. Taken all together these factors created an intense feeling of belonging. 'Do you own the church,' she wondered, 'or does the church own you?'

It was a good question, one I carried north.

The day before Clemmie's baptism, I had spent time examining the font in the company of Dr Louise Hampson, an art historian from the Centre for the Study of Christianity and Culture at the University of York. She has an interest in the North Grimston church both as an academic and as a member of the congregation, and has been looking at and thinking about the font for twenty years. She believes it dates from around 1100: a prestige object made in post-Conquest England by people still working in an older Anglo-Scandinavian tradition, which would explain why it looks Viking as much as Norman. The font is likely to have been painted originally, she said, and would therefore have been even more striking than it is now.

She is fascinated, in particular, by the carving of Christ being brought down from the cross, a scene known as The Deposition. This is an unusual subject for a font, perhaps unique in England, and she had thought deeply about its presence and meaning here. To Christ's left, his arms gripping the thin body, is a figure who has been identified as Nicodemus, a Pharisee. To Christ's right is Joseph of Arimathea, a wealthy disciple; he supports the crucified man's right arm which he has freed from the cross, the wound left by the nail visible in the palm. It is a frozen moment of physical and mental suffering, despair and defeat. These two men have no thought or hope that their friend and leader can live again. Their task is to manhandle a corpse from the place of execution and take it for burial. 'This is death,' said Dr Hampson. 'There's no holy spirit, no trinity, no Jesus rising from the tomb.'

Why carve this portrait of trauma on a font? Possibly because the people who made it were themselves traumatised. 'I think,' said Dr Hampson, 'this is an expression of local distress.' If the font was made in the aftermath of 1066, then among the villagers there may have been men, or their fathers, who had fought in the bloody battles of Fulford and Stamford Bridge, and this place would surely not have escaped the Harrying of the North, the violent oppression by William the Conqueror which has been described – though the term is disputed – as a genocide. 'So maybe people had first-hand experience of unhooking dead bodies from trees.'

The font, then, is a mirror: darkness reflecting darkness. But it is also a torch: offering the light of salvation through immersion in its waters. 'I think that the people who carved this imagery,' said Dr Hampson, 'used it to cling to the idea that, even though they were living in incredibly dark times, there was the eternal life to come.'

That feeling was present at Clementine Hartshorne's baptism. This was no great national event. This was no grand cathedral. It was a family occasion in a little church in a little village in a summer of tentative pleasure. And it wasn't about getting back to normal. There is no normal. Time passes and the world gets better and worse in its different ways. But it was a moment of hope, and I was glad to be there to witness it.

Now, as the time came for the sacrament, Catherine held her daughter in her arms. The priest dipped his right hand into the font and wiped water across Clemmie's head three times. 'I baptise you,' he said, 'in the name of the father . . .

. . . and of the son

. . . and of the holy spirit.'

Clemmie, startled, perhaps even a tad put out by this unexpected touch, lifted an indignant hand to wipe her forehead dry. We all laughed at this, and that sound, the simple happiness of people who had come together in a room to celebrate a child, was itself a kind of blessing.

'Amen,' said the priest. 'Good girl.'

*

I turned right at the gothic gift shop, walked down a little street zigzagged with bunting, paused to admire the house where Beatrix Potter set her *Tailor of Gloucester*, squeezed along the narrow passage of St Michael's Gate, through which pilgrims and tourists have for centuries made their way to the tomb of Edward II, and was just beginning to take in the splendid south face of the cathedral when a bicycle bell dinged twice and a French voice sang out: 'Peter Ross, I presume?'

Pascal Mychalysin is master mason at Gloucester Cathedral. He is in his early sixties and has worked here since 1990. He had agreed to meet and talk about stone.

'We have inherited this building,' he said. 'It is of huge historical and human significance. My mission, very simply, is to make sure it will pass to the next generation in, I hope, a better state than when I started.'

Gloucester Cathedral dates from 1089, but has been reworked over a long period and therefore represents distinct styles. This is experienced most dramatically when passing from the nave into the choir. In architectural terms, this is a three-hundred-year step from the Romanesque into the Perpendicular, but that does not convey what it actually feels like. Visitors should be supplied with popcorn for this is pure cinema. Think of that moment in *The Wizard of Oz* when Dorothy walks out into a new world of colour. The chief causes of this effect are the choir's high roof – a constellation of golden bosses and angels – and Great East Window. The window ('The glory of Gloucester,' said Pascal) is seventy-two feet tall by thirty-two wide, the largest in the world at the time of its completion in 1350. Its size is often likened to that of a tennis court, but a better comparison is a cinema screen. To fourteenth-century eyes it must have been a thing of astonishment and wonder, a medieval blockbuster, a wide-screen epic of apostles, bishops, martyrs and saints. Nor are the cinematic qualities of this cathedral lost on our own age. The cloisters, famous for their fan-vaulting, were used as a location in the Harry Potter films, representing the interior of Hogwarts, and even now this connection draws many

tourists. On the day of my visit, a little boy was running to and fro, wizard cloak flying behind him; his dutiful parents, in close pursuit, had been pressed into service as trolls.

Most cathedrals have been built and rebuilt over centuries. From the moment a new stone is set in place it begins to weather and decay; therefore these great buildings are, in a sense, never complete. And, of course, the worship and glorification of God is an endless business. All of which means that cathedrals require generation upon generation of human lives for their construction, maintenance and daily ritual. A cathedral is a sort of oak tree – vast, ancient and alive, drawing into itself the thoughts of many minds, the work of many hands, the songs of countless throats. The mason's mark of Pascal Mychalysin is an oak leaf. This is the signature he inscribes into the objects he carves. You see these here and there, an autumn carpet of stone. 'I love the architecture of the oak,' he explained. 'I am completely in awe of that tree.'

Gloucester Cathedral was built from oolitic limestone, known as Painswick stone, quarried locally. This suits Pascal, who admires the way the sunlight plays upon it, but, more than that, he has an affinity with the material. It is a sort of birthright. He was born in Burgundy, a limestone area, and so feels at home – indeed, at one – with the stone. 'It is my mind and my spirit and it has made me a human being as I am now.' It would be difficult for him to live, he says, in an area of sandstone or granite. This is not just a building material. There's something about the way it feels under his hands, and as he turns it in his thoughts, that is vital to his identity and well-being. The way he tells it, this feeling for stone is not unique to him; it's a mason thing.

'When you work a stone, there is a physicality to it that goes both ways,' he said. 'You shape yourself in shaping the stone. It is incredibly intimate. After many years, you are not only you, but something that the material has shaped. It changes your body and your mind. You are marked in your muscles and in the way you behave and think. You can recognise stonemasons. You can distinguish them from carpenters and joiners. We have a different mindset, a different psychology, a different attitude – because we have been profoundly marked by what we do.'

I can understand how working with stone shapes the body: building muscle, roughening the hands, bending the back. But, I asked Pascal, how does it change the way you think?

'A lot of masons are reflective people,' he replied. 'They are not bragging. They are unusually modest and humble. Working with stone gives you the gift of reflection. You think slowly and with purpose.'

Because the material itself is hard and heavy and slow and demanding?

'Yes. You cannot ply stone to your will. It is impossible. You have to accept what the material is ready to give you. Some people cannot accept this. They are too impatient and want the result they want.' He shrugged. 'They will move into some other work.'

Pascal heads a team of six masons based at the cathedral, three of them apprentices. They are based in a brick workshop beside the cathedral with a yard in which newly quarried limestone sits gleaming next to worn-out lumps of nineteenth- and fifteenth-century masonry brought down from the roof, all of it formed at the bottom of the Jurassic sea 160 million years ago. During the medieval period, the stonemasons worked within a wooden structure, known as the lodge, leaning against the side of the cathedral. It is not difficult to imagine the noise and stink and strong-arm glory of such a place. William Golding, in *The Spire*, presents a portrait of an army of journeyman masons, 'strange creatures from every end of the world', as they went about their work in the fourteenth century:

> The yard was full of stacks and piles of cut stone. They reached up to the windows between the buttresses. What space the stones left was filled with baulks of timber and the passage between them was no more than a catwalk. On the left of the entrance was a bench against the south wall, with a thatched cover. Glass, and lead strip was heaped up under the thatch, and two of the master builder's men were working there, chink, snip, snip . . . The two men breaking up the pavement were working out of sight to their thighs, and the dust was so thick in that part of the air, he thought their faces

were monstrously deformed, until he saw that they had drawn cloths over their mouths; and these cloths were caked with dust and sweat.

Engineering and artistic advances in church-building from the twelfth to sixteenth centuries feel exciting even in long retrospect. It is akin to polar or space exploration: human intelligence and will working at their limits, the body labouring to realise the vision of the mind. Except, unlike the missions to the poles or the stars, the builders of cathedrals were expressing their genius right here, where their creations – these giant buildings arrowed toward heaven – could be seen and marvelled at by everyone around. Andrew Ziminski, in his book *The Stonemason*, speculates that 'it must have felt as if something supernatural had seized the earth'.

There is no longer any need for travelling armies of stonemasons. However, Gloucester's workshop as it is now would probably seem familiar to a medieval craftsman, or so I thought when Pascal showed me round. There was the percussive sound of mallet and chisel as an apprentice carved the horns of a fawn. There were gargoyles modelled in clay, gurningly ready to be rendered in stone. There were the bankers – the heavy blocks used as work benches – and the racks of tools, and everything covered in dust.

Pascal's tools come with stories. He hefted a pick-axe, made before the First World War, which he had been given, in 1984, by a mason with whom he worked at a quarry in Germany. Next he lifted an axe – a *taillant champenois*, he called it – also dating from the early years of the twentieth century, that he uses for roughing-out stone; marks made by just such an axe are visible, by torchlight, on the underside of the vault above the Lady Chapel, left by masons during its construction in the fifteenth century. Finally, Pascal brought down from its

shelf a drawing compass that he had inherited from his father.
'When he came back from the war, after five years in a stalag
for Polish army prisoners, he could no longer make a living as
an agricultural labourer, so he became an apprentice black-
smith. This was the compass he forged himself to use in his
work. It's still got the end of his name on it, look – Z-Y-N.'

Mychalysin is a French adaptation of a Ukrainian name.
Just as Gloucester Cathedral, where one king is buried and
another – Henry III – was crowned, contains geological layers
of English history, so the stonemason who cares for the cathedral carries within him strata of Europe's turbulent past.
His French maternal grandfather, Robert, a survivor of the
Battle of Verdun, was a prisoner of war in Westphalia. His
maternal great-great-grandfather, François, was a veteran of
the siege of Sebastopol and a member of Napoleon III's imperial guard. The blood in Pascal's veins is French, German,

Russian, Polish, Czech and Baltic. 'He never spoke about it to us,' he once wrote of his grandfather's experience of Verdun, 'except to say that the shelling reverberated and resonated in his head long after he left the battlefield . . . I believe it is still with us, reverberating through us, we just don't realise it.'

Pascal had become a stonemason, he once told me, 'to try to bring back a little beauty in this ugly world'.

We took a walk around the cathedral, outside and in. 'Hello!' he called up to a pair of hard-hatted colleagues waving down from exterior scaffolding. They were removing a dark crust of calcium sulphate that had scabbed over the stone. 'The legacy of the industrial revolution and all the pollution in the atmosphere,' Pascal explained. Up there somewhere, chiselled into a pinnacle of the north ambulatory parapet, was the date 2020, the final zero made to look like a spiked blob of Covid-19. Few would see it other than gulls and future masons, but the virus had carved its way through the world, so Pascal had felt it appropriate that it should leave a mark on the stone.

Some of his work is much more visible, such as the statue of St Kyneburgha, abbess of Gloucester from 679 to 710. Other works made by the team of masons are pragmatic rather than beautiful. A new lintel above the entrance to the Lady Chapel has allowed that sacred space to be accessed by wheelchair-users; it was made by one of Pascal's colleagues who left his mark, a salamander, on the back. This was meaningful work, Pascal said, because it showed that the building was alive – not a museum, fixed forever, but a welcoming place of growth and change.

'And this is one of the most important monuments in the cathedral,' he declared. We stopped and looked up at a strange sculpture, jutting from the wall of the south transept about fifteen feet from the ground. It had been carved with a dreadful scene: a young man in robes, thought to be an apprentice mason, plummeting from the vault of the cathedral, while his master, looking up from below, roars in horror. 'Nobody knows exactly,' said Pascal, 'but it is probably to commemorate the death of an apprentice who really did fall from scaffolding. The ceiling of the south transept is completely devoid of decoration, which is very unusual, and that could be a sign of mourning.' The sculpture is in the shape of a set square, a mason's tool; grief expressed as geometry. 'It shows how much the life of an apprentice was valued, because it is the life – and the future – of the craft.'

Pascal has, of course, been both figures: apprentice and master. In one sense it was destiny that he become a stonemason. He was born in a fifteenth-century hospital, Les Hospice de Beaune, which is now a museum – and feels that being 'born in history' predetermined his lifelong interest in art and the past. However, in another way, he came to his calling by chance. An art teacher at school was married to a mason, Claude Chevènement, who took him on and later sent him to train with Les Companions du Devoir, the medieval craft guild. Pascal, every bit as much as a priest, is both an inheritor and bequeather of tradition.

What, I wondered, is his relationship with Christ – as a workman in his house? 'I'm not a practising Christian. I'm a lapsed Catholic. I hated the church when I was growing up. I hated the hypocrisy and the sanctimoniousness. So I left the church, but I've never left God.'

'Work,' he said, 'is my form of prayer.'

Back outside, Pascal drew my attention to the exterior of the south aisle. Over a period of eight years, he and his team worked on this part of the building, which was badly eroded and had been damaged by musket balls. They repaired statues, made several new gargoyles, replaced the decorative facings of buttresses worn featureless by time, and – like dentists extracting old fillings – removed hundreds of Victorian clamps that had rusted and so fractured the window tracery.

There is an argument that ancient buildings should be conserved rather than restored. John Ruskin denounced restoration as 'the most total destruction which a building can suffer' and declared that 'it is impossible, as impossible as to raise the dead, to restore anything that has ever been great or beautiful in architecture'. Pascal does not agree. The south aisle, he said with satisfaction, has not been seen as it is now since the English Civil War.

The limestone they use, like the man who carves it, comes from France. It is a better match with the medieval stone than is now available locally. Pascal, in the yard, had demonstrated its quality by knocking a large block with his hand. 'See how it rings?' he said. 'If it rings like that, like an anvil, that means there is absolutely no fault, no micro-fracture, no vents.' Good limestone like this, he estimates, will erode at the rate of one millimetre every four generations. A very slow process, yes, but Pascal knows that even his most careful carving can only ever be temporary. On this matter, as in all things, he is philosophical. He takes the long view, though not too long. He thinks in centuries, in oak trees, but not in millennia, in yews.

'There are gloomy predictions about our predicament with the climate change,' he said. 'But I hope that we will survive and that in five hundred years our children's children's children will be able to come and see this. That's what I am working for. What will happen to the human species in tens of thousands of years, that's another matter. But let's not think about that, because what's the point? That cathedral is part of our civilisation.'

He nodded up at the south aisle, at the gargoyles showing

the diversity of creation, based on Psalm 148: a boar playing the bagpipes; a lion playing the lute; a young woman, pregnant, hair cascading over her belly, as rainwater flows from her jug.

'I have played my part,' Pascal said. 'I have put my little stone down.'

*

As I ARRIVED in Kilpeck one bright May morning, the old house across from the church was being cleared. Solid-looking furniture, the sort you inherit rather than buy, was being taken out of the handsome timber-framed property and loaded into the back of a van. George Meadmore, who had lived there since he was an infant and looked after St Mary and St David's for much of his life, had died at the age of eighty-eight and was now buried in the pretty church-yard that he had for so long tended. Daffodils and tulips that he had planted some months before his death came up, an honour guard, for his funeral.

'This is a sad day,' his niece, Gill, told me. Born in the house sixty-seven years before, she had been baptised and married in the church. Now she and her sister Val – who had also received those sacraments there – were overseeing the clearance. They had found a box of family photographs showing generations of weddings; brides and grooms in black and white and fading colour standing in the church door-way, after the service, as an arch of twelfth-century carving curved above their heads.

Val well remembered the church key which had hung on a nail just outside the front door. How it seemed huge in their little-girl hands, and how, when allowed the treat of locking the great wooden door, they would hold tight to its dull cold weight for fear of losing it. Now the house was empty, and all those small moments of family life existed only as memories, unlocked on occasions such as this and brought out to be admired. 'It's the end of an era,' Gill said.

Yes, and in more ways than one. I had turned up just in time to see a fraying of the ties between church and community. This process is going on all over Britain, but it seemed a particular sorrow here. Kilpeck is extraordinary. The best small Norman church in England, say the guidebooks: 'An extremely modest building but one of the high points of English architectural sculpture.' That is a reference to the luxuriant, almost psychedelic Romanesque carving around the south doorway and the fabulous bestiary of the corbel table – the line of carved blocks helping to support the roof.

The church was built around 1140, possibly incorporating part of an earlier Saxon church, and has been part of the life cycle of this Herefordshire village for centuries. But now Sunday worship was being held just once every third week for a congregation of around ten to fifteen people, and the likelihood was that it would become even less frequent. One needn't listen very hard to hear the 'melancholy, long, withdrawing roar' that Matthew Arnold identified as faith's tide going out. Could these really be Kilpeck church's last years?

Not if Hesketh Millais can help it. The churchwarden is a tall man of seventy, rather patrician in appearance. The painter John Everett Millais was his great-grandfather. 'Like so many churches, our congregation is pitifully small these days and very elderly,' he said, 'but it's a working church still, thank goodness, which gives it life. Otherwise it would just be a monument and rather sad.'

This is key. Churches are more than their stone, no matter how beautifully carved. The solemn loveliness of being inside a country church comes from decay and use held in perfect balance. On the one hand: cool damp air, peeling plaster, spiderwebs on the hymn board. On the other: those old songs sung, the bread broken, the wine sipped. T. S. Eliot said it well: 'You are here to kneel / Where prayer has been valid.' There is a seriousness to an ancient church where people still gather; a weight, but a lightness, too. The weight, in Kilpeck, comes from centuries of worship, the lightness from the knowledge that the prayer books on a shelf at the back of the nave have not – yet – been closed for the final time. There have been an awful lot of yesterdays; but there will be a tomorrow.

'We're very lucky,' Hesketh explained. 'We can survive because we get over a thousand visitors every year.'

There is no charge for entry, but donations are welcome, and there are guidebooks and postcards for sale. The proceeds cover the cost of repairs and subsidise the stipend of the vicar. Kilpeck is part of a benefice of ten rural parishes with small congregations; the sister churches of Wormbridge and St Devereux are listed in one official document as having a combined Sunday flock of twelve people and a dog. All ten churches are served by one vicar supported by retired clergy and lay readers. The impression is of a tradition worn thin, stitched together by a mixture of faith and sheer bloody-mindedness. 'Whether all the other churches will be able to keep going, who knows?' Hesketh said. 'This will be the last to fall, probably.'

The last to fall. Quite a thought. I suppose that one day, unless there is some extraordinary revival, there will be a church in England that is the last of its kind still in use. Imagine that: the last English parish church, the last candle burning.

Kilpeck, if it should be that candle, would certainly be illuminating and delightful. It only takes a minute to walk the perimeter. It is made of red sandstone, 'the colour of newborn children' as Fleur Adcock's poem has it. This place attracts poets. It's not enough to see the church, you have to somehow get it down on paper. Even the birds and beasts are prone to mimesis. Swallows, I saw, had built their own corbel, from mud, on the exterior of the apse, and darted in and out to tend their young. Moles raised mottes among the graves. A fox, harking back to an earlier tradition of sacrifice, had made an altar of the churchyard; the severed wing of a pheasant seemed a dainty offering to some ravening vulpine god.

'The church was built by a chap called Hugh de Kilpeck who was given this area by William the Conqueror,' Hesketh explained. The stony stump of his castle is on a man-made mound just to the west of the church. Once a stronghold raised by an invading culture, it is now the fiefdom of sheep that take their ease in the cool shadows of ruined walls. Medieval Kilpeck was a six-acre site that can be discerned as a series of humps in the fields. That old settlement had a population of around six hundred, but famine and plague in the fourteenth century all but wiped the villagers out. Now, two hundred or so people live here and think fondly of those they have lost; an unopened can of cider, placed on a recent grave, had 'Love you, mate' written on it in marker pen.

Hesketh led the way around the church. He pointed to a row of carved faces, animals and monsters, each around a foot tall and set into the south wall, about a dozen feet up. 'These are what people come to see, these corbels,' he said. 'I think the stonemason was having quite a lot of fun.' There are eighty-nine of them, all different, peering down from just below the roof line. A few have been smashed off or badly damaged, but those that remain include: knights, fanged beasts, a bear devouring two unfortunates; lions and lambs, pigs and rams, and a couple of those unclassifiable chimeras known as beakheads, typical of Romanesque sculpture, that inhabit the liminal zone between charming and sinister. Although the carvings are twelfth century, their style and mostly good condition make them appear much more modern; a cutesy hare and hound, sharing a corbel in cheerful companionship, could be the work of Disney.

'And this,' said Hesketh, 'is the one that gets all the attention: Sheela-na-gig. When we have school parties we have to walk on quickly when we get to this bit.' He stopped below a rosy carving of a naked woman with bald head, saucer eyes and a smirk. She is sometimes described as an exhibitionist, and – as we looked up at her – it was obvious why. Her vulva, mandorla-like, gaped to public gaze. She held herself open with little stone hands as she has done for almost nine hundred years.

\*

The first time I ever heard the words 'Sheela-na-gig' was in 1992 when PJ Harvey released her song of that name. 'Look at these my child-bearing hips,' she sang. 'Look at these my ruby-red, ruby lips.' Harvey is from Somerset and so may have had in mind, not the famous Sheela at Kilpeck, but the much more roughly carved example at the church in the village of Fiddington.

Sheelas are at their most numerous in Ireland. There are around sixty in England; far fewer in Scotland and Wales. They are a fugitive art form. They are discovered from time to time during building and renovation works, lost for centuries, prevented from showing themselves off, and then someone turns over a slab or takes a pick-axe to a wall or notices something odd about a chunk of rubble in a skip, and suddenly there's Sheela, bless her, brazen as ever.

Their meaning, too, is fugitive. One of the frustrating and yet beguiling things about these carvings is that no one knows for sure what they meant, what they were for, or – in many cases – how old they are. There are competing theories. Feelings can run high. A visitor to Kilpeck once took such exception to the interpretation offered by a guidebook on display that they crossed out the terms they considered ignorant and offered, in blue pen, their own. The word 'exhibitionist' was struck through and replaced by 'goddess'. The assertion that the figure represents 'low morals' was deleted. No, the visitor insisted, it is a symbol of 'female creative power'.

Even the name, Sheela-na-gig, is a will o' the wisp. Its use is first recorded in connection with the stone figures in a letter of 1840 written by a man engaged in recording antiquities of County Tipperary as part of the mapping of Ireland. He had heard the name from locals in reference to a carving, since stolen, on the ruined church at Kiltinan. So, it may derive from Irish, although there is no direct translation. 'Sheela', among other spellings, is said to have been the wife of St Patrick, and 'gig' an old slang term for the female genitals or for a sexually promiscuous woman. It could be, however, that those in England were known as something else entirely by the people who carved them and to whom they were meaningful. Certain individual figures have been known as the Witch, the Idol and the Hag of the Castle. Although the Sheela at Kilpeck seems rather too jolly for such titles, she has a confrontational power undimmed by age.

'I think she's absolutely wonderful because she's unapologetic and she doesn't give a damn,' Professor Emma L. E. Rees told me. 'Like the word "cunt", she has all that power to shock, intrigue and amaze.'

Rees is director of the Institute of Gender Studies at the University of Chester. It was an encounter with the Kilpeck

Sheela that inspired her book *The Vagina: A Literary and Cultural History*. Rees had never heard of Sheela-na-gigs until she chanced upon the carving during a visit to the church with her husband in the summer of 1995. 'We spotted her and were absolutely dumbfounded,' she recalled. What on earth was that doing on a church? Even more significant for Rees was the guidebook she bought inside. It contained extracts from an 1842 illustrated book on Kilpeck and its carvings by the artist George Robert Lewis. To her amazement, Rees read that Lewis had interpreted the Sheela as 'a fool – the cut in his chest, the way to his heart, denotes it is always open and to all alike'. Even more troubling, his drawing of the carving departed significantly from reality. The arms and hands were shown pointing away from the body and the vulva – or 'cut' as he had it – was shaped more like a heraldic shield. 'It was totally wilful,' Rees thought. 'As a nineteenth century man, he felt he needed to eradicate her, needed to pretend that she didn't exist.'

But why do Sheela-na-gigs exist? Some who have studied Sheelas see them as representations of a pre-Christian goddess, others as warnings against the sin of lust. They have been classified as belonging to a class of imagery known as 'apotropaic' – images with the power to avert evil influences. In *King of Dust*, a book about his fascination with Romanesque sculpture, Alex Woodcock explains how apotropaic imagery is thought to have worked:

> First, the image could repel malevolent spirits by using concentrated images of abundant life force: impossible monsters (themselves understood to be generated by sexual transgressions), images of violence, exaggerated body parts such as the head or genitalia, and so on. Much of what we describe as grotesque now falls into this category. Then there are the complex and repeated patterns. These, as the anthropologist Alfred Gell has suggested, slow perception down, rendering demons harmless by trapping them in the complexity of the design. Either way, apotropaic images were intended to charm the viewer, human or otherwise, into a kind of paralysis, and by doing so avert any potentially harmful outcomes.

The church at Kilpeck can thus be seen as a kind of dazzle ship, confusing the devil and allowing worshippers to enter safely and pray unhindered.

Dr Barbara Freitag, a former lecturer in intercultural studies at Dublin City University, is the author of *Sheela-na-Gigs: Unravelling An Enigma*. She has travelled throughout Ireland and beyond, including to Kilpeck, studying most Sheelas known to exist and identifying a number of examples that hadn't been recorded before. She regards the carvings as folk deities, used by the medieval peasantry to help with both conception and the perils and pains of childbirth; not pagan as such, but a tradition and belief system that operated alongside Christianity and was, at least at first, tolerated and co-opted into it – as evidenced by the many Sheelas that appear to pre-date the churches into which they were later built.

By the seventeenth century, however, clergy seem to have become far less comfortable with this folkloric imagery; there are records of orders being given that Sheelas should be destroyed, and of priests attacking them; a number of surviving carvings have obvious damage to the genital area. That Sheelas have been found buried in churchyards or turned inward and hidden in walls and gateposts suggests that they were concealed by people who knew that they could not be left on display but were unwilling to see them smashed up. Outrage and disgust, a feeling that Sheelas have no place in a church – such reactions are, unfortunately, not entirely historic. In 2004, a Sheela was chiseled from a wall of All Saints, Buncton, a twelfth-century chapel in Sussex, and smashed to pieces on the floor. One parishioner, quoted in the press, admitted that 'it is not something I'll miss because, after all, it's a pagan symbol in what is a Christian building.'

This point of view may be wrongheaded in more ways than one. First, as we have seen, Sheelas – whatever their origins – were certainly part of the iconography of medieval Christianity. Moreover, they may not be about sexual desire per se. Barbara Freitag feels certain that the display of a Sheela-na-gig is not erotic exhibitionism, but an image of a cervix dilated to such a degree as would make birth go easier. She believes that pregnant women, in the course of some kind of ritual, touched or even placed pebbles inside

the vulva of the carving as a form of sympathetic magic –
desiring that their own bodies would open as easily. This,
remember, was a period when mother and infant deaths
during labour were common. 'Since mortality rates were so
high, women simply had to rely on something,' Freitag told
me. 'If you do what your ancestors have done, and what the
women before you have done, you feel good about it, I think.'

The Kilpeck Sheela is an outlier in the quality of its
workmanship. It is self-evidently the work of a professional
sculptor employed by a wealthy patron as part of a sophisticated and expensive construction job. It could not easily have
been used in the sort of ritual Freitag describes, in that it is
too high up on the wall to reach, and therefore should perhaps
be seen as a pastiche or parody of that tradition, an incorpor-
ation of its imagery, but not its purpose, into the authority of
the church. Most Sheelas, at least those that have survived,
look very different to the one at Kilpeck. They appear to have
been gouged into shape using whatever tools were available
to people who had not been trained to work stone. They are,
to this extent, a sort of folk or outsider art, and they have the
wild energy, the rough magic, that comes when a self-taught
individual creates an object with serious intent but only
native skill. They remind me of early blues field recordings –
all hiss and slur and scratch, but so much more exciting than
later, polished studio versions of the same songs.

Take, for example, the Sheela that Freitag visited in
a farmhouse in Ireland, with its jug ears and incised ribs,
its tiny breasts and chiseled cleft between splayed thighs.
Primitive, talismanic, made with no thought of being pretty
and decorative, it seems more like a manifestation than
something made. 'When I arrived at this village there were
at least four or five other women who the farmer's wife had
invited,' Freitag recalled. 'The Sheela was in a broom cup-

board. She kept it there, hidden away from her husband, and she only wanted me to see it in the presence of other women. So there's still a strong connection with life-giving powers.' These women, she noted, were Christian. This wasn't some neo-pagan gathering. They could respect the Sheela in their midst and still say their prayers. 'What I found was that in Ireland a lot of people still stood in a kind of awe,' she said. 'They considered the Sheela to be something that had to be revered. And the general context always was fertility.'

On another occasion, about ten years ago, in a pub in the suburbs of Dublin, Freitag was present with the permission of the landlord who owned a replica Sheela-na-gig made to look like the old rough kind. He had agreed to help a couple who were having trouble conceiving a child. 'The young woman, who was in her twenties, arrived with her husband,' Freitag remembered. 'The pub owner unveiled the Sheela and she touched the vulva. Then she thanked him, embraced him, and, when she and her husband had left, he put a cloth back over the figure. It was like observing something mystical. I never thought, "How pathetic in this day and age that somebody should want to touch a Sheela." I was moved by the whole scene.'

Perhaps it is little surprise that the power of the carvings has persisted into the twenty-first century. Ambiguity around their meaning and purpose allows us to lay our own preoccupations, anxieties and desires upon them. Sheela makes a holy show of herself and we see what we want to see.

'The Sheela-na-gig has become a symbol of feminism here in Ireland,' one of the street artists behind Project Sheela told me. 'People are really connecting with the ancient traditions.'

Project Sheela is the name given to the activist art of two Dublin women in their early to mid thirties who prefer to remain anonymous. The identities of those who carved the original Sheelas are lost in time, the names of the Project Sheela street artists are deliberately withheld, but the effect is the same: all the power comes from the object and not the individuals behind it. Inspired by the successful campaign to repeal the legislation that had made abortion illegal in Ireland, Project Sheela mark each International Women's Day, 8 March, by making and leaving their own versions of Sheela-na-gigs at sites in the Irish capital and beyond that are significant to women's rights. Their small ceramic Sheelas are made of crank clay, intended to resemble stone when fired, and decorated with glass and gold lustre. The finished objects are then glued into place, secretly, at the chosen location. 'All our Sheelas are confident and strong,' one of the artists explained. 'We use them to draw attention to certain issues, but also to act as a healing.'

Their Sheelas are sometimes meant to shame, such as the one left at the entrance to a former Magdalene laundry – the notoriously cruel workhouses, run by nuns, for so-called 'fallen women' – that had closed as recently as 1996. Others are intended as gestures of sisterly respect; one attached to a wall inside Neary's, a historic pub, is a tribute to an act of civil disobedience carried out in the early 1970s by members of the Irish Women's Liberation Movement. Pubs in Ireland in those days could refuse to serve women a pint of beer unless they were accompanied by a male chaperone. To protest this, thirty women entered Neary's and asked for brandy. When these were poured and lined up, they ordered a single pint of Guinness. The barman refusing, they downed their brandies, turned heel and left without paying.

'The Sheela-na-gig has become the symbol of Irish women reclaiming some power,' the Project Sheela artist told me. 'As an Irish woman, I'm using it as a symbol of empowerment. Sheela is unashamed of her body and sexuality, and confident in herself. There's a lot of shame in Ireland. Even my generation that grew up in Catholic schools, there was a lot of oppression. We've got to the point now where we're ready to let go of that, we're ready to celebrate our bodies and to be more confident in ourselves.'

Sometimes it takes an outsider to see such things. In Kilpeck, Gill and her sister Val had had little to say about the carvings. They were just normal, part of their everyday lives. Gill seemed to have no idea that the Sheela-na-gig even existed. For them, the church is special not because of the way it looks, or its national reputation, but because of its long connection to the family. They belong to it and it to them. They are like those swallows that build their mud nest alongside the corbels, returning season upon season, seeking shelter and the comfort of the familiar, clinging to the time-worn, sun-warmed stone.

# DUST

I crossed the border into Wales and, moments later, pulled off the road at the side of fields. Three farm gates faced me. Those to the left and right bore hand-painted signs warning, 'Beware of the Bull.' The gate in the centre seemed more promising. I could see a little church at the foot of a rutted grassy track: white bellcote rising above trees, cockerel on the weathervane black against the blue sky. Three buzzards circled overhead. Here was St James's, Llangua, at the end of its working life. It was badly in need of friends, and I was glad to make its acquaintance.

Close to, it became obvious that the church was in trouble. It sits in a bend of the River Monnow, which often floods, and the porch was crusted with silt. Scaffolding held up the roof. Headstones poked above long grass like mountaintops through cloud.

'I don't think anyone's been in here for a while,' said Rachel, unlocking the door. 'This church is on my mind a lot. I'm really worried about it.'

Rachel Morley, an Irish woman in her thirties, is director of Friends of Friendless Churches, a small charity dedicated to the rescue, repair and reopening of churches in England and Wales. Since its foundation in 1957, Friends has taken on sixty places of worship that were no longer in use. These churches haunt the countryside. Stone revenants, relicts of villages that have vanished or all but vanished, they sit on salt marshes, in the shadows of mountains, on headlands overlooking the sea. They enclose the deep past; keep the centuries penned in like sheep. Often, these churches are

looked after by a local volunteer, fiercely dutiful, who sees –
or, rather, feels – their importance and has decided to care
for them. That name, Friends of Friendless Churches, says
a lot. These aren't guardians or champions. The tender but
powerful idea of friendship better describes the relationship between people and place that is so much a part of the
charity's ethos. Think of the finger-rhyme: 'Here's the church
and here's the steeple' – well, that's the Friends; taking old
churches in hand.

We went inside. Light angled through diamond panes.
Services were lit by candles in the darker months. But it
had been two years since worship was last held, and by the
end the congregation was down to two; a husband and wife.
Now, the resident population consisted of a great many bees –
an inhospitable order, hostile to visitors – that had made a
cloister of the mossy uneven roof.

'I love these places because they are full of traces of the
people who used them,' Rachel said. 'The greasy timbers,
the threadbare hassocks. When you see a worn step, like that
one there, you think of the feet that went over it. Some of
our churches are on pre-Christian sites; people have found
something important about the spot for thousands of years,
and so I think it's very important that we acknowledge that,
and don't demolish them, and don't sell them off as private
spaces where no one else can go.'

Rachel would like St James's, which dates from the fourteenth century, to join the Friends' portfolio, but the matter
must be weighed. The case for: without proper attention, and
soon, the church could fall down. The case against: it will
cost £300,000 just to fix the roof and make the site safe, more
income than the charity has in an average year. Rachel is
alert to the poetry of old buildings – 'It would be so beautiful
to put thatch on it, and a lovely white render on the walls.

It would just glow. It would be such a happy church.' But she grapples daily with the prosaic realities of the balance sheet.

Money is a constant and increasingly painful headache. The Friends receives no state or church finance in England and only a little in Wales. Yet the qualities that make ancient churches special are difficult to reconcile with the priorities of external funding bodies. There is no tick-box marked 'intangible', nor one marked 'numinous', and Rachel is often frustrated at being asked about a business plan. 'Give me a break,' she sighs at such moments. 'It's a church in the middle of a field. It's a stone box with six benches. It doesn't need a business plan. We're going to gently, quietly look after it, and you can go and visit it. But that's not fundable. That's never enough. I find that so infuriating and lonely.'

Lonely. An unusual expression to use in relation to the position of a charity within the heritage sector. Yet it does not feel inappropriate. Loneliness is a quality that these friend-less churches often embody and emit. There is a particular elegiac pleasure to be had from visiting a church that is no longer in use, or used – as some are – for just one service a year. To walk into one of these buildings, especially alone, is to ache with a kind of exquisite sympathy: one solitary meeting another.

Is that sadness something that Rachel often feels? She nodded. 'Somebody said to me the other day that the Friends of Friendless Churches occupy a space between awe and melancholy. I think that sums it up perfectly. Our work is really melancholic. I see so many parish churches at the end of their life. They are venerable buildings and it's important to treat them with dignity and respect.' She laughed. 'I'm talking about them almost as if they are people.'

They are in a way. What makes them worthy of esteem and attention – their great age – also makes them vulnerable, especially those that are isolated. Most churches looked after by the Friends are in the countryside. These were built before the Industrial Revolution, serving large agrarian populations. The people have long since moved to the towns and cities and, in an increasingly secular society, have moved away from God.

Worshippers in historically significant rural churches are likely to be elderly and shrinking in numbers. But it is up to these people, not the ecclesiastical or civil authorities, to raise the money to fix the guttering, renew the roof, pay the energy bills and so on. This is a financial burden – it is estimated that it will cost £1 billion to fund repairs to the 16,000 Church of England churches over the next few years – but it is also emotional and psychological. It must feel to congregations as if the weight of history is pressing upon their weary shoulders. No one wants the local church to close on their watch, and yet close they do.

The Church of England has a formal process that governs how churches are closed and their futures decided. Attempts are made, for a period of two years, sometimes more, to find an alternative use for the building. It may be sold or leased for housing or commercial use, generating important income. If no use can be found, the building may be vested in the Churches Conservation Trust or demolished. The Friends, as an independent charity, can choose to take on churches which, for one reason or another, do not go to the CCT.

Between 1969 and 2021, the Church of England disposed of 2,013 churches, of which five hundred were demolished. However, there are widespread fears that the pandemic and its aftermath will accelerate closures and selling off. The Friends estimates that a further 368 churches could close by 2026, and that is just the C of E. Some 2,000 or so churches across all denominations have closed in the last decade. For years and years there has been pessimism about the future of churches, but there is now a widespread feeling that the moment of crisis has arrived. We could call this a tipping point, but church people favour eschatological language. 'We're heading for the apocalypse,' one well-informed observer told me.

Across most of the UK these buildings feel precarious and vulnerable. The exception is Northern Ireland, where, although there are declining congregations in both Catholic and Protestant traditions, the point has not been reached – yet – that the threat of closures is widespread. As a result of its particular history, almost all of Northern Ireland's medieval churches are in ruins, and are often found in the churchyards of their nineteenth-century replacements. Only two parish churches of the period – St Nicholas, Carrick-fergus and All Saints, Antrim – are roofed and still used for services.

Brechin Cathedral, in Scotland's north-east, closed for worship in 2021, a year after its eight-hundreth anniversary, facing debts of almost £170,000. In Glasgow, two import-ant Victorian churches reached a crisis within the space of three months. St Simon's in Partick was gutted in an arson attack, and the congregation moved out of Alexander 'Greek' Thompson's St Vincent Street Church after part of the ceiling fell in. 'That was devastating,' said Niall Murphy of Glasgow City Heritage Trust. 'One of Thompson's three churches was destroyed during the war. Another is a stabilised ruin. To lose this third would be a real tragedy.'

It has been estimated that Wales could lose up to 70 per cent of its places of worship over the next twenty years. The valleys are full of empty chapels; the chapels full of rotting organs; the organs full of ghost notes and dust. The problem is acute in that country because a huge number of churches were built in the late nineteenth and early twentieth centuries by non-conformist congregations that have since disbanded or steeply dwindled. Closures are so many and so frequent that even the heritage bodies cannot keep up with them. 'Too often,' writes Christopher Catling of the Royal Commission on the Ancient and Historical Monuments of Wales, 'the first we know of a disposal is when we drive past a chapel and see the broken-up pulpit and pews being piled into a skip or the archives being heaped onto a bonfire.'

Inside the church at Llangua, which is Church of England even though it is in Wales, Rachel gave me the tour. We admired a medieval screen on which is painted a rather wonky Virgin and Child, and the statue of St James wearing a jaunty cockleshell in his hat. Her concern for the building and its contents was palpable: 'This lovely wagon-roof is sixteenth-century, but you can see the whole thing is moving. Look at the massive cracks across that beam. Every single timber has snapped. We need to take it off and rebuild it. But I feel duty-bound to take it on. This is Ivor's church. Our story starts from here.'

Friends of Friendless Churches is not a faith organisation, but it was founded by a man of great faith, Ivor Bulmer-Thomas, who saw these buildings themselves as holy. 'An ancient and beautiful church fulfils its primary function merely by existing,' he believed. 'It is, in itself, and irrespective of the members using it, an act of worship. A beautiful church, whether standing alone in the countryside, or surrounded by wharves and warehouses, offices and houses, is a perpetual reminder of spiritual values.'

There is, in other words, something in the stones. Such churches will have been consecrated – made sacred – by the priest or bishop who blessed them, but they have been anointed by human activity and emotion too, over a long span of time. That people have come to pray, that they have brought their hope and anguish, their boredom during long services, their young to be baptised and their dead to bury – all of that has been absorbed by the building. Break open a piece from an old church wall and you might find joy and grief spiralling, ammonite-like, through the stone.

Ivor Thomas (Bulmer, the maiden name of his second wife, Joan, was added later) has rather fallen out of history and deserves to be put back in. He was born in Cwmbran, Monmouthshire in 1905, the second youngest of four children in a working-class family. His father, a stoker in a brick factory, died in the flu pandemic of 1919. It was expected that Ivor would have to leave school and get a job, but his older sister Beatrice, a seamstress, recognising that he was very bright, offered to do more to support the family so that he could continue his education. He won a scholarship to St John's College, Oxford, taking a double first in mathematics and classics, and making a name as a middle-distance runner of international standing. He also had a gift for languages; Dante, in medieval Italian, was his idea of bedtime reading. Having given serious consideration to joining the Anglican priesthood, he became first a journalist and then a Labour MP. He entered Parliament in 1942 and went on to join the post-war government of Clement Attlee, whom he loathed. In 1948, unwilling to support the nationalisation of steel, he resigned from the party. After a period as an independent, he switched to the Conservatives, but was not re-elected.

Were one to draw a family tree of European politics and culture during the twentieth century, Bulmer-Thomas would be an important point of connection. He met Mussolini in Rome (he did intelligence work during the war, writing anti-fascist propaganda leaflets that were flown over Italy and dropped from planes) and Einstein in London. His children remember T. S. Eliot and John Betjeman coming for tea, and Roy Jenkins playing croquet in the garden. He was a romantic figure, given to the grand gesture. After losing his seat in the House of Commons in 1950, he and a couple of pals drove from London to Dakar, crossing – or, almost crossing – the Sahara in a Ford V-Eight. When the car broke down on the last leg, they were marooned in the desert for four days, keeping themselves going on tea and oranges until the rescue party arrived.

Raised as a Baptist, Thomas joined the Church of England while at university. In April 1932 he married Dilys Jones, the daughter of a surgeon from Merthyr Tydfil. A black and gold plaque on a wall inside the church at Llangua records, in Latin, that she died on 16 August 1938. She was twenty-eight. She had given birth to a son, Michael, in the early summer of that year. He was adopted, following his mother's death, by a Scottish couple, Charles and Isobel Walker, a doctor and his wife.

Michael Walker is now a retired teacher. When I contacted him, he told me that his birth mother had been suffering from post-natal depression – 'which, of course, wasn't understood in the 1930s'. Newspaper reports record the result of an inquest: she had fallen forty feet from the window of a nursing home in Hampstead where she had been a patient for the previous ten days. The doctor who treated her testified that she had been suffering from delusions. Ivor Thomas told the coroner that his wife had a breakdown following childbirth. 'No darkling fears,' he later wrote, 'Can touch her now.'

Grieving, he found consolation in English and Italian poetry, and began to write himself. His poem, 'Dilysia', from which the above quote is taken, was circulated privately among friends in 1939. In 1954, by which time he had remarried, he rescued St James's from dereliction, intending that act as a further tribute to his first wife. She was thus twice memorialised – first in paper and then in stone.

'He was very badly affected by her death,' Victor Bulmer-Thomas, Ivor's son from his second marriage, told me. 'The poem is beautiful. He never wrote any other poetry, but it's extraordinary. And he would always go and put flowers on her grave every year. I think he was very much in love with her.'

Victor's sister Miranda added: 'I think my father sancti-fied Dilys.'

Out of this moment of personal sorrow came the modern church conservation movement. Bulmer-Thomas's restor-ation work at Llangua can be seen as a dry-run for his establishment, three years later, of the Friends of Friendless Churches, and, in 1969, what is now the Churches Con-servation Trust – the two principal organisations that save churches in England and Wales. It is as if, having already lost so much, he was unwilling to accept further losses. When, in 1957, he witnessed the demolition of the church of St Peter the Less in Chichester, he could not help but weep.

The Friends took on its first building in 1972: the surviv-ing tower of Old St Matthew's in Lightcliffe, West Yorkshire, the rest of the church being demolished. Those early years were exhilarating. There was a certain feeling of knightly quest: the chivalric thrill of rescuing a building in distress; the sense that you were on the side of civilisation and against barbarism. An outsider's brag, too, perhaps, that they, the Friends, could see something in these decaying churches that others could not. Father Philip Gray, a priest in his eighties, has been a member of the organisation since he was sixteen years old, when he wrote to Bulmer-Thomas that he was worried about a church in Suffolk at risk of being knocked down. 'I take the view that a church is a sacrament of stone,' he explained when we spoke on the telephone. 'It absolutely points at things of God, much more than a priest does in his sermon. If you lose your church, something goes in your community.'

Ivor Bulmer-Thomas died at home in London in 1993, aged eighty-seven. His legacy? 'Some of the most glorious buildings in the country are safe because of what he did,' Matthew Saunders, a former director of the Friends, told me. Among the notable successes is St Mary the Virgin at Llanfair Kilgeddin, Monmouthshire, with its extraordinary Arts and Crafts sgraffito panels; once threatened with demolition, the church has been looked after for the past thirty years by a farmer who worshipped there as a child.

Then there is St Mary's, Mundon, on the Dengie peninsula in Essex. The window behind the altar looks out toward a field of dead oaks, jutting from the ground like the antlers of some prehistoric herd. This fourteenth-century church closed in 1970, and was acquired, close to collapse, five years later. It was in the worst condition of any property taken on by the Friends. Christine McDonald, a local woman who now looks after the church, remembers climbing in through a broken window with other kids, daring each other to spend ten minutes in there alone. The place was rumoured to be haunted, so this took some steel: 'It was totally overgrown, it smelled of mice and damp, and a sign said Danger – Keep Out. Well, there was nothing more likely to entice Enid Blyton children like us.' Tolstoy – according to popular yarn – had visited St Mary's during his stay in England in 1861. That he would have seen what we still see now, a remarkable little church with timber bell-tower and red pantiles, is thanks to the continuing efforts of people who lose their hearts to these lost causes. Christine, meanwhile, has her own reason to be thankful. She married the boy who, long ago, dared her to go inside.

Rachel Morley keeps on her desk, in a clear 1950s butter dish, a piece of supporting timber from St Mary's, Mundon. She had brought it with her to Llangua. 'Maybe I'm sentimental,' she said, passing me the dish, 'but this I really love.' The wood looked crumbly, more air than tree, honeycombed by the larvae of deathwatch beetle. This artefact once belonged to Ivor Bulmer-Thomas, who had kept it on his desk. It acts now as a reminder to the present director of the scale of the challenge facing the organisation she leads. The work is never-ending and is likely, over the next few years, to become more pressing and intense. Rachel is in the salvation business and there are a great many churches to save. This takes cash, of course, and energy and will, but also a willingness to attend to the small fond duties that keep a place going. After she was finished at St James's, she planned to head over to St Peter's at Llancillo and sweep it out. Then it would be on to the twelfth-century chapel at Urishay, where the grass needed cutting. Unglamorous chores, but she was in no doubt about their necessity and worth.

'These buildings transcend time,' she said. 'They are the spiritual investment and the artistic legacy of generations, and a community's greatest expression of itself over centuries. There's a concentration of shared human experience within their walls, which means that churches like this are a monument to the lives of thousands of ordinary people who have been completely forgotten about. This is their gift to the future. I think that's really powerful and we need to protect it.'

*

GOD IS DEAD. So said the graffiti. Also: Hell Awaits. A vandal had daubed a crude saltire high on an exterior wall; a cross of sorts, I suppose. Above an altar, a huge grinning skull – bright green, a lurid memento mori – had been spray-painted by someone with real skill. A tree was growing from the chimney, and the main chapel, roofless, lay deep in a forest of scaffolding.

This was my first visit to St Peter's Seminary, which can be found, with only a little difficulty, in woodland about twenty miles west of Glasgow. It has been called 'a secret masterpiece', yet it is not so much secret as hidden; indeed, it has become a kind of cult. It is the haunt of graffiti artists, urban explorers and anyone who ever felt drawn by the eerie call of ruins.

I had been meaning to come here for years, intrigued by a building that provokes such love and hatred. 'A masterwork of hideousness and of delusional hubris,' a stonemason had commented when I shared a picture online. Others regard the seminary as Scotland's best post-war building and its decay as a sorrow. There is a third group, to which I belong, who fall into neither camp with regard to the architecture, but are drawn to St Peter's by a sort of gingerbread-house *unheimlich* that both seduces and disturbs. As one of the building's would-be saviours has said, 'There is a sense of it being a netherworld where dark things happen.'

Somehow, though, the opportunity to visit had never arisen until I got to know Father Rafal Sobieszuk and he offered to show me the place. The young Pole is priest at St Bride's, a church in East Kilbride which had been created by the architectural practice Gillespie, Kidd & Coia, that had also designed the seminary complex. While many regard St Bride's as boxy and ugly, Father Rafal thinks it strong and beautiful, and so is inclined to defend those other religious buildings that had been dreamed into life by the same archi-

tects. 'Okay, let's go,' he said, leading the way through the security fence.

St Peter's was built as a training college for Roman Catholic priests. It is Scotland's best-known example of brutalism: the confrontational style, notable for its use of unadorned materials and exposed structure, that has been described as 'a brickbat flung in the public's face'.

Before setting off on the short drive from my home to the site, I had watched an old documentary called *Space and Light*. Without recourse to voiceover or formal interviews, set to harpsichord and flute and the incidental sounds of birdsong and wind in the trees, it shows the seminary as it was in 1972: more spaceship than building. The camera drifts across its jutting angles in a manner that recalls Kubrick's *2001* (the grip, Tony Cridlin, had worked on *A Clockwork Orange*). Seminarians in black soutanes walk, whistling, to Mass and to class, in sunlight and shadow, footsteps echoing in concrete caverns. 'That was a good lecture on the origin of life, wasn't it?' says one. 'I think I'll go and have a shot on the piano.' Here is a world set apart, of young men not in a hurry, filling their days with table tennis and Thomas à Kempis. *Space and Light* is a celebratory film that has become a kind of lament. 'It's tragic, really, the story,' the director, Murray Grigor, had told me.

Father Rafal pointed out the rooms where the students had dined and worshipped and slept. The seminary, even in its ruined state, perhaps especially in that state, seemed vast, weird and magnificent. Just as the great cathedrals of medieval Europe were at the cutting edge of architecture and engineering, so the churches of Gillespie, Kidd & Coia represented a radical vision and, certainly in the case of St Peter's, could inspire feelings of awe.

The practice built fourteen modernist Catholic churches in Scotland between 1957 and 1972. St Peter's Seminary was inaugurated on 30 November 1966 – St Andrew's Day. The architectural historian Diane M. Watters has identified Isi Metzstein as the lead architect, with significant input from Andy MacMillan and John Cowell. Jack Coia, partner in the firm since 1927, secured the commission and led financial and other negotiations with the Archdiocese of Glasgow.

New churches were needed for new places: the New Towns and large peripheral housing schemes planned to accommodate those moving out of overcrowded city centres during the clearing of the slums. It was a moment of cultural optimism, and the forward-looking architecture reflected this. These were churches for people who had faith in the future.

Not all have survived. St Benedict's in Drumchapel, Glasgow, was demolished, controversially, in 1991. The ninety-foot campanile, or bell tower, of St Bride's was knocked down in 1987, twenty-two years after the church opened, because it was cheaper to do so than to repair the deteriorating brick-work. 'I dream about having it back,' Father Rafal told me. Those churches still standing are not as well known and nowhere near as celebrated as they should be. Take Sacred Heart, Cumbernauld, tucked away at the end of a road on a council estate, which just happens to have some of the most beautiful *dalle de verre* windows – by Sadie McLellan, show-ing the Stations of the Cross – that you will see anywhere in the UK.

There really ought to be a trail which would allow people to travel around the country bagging these churches as hill-walkers do with Munros. But Scotland's romantic idea of itself seems for the most part to end with the Second World War, and the sneering attitudes that have made Cumbernauld in particular a byword for ugliness can make it difficult to see these buildings as the treasures that they are. They also have a reputation for being impractical and expensive to maintain. 'I'm one of the few priests who like the work of Gillespie, Kidd & Coia,' Father John Campbell of Sacred Heart said, when I called to arrange a visit. 'Most hear that name and go bonkers and start talking about leaks.'

Even before its formal opening, St Peter's had problems with water ingress. 'This morning flood waters greeted our arrival in the chapel,' reported the college magazine in Octo-ber 1966, 'but there was no Moses to conduct us through dry shod . . .' By the winter of the following year, rain was observed falling into the sanctuary through fifty-three leaks in the lantern. 'Visually, I loved the building. It was brilliant – but utterly useless,' Father John Fitzsimmons, a lecturer at the seminary, once recalled. 'I talked to Jack Coia about the prob-lems, and he answered, "God did not create a perfect world!"'

A few months before our visit to St Peter's, I had attended Mass at St Bride's and then, at Father Rafal's invitation, gone up to the roof. He sometimes climbs there to take tea and take in the view. He led the way up the spiral staircase and along a narrow ledge. Far below, through the pine slats of the false ceiling, I could see the interior of the nave: an immensity of brick and granite. The priest opened a small door and we walked out into daylight. Up a final ladder and we were on the same level as the steel cross, a scabbed-blood brown, that is the roof's only adornment. It is also the sole clue, for those passing on busy roads, that this is a church; you might otherwise take it for a warehouse or factory, some great industrial hulk. The cross proclaims its business, its manufacture of prayer. Looking down the hill, I could make out East Kilbride's parish church, built in the eighteenth century. It is a church that looks like a church, a church that needs no advocates or intercessors. Father Rafal admired its crown-like belfry, but his deepest love is for his own place, St Bride's. 'This is extraordinary,' he said.

St Peter's had been extraordinary, and still is in its way, but its lifespan was just fourteen years. Its problems were numerous and serious, but among the most damaging were an abundance of rain and a scarcity of men. While the seminary was letting in water, it was also failing to retain students. Insufficient numbers wanted to become priests. Some found the life was not for them, and left. Others who, in an earlier generation, might have seen it as an honourable duty to enter the priesthood, were following other paths.

The seminary has now been dead for far longer than it was alive; what one sees are its bones. All the glass is gone, and the metal and wood, and the rain in the west pours down inside. The large concrete cross that was the base of the altar has been exposed, but the holy table itself lies in eight great granite blocks. It was smashed apart quite deliberately so that this most sacred part of the building could not be used for profane purposes; a retreating army salting the fields to deny their enemy nourishment. Even the coffins of Archbishops Eyre and Campbell were exhumed and reinterred in St Andrew's Cathedral. Abandoned by both the living and the dead, unmoored from its mother church, but not yet sunk, St Peter's drifts onward through a kind of purgatory. 'Ach, it is a pity,' Father Rafal said, frowning at the state of the place, 'that they gave up on this building.'

It is a strange pleasure for anyone who has ever walked through these ruins to consider the architectural drawings from which the seminary was built. Before its short life, before its long afterlife, it was an idea – and this is what the plans show. There are 15,000 drawings relating to the work of Gillespie, Kidd & Coia in the Glasgow School of Art archives, a significant proportion of which detail the gestation of St Peter's. They are on tracing paper, in pencil and ink, mostly black, sometimes red. These are precious documents, curated and protected, but they carry evidence of their working life in the form of finger smudges, ragged edges and mug rings. Some appear a little brittle, as if caught in the rain many years ago. It is easy to imagine them being rolled out in a site office, perfumed by fag smoke and coffee breath. I like their bathos: the way they detail the toilets and the tabernacle, the high altar and the drains. I also like the boxes of photos in the archive. Most show the newly built seminary empty of people, but a few hint at the lives led there: an ice-cream van parks by the side-chapels; rosary beads lie on a neatly made bed; a sepia priest, face blurred, walks down the ramp away from the sanctuary and into obscurity.

These photos and the documentary *Space and Light* had left a sort of after-image so that, as we explored the seminary on that day of autumn showers, I could sense the bright sky of a Clydeside summer and the fluttering presence of those fledgling priests, corvine-robed, making their way from room to room. They would be old men now, some dead, but they remained nested in the building's memory.

Later, as the months passed, I spoke with men who had studied there. One, now in his eighties, turned the pages of a book about St Peter's, old photos prompting recollections. There he was in the common room, playing chess. And there, in the background, was a fellow seminarian who, decades hence, would make a terrible mistake: offering the shelter of his church to a homeless man who went on to kill a young woman who also lived there. I had attended the trial and cannot forget the sight of the murderer, a bland demon in a lilac jumper, head bowed in the dock as if in blasphemous prayer. It is extraordinary how the power of a photograph, so mundane in the moment it was taken, can defibrillate the memory and jolt the soul.

Another priest with whom I discussed the seminary, Father Gerry Chromy, was a student there from 1970 until his ordination in 1976. He was seventeen when he arrived. He knew St Bride's, which everyone called Fort Apache for its citadel bulk, but St Peter's was on another level in grandeur and scale. The first time he saw the place was the day he moved in, driven there by his father. It must have been disorienting – and this would have been the experience of many – to go from being a schoolboy living at home to being part of a community of trainee priests living in a giant building in the woods. The seminary had been overwhelming at first, but he got used to it: the monastic rhythm of prayer and study; the perfect choreography of the liturgy; Sister Lucy's cooking; the cold and noise and leaks. Those in their first two years were known as Philosophers, because they studied philosophy, and the more senior students were Theologians. The priest-lecturers were referred to as the Profs. In Chromy's first year there were fifty-four seminarians living at St Peter's and by his final year only twenty or so. The building had capacity for just over a hundred. 'There was a sadness,' he recalled, 'that it was coming to an end.' He has walked around the ruins and peered in the glassless window of his old bedroom, seeing all the time, in his mind's eye, the way things used to be. 'Who could have foreseen what happened?' he said.

In February 1980, the remaining students left St Peter's and transferred to a former convent in Glasgow, later moving again to Scotus College in Bearsden, an affluent town west of the city. Now, each year, around ten Scots begin their studies for the priesthood, but they no longer do so in their native land. The last seminary closed in 2009, bringing to an end three hundred years of tradition. Scotland's priests, these days, are made in Rome, most studying at the Pontifical Scots College, though a few receive training at seminaries in England, such as Oscott on the outskirts of Birmingham. None of these buildings resemble interplanetary craft.

What to do with St Peter's? There has been talk of converting it to a conference centre, a hotel, a nursing home, an apartment building and of demolishing it altogether. Between 1983 and 1987 it was a drug rehabilitation centre. In 1992, Historic Scotland gave it Category A status, the highest level of protection available. Over ten nights in March 2016, the arts organisation NVA staged a promenade event, Hinterland, using music and light to intensify the widdershins drama of the site, but was unable to secure the funding to effect a permanent transformation into an arts venue. In 2019, the Scottish government declined to take St Peter's into state ownership.

It was clear, as the years passed, that the Archdiocese of Glasgow was growing ever more frustrated with the costly problem. The seminary was, a spokesman said, 'an albatross around our neck'. They felt burdened: unable to sell the building, give it away or knock it down. A year later, however, the ownership was transferred to Kilmahew Education Trust. The charitable body hopes to see the 140-acre estate achieve UNESCO World Heritage status by the 2030s, and attract upwards of 375,000 visitors annually.

For now, as I write, the seminary lies empty and fenced-off. A notice on the owner's website warns that it is closed to the public, and that those who enter risk falls and fatal injuries. It did not feel safe when I visited. I would not like to have been there on my own. But then it is not a place where one ever does feel alone.

I am reminded, whenever I come to think about the seminary, of an expression by the writer David Southwell: feral churches. These, he has written, are 'places without regular congregation, places returned to older ways, green prayers. Most guidebooks call them abandoned, deconsecrated or empty. Yet they never feel any of those, rather filled with spirits and the holiness of wild things.'

That seems about right for St Peter's. It is consoling – and perhaps a little unsettling – to think of it as not unused but untamed.

*

ONE WARM AFTERNOON in the summer of 1992, Gloria Davey returned home to North Pickenham, Norfolk, with news for her husband Bob. Her ramble with the local Women's Institute had taken an unexpected turn. She had discovered, on a low hill near Swaffham, an old ruined church, its tower draped in ivy like a bird cage beneath a sheet. Forcing her way inside, through thickets of thorns, she had seen, in the gloom, something troubling.

'What did you find?' asked Bob.

'A Satanic temple,' Gloria replied.

Well, Bob was straight over there, all in a rush, and what he found upset him: a pentacle drawn on the floor, inverted crosses daubed on the walls, and an altar laid out for a black mass. There were human bones; an old grave shucked. 'I'm not having the church abused in this way,' Bob said to himself. 'I've got to take this on.' He had a sense, as soon as he entered the building, that he was supposed to be there, that this was God's plan. It was the feeling a key has for a lock: the just-rightness of proper place and purpose, the turning moment of a life. He set to work.

'From then on, he came here every single day, including Christmas Day,' Delna Barrett, a close friend of Bob and Gloria, told me. 'Oh, it was more than an obsession. There was nothing else left in his life. Nothing else mattered. The church came first.'

Bob Davey was a little old man with a great white beard, which saw him compared, variously, to a garden gnome, an Old Testament prophet and Father Christmas. He grew up on the Sussex Downs, falling into ponds and out of trees, spent his working life as a superintendent in charge of sewage works, and moved to North Pickenham in 1987 with the idea of becoming an antiques dealer. He was seventy-three when Gloria discovered St Mary the Virgin and ninety-one at his death in 2021, by which time the church had not only been restored, but had come to be regarded as internationally important. 'I could recommend this to anyone,' he once said. 'When you retire, take on a ruined church. You'll never look back.'

I visited St Mary's on the hottest day of the year. Poppies blazed along the edges of cornfields and turbine blades stirred the soupy air. As I arrived, Delna was bringing supplies of water to a woman who had been evicted and was now camping in the churchyard. Delna agreeing to meet me was another kindness; she is in her late eighties and finds it strange being at the church now that Bob's not there. Still, she was glad to talk about him, and had asked along another couple of old friends who, like her, had been both participants in and witnesses to his saving this place.

'Oh!' said Janet Oxborough, walking into the sudden cool of the nave. 'Ain't this a blessing?'

She had come with her husband, Peter, who had brought files of photographs showing the way the church used to look. In a word: unsettling; no door, no roof, no windows, the walls a sick dank green. The doorway was a dark pit, like the lair of some beast. Glossy leaves shrouded the stone. 'I thought if we took the ivy off, it would all fall down,' Peter recalled.

St Mary's is thought to date from about 1090. There is some evidence that a wooden Saxon church was on the site before that, said to have been established in the seventh century by the missionary St Felix, who had been saved from drowning by a colony of beavers. The church served a small village, Houghton-on-the-Hill, which was abandoned in the 1940s. What homes remained were cleared, and St Mary's now sits amid trees and farmland. Its square tower, said by some to be the highest point in the county, rises from the pretty churchyard where Bob planted thousands of flowers. Just inside the west door is the block of wood, a rough chunk of the old rafters, on which he used to place his hat before starting the day's work.

His first priority was to stop Satanists using the church. He was a forceful character, not afraid of confrontation, indeed he seemed to rather enjoy it. He worked out when the group were having rituals and began camping out to prevent access. The devil-worshippers weren't happy. One night, as he was standing in the road to block their way, they tried to run him down. 'Somebody even came to my front door and threatened me with death if I carried on working here,' he once recalled, cheerily. A Christian all his life, he regarded himself as being engaged in a battle between good and evil, and to make sure that his side triumphed he had no hesitation in calling upon earthly powers. These arrived in the form of men from the local Territorial Army. On Hallowe'en 1996, the Satanists turned up at St Mary's, expecting to find Bob alone, and instead found themselves faced down by a group of soldiers. They fled and did not return.

All this time, Bob and his friends had been busy clearing the church of ivy and blackthorn and brambles and fallen timber and rubbish of all kinds.

'I was the bonfire queen,' laughed Delna, looking at a photograph of her younger self.

Following the initial clear-up, Bob began restoration, funding it himself at first, and doing whatever work he could with his own hands. He used a barrow and shovel to build an access road almost a mile long. 'This place has cost me a fortune,' he said, 'but the good thing about that is: once you put your own money in, people know you're serious.' He and Peter found the original stone altar being used as a step outside. Other fittings, dispersed around nearby villages, required detective work. The font was a garden planter. The holy water stoup was a bird bath. The floor tiles were found laid in a kitchen. Bob even recovered the eighteenth-century parish chest and a sixteenth-century silver chalice. He had let it be known that there was an amnesty: return what belongs to the church and he would say no more about it.

The greatest treasure, however, lay within the walls themselves. Bob was in the church one day when some plaster fell. He saw a patch of red and went over for a closer look. Revealed on the east wall, for the first time in five hundred

years, was the face of an angel. It had large eyes, three sets of wings, and was blowing a trumpet to raise the dead. Experts were called in, and it was discovered that the nave is covered in paintings, concealed and forgotten, thought to date from the foundation of the church in the late eleventh century.

Those angels blowing their trumpets are part of the earliest surviving depiction of the Last Judgement in English painting. On the north wall is the only surviving representation of Noah's Ark, and on the same wall one can see Eve created from Adam's rib. The original painting scheme was covered with limewash, and a number of layers have been applied over the centuries as doctrine and fashion changed. What has been uncovered is fragmentary and confusing and has lost much of its colour, but it offers a glimpse into a deep past of deep faith. My grandmother, in her last years, recalled moments from her childhood with great clarity, but the present left no mark on her at all. This old church seems to me the same. Those jumbled ochre images of faces and scenes – it is as if St Mary's is remembering her own earliest days.

How thrilling to think that these paintings were hidden in the church all this time. They were there when the Black Death raged and Julian of Norwich, thirty miles east, had her sick-bed visions of Christ. They were there when a Zeppelin dropped a bomb beside the tower and lumbered back over the North Sea to Germany. And it is likely that they would never have been discovered had Gloria Davey not taken a notion that summer day to see what lay within a dark and forbidding doorway.

Outside in the churchyard, in a sunny spot surrounded by flowers, are two unfussy stones. Bob and Gloria are next to one another, close to the place that was so important to them. Churches outlive people. A human lifespan, to a church, must seem a passing season. Yet just as the seasons provide markers and definition in our lives, so do those lives mark and define the churches they attend. A man paints an angel on a wall. Nine hundred years later another man uncovers it. The church, through the actions of both painter and restorer, is found to be important and saved for the future. The story of St Mary's is therefore about friendship and kinship: between the many generations who saw value in this place, and the group of pals who decided that value was worth their time and work and sweat.

'We were a good gang, actually, weren't we?' said Delna.

'Good old buddies,' Peter replied. 'Oh yes.'

# PAINT

*Stanley Spencer painting Holy Trinity,
Cookham, May 1953*

COOKHAM CHURCHYARD on a day of spring showers. A rabbit jinked between headstones; a St George's Cross flew from the tower; a cormorant inked the air. It was easy, in this Thameside nook, to imagine the dead rising from their graves.

What made it easy was that Stanley Spencer had painted it. *The Resurrection, Cookham* is one of England's strangest and most celebrated paintings. Spencer completed it in 1927 and it was bought, before long, by the Tate – where it can be seen to this day. Across its eighteen feet, villagers climb sleepy-eyed out of the earth and take their ease among the ivy and daisies; a wife brushes soil from the shoulders of her husband; a woman, still half-sunk, takes a moment to sniff a flower. Spencer put himself in the picture – lying back on a broken tomb – and in a way that was prophetic. His own grave is in the churchyard, just off the main path, a simple stone for a complicated man.

Where else could he have been laid to rest but here? The Berkshire village was more than his home and more than a muse, it was an object of devotion. 'Places in Cookham seem to me possessed of a sacred presence,' he wrote, 'of which the inhabitants are not aware.' It felt quite natural to him that the Annunciation would have taken place in the sheep field below Cliveden woods, and that Christ would preach from a barge on the Thames – the latter the subject of a large unfinished painting in Cookham's Stanley Spencer Gallery.

An exhibition was on when I visited, called 'Love, Art, Loss: The Wives of Stanley Spencer'. His work would be ever in danger of being overshadowed by the drama of his marriages were it not for the fact that his painting is so often obsessively about those women, Hilda Carline and Patricia Preece. Spencer's trinity of love and sex and faith is indivisible. Hilda, his first wife, died in 1950 and he continued to write letters to her until his own passing in 1959. Death was something that Spencer felt he could, if inconvenient, ignore.

Also in the gallery was a wondrous relic: his daughter Shirin's pram, ragged and rusty now, which he used, once she had outgrown it, to wheel materials to places he wanted to paint. The pram contained an umbrella, to keep off the rain, and a sign to keep off the curious:

> As he is anxious to
> complete his painting
> of the churchyard
> MR STANLEY SPENCER
> would be grateful if
> visitors would kindly
> avoid distracting his
> attention from the work.

Spencer, as the sign suggests, was a public figure and a local landmark; five foot two of artistic eccentricity. 'To know intimately, as I did, he was most strange and a little mad,' one friend recalled. 'Seen with his long shabby coat, his package under his arm, his curious gaze, his rodent-like scurry, he was a fantastic figure in Cookham High Street. When he passed the shop girls used to titter.' The same friend thought him 'of monkish temperament' – not in his sexual desires, certainly, but in his appetite for solitude and the pleasures of the inner life.

I walked to Holy Trinity Church with Ann Danks, the archivist at the gallery, and we sheltered from a downpour in the wooden porch. She had brought along a reproduction of the *Resurrection* but it wasn't possible to map the image on to the churchyard. Spencer had painted it in Hampstead and taken a few liberties. The general look of the place was the same, though, and someone, we noticed, had marked their own recent loss by laying a bouquet of lilies and white roses, like those in the painting, on top of an old chest tomb. The world between the wars did not feel far away.

'As a child, this was almost his playground,' Ann said of the churchyard. 'He would have known it intimately. He called Cookham a village in heaven, and it was very much part of his psyche.'

Stanley Spencer was born in the summer of 1891, the second youngest of nine surviving children, in a house that is still there on the High Street. The hour of his birth was marked by an omen: a crow fell down the chimney, flew out into the dining room and through an open window. Spencer cherished the nest and would never quite be fully fledged. He spent most of his life in Cookham. The first time he left was to go to war.

He joined the Royal Army Medical Corps as an orderly in July 1915 and was posted to Beaufort War Hospital in Bristol. His father called through the window of the departing train of recruits, telling the soldier in charge, 'Take care of him, he's valuable.' Just over a year later he was sent to Macedonia with a field ambulance unit. In August 1917, he volunteered to fight and was accepted into the Royal Berkshires. He joined his battalion on the Salonica front in February 1918 and was with them until the end of the war. He survived, but his family – like so many – suffered a terrible loss. His brother Sydney, who had planned to become an Anglican priest, was killed while fighting in France.

Many of Spencer's experiences of the war, and his feel-ings about it, are expressed in the scheme of wall paintings that are regarded as his masterpiece and which have been described as Britain's Sistine Chapel. 'You walk in there,' I was told ahead of my visit, 'and you are about as close as you're ever going to get to the mind of Stanley Spencer.'

Sandham Memorial Chapel in Burghclere, Hampshire, is around an hour's drive south-west of Cookham. It was a dull morning when I arrived, but no chances were being taken. The blinds were raised so that I could see the paintings by grey mizzled light, but lowered again at the first sign of sunshine. Spencer's pictures, many of which show the wounded being treated, are approaching their centenary and are themselves patients in need of gentle handling. 'Take care of them,' one might beg. 'They are valuable.'

The building, now a National Trust property although still used for occasional services, was constructed of red brick and is rather functional in appearance. Spencer called it his 'holy box'. He first had the idea of a sequence of war paintings while serving in Macedonia, and was fortunate, in the early 1920s, to meet patrons – Mary and John Louis Behrend – who were willing to fund the work and build a small chapel to display them in perpetuity. Like Spencer, Mary Behrend had lost a brother, Harry Sandham, to the war, which must have been a point of sympathy between them, and the chapel would also serve as a memorial to him. First finishing his Cookham resurrection painting, Spencer moved to Burghclere in the summer of 1927 and got to work.

You pass through the oak door and into the Great War. You take a few steps and reach eternity. From floor to ceiling, the north, south and east walls are covered in pictures, and it is the east wall, directly across from the door and windows, that you see first. This is an enormous painting, twenty-one feet high by seventeen or so wide, called *The Resurrection of the Soldiers*. The English dead have risen, but this time it is from a foreign field: one of those battlefield cemeteries in which white wooden crosses sanctify and sanitise violent death. The soldiers pull their grave markers from the ground, by the walled village of Kalinova, making a firewood jumble in the foreground, or else, much further up the picture, presenting them to the quartermaster, Christ.

'The crosses mean as much to a dead soldier as a rifle to a living one,' wrote George Behrend, the son of John Louis and Mary, 'and, like a rifle, they have to be handed in when done with, or so it seemed to Spencer.' It is not a painting of rotting horrors, as the subject might have been in the hands of, say, Otto Dix. Spencer's infantrymen seem better for their rest. They wind their puttees, polish their buttons, shake hands as if at a regimental reunion. If there is a hell, they have left it behind; all the devils are elsewhere. The painting is the supreme example of Spencer's ability to perceive the divine and benevolent in the everyday, to see God in mud.

As Christopher Neve observes in his book *Unquiet Landscape*, 'art is the natural ally of religion'. Both require thought, focus and a sense of wonder. The intense noticing of a painter, or indeed a poet, is a form of worship, and the act of recording the world in oil paint or ink a transfiguration. The other paintings in the Sandham Memorial Chapel reflect this idea. These are war pictures without war in them, or at least without conflict. While the altarpiece on the east wall is a work of imagination, the rest depict experiences Spencer himself had, and chores he performed in the war hospital and elsewhere during his service. A sample of titles gives a flavour: *Ablutions; Kit Inspection; Frostbite; Tea in the Hospital Ward; Scrubbing Floors.* If these paintings had an odour they would smell of iodine, damp washing, fried bacon, jam and feet.

War consists of months of boredom and moments of terror, and here was a painter who hallowed boredom and consecrated the mundane. Terror was never his subject. 'I am on the side,' he said, 'of the angels and dirt.' He was drawn to litter and clutter, bits and bobs. Even a mouldy cabbage could be holy. 'Sometimes it seems as though Spencer possessed an extra sense, as though he had access to a secret language of objects, an arcane music of tea-urns, bed-pans and railings,' Kitty Hauser has written. 'Certainly things and places seemed to him to possess a double identity, corresponding both to this world and another, heavenly world.'

In 1947, reflecting on the war, Spencer's thoughts turned to the brick kilns that the Royal Army Medical Corps would build to burn refuse such as soiled bandages – and how these unlovely objects seemed to him: '. . . every incinerator was an altar.' His paintings are not evangelistic, he wasn't that sort of Christian, but they allowed him to show the world as he saw it. More than that, his work is deeply redemptive. These paintings were a way of processing the trauma of war and getting back to the person and artist he was before he left Cookham. 'By this means,' he explained, 'I recover my lost self.'

On my visit to the chapel, I met Alison Paton and we looked at the pictures together. The chapel had been closed as a result of the pandemic, and had only now reopened, which meant this was her first visit in a year. What was it like to be back?

'Lovely,' she replied, quietly. 'It's such a special place. There's a feeling of safety here, and you cannot but be moved by the power of what you see.'

She had started volunteering in 2009, in her forties, went on to be operations manager, and since 2018 has been a volunteer again. 'When I started here I was struggling with mental health issues,' she explained. These included feelings of worthlessness and panic. She subsequently had to retire from her professional life as a lawyer. Working in the chapel and its garden was an instrumental part of her recovery – it brought peace. 'It was a salvation,' she said.

What was in Spencer's work that made it so? It was something to do, she thought, with the modesty of what he had portrayed – the solace of performing small tasks, of just getting through the day – alongside the vision and grandeur of the execution. The chapel has the power both to enthral and console. Churches are places of transubstantiation – bread into flesh, wine into blood – and so it is fitting that a man's pain should become art here, and that the pain of others should, on seeing that art, be soothed.

'Did you recover your own lost self in here?' I asked.

Alison shook her head. 'I think I changed. I changed very much for the better because my life was no longer dictated by the constant depression, anxiety and lack of confidence that had built up over years and years.'

Many people have found the chapel and paintings a solace, in particular veterans of conflict – some suffering with post-traumatic stress disorder – who discover in these pictures from the First World War a reflection of their more recent experience in Afghanistan, Iraq and so on. Alison has seen them in tears. One wishes, hearing this, that it was possible to call back through time and let Spencer know that, more than a century after he painted them, these works are not only admired but actively helpful in people's lives. He would surely be chuffed at such news. Art, he felt, was a way of saying 'ta' to God. Well, there are lots who have cause to say 'ta' to Stanley Spencer.

He spent almost six years in this place, dedicating himself to the chapel until 1932. He worked from scaffolding; wire netting kept him from falling backwards. He listened to Bach on a wind-up gramophone. He wrapped his baby daughter Unity in a shawl and laid her on a chair while he painted.

New life in a room full of the dead. He had seen so many bodies. He had lost a brother. Now, here in Hampshire, he remade the war and made himself immortal.

'Good morning, Stanley,' Alison used to say to the air when getting the chapel ready for a new day. He was there, of course he was, in the paint and the silence and the pale resurrected light.

\*

IT HANGS LIKE a fading memory, like a fragment of a dream, in the dim and dark and dust. It is a painting made of four paintings. Together, they show loose folds of white cloth. The paintings do not quite touch, and the space between them forms, in shadow, a cross.

This work of art is called *Still* and is by the painter Alison Watt.

*Still* has been part of Old Saint Paul's, Edinburgh, since 2004. I almost wrote that the painting had been 'on display' since then, but that would be the wrong way to put it. Is a shaft of light in an empty room on display? Is a guttering candle? *Still* is a large work – twelve feet square – that commands attention but does not crave it.

'There she is,' said Richard Holloway, leading the way into the chapel, when I met him at Old Saint Paul's one cold morning in November.

Holloway, a former Bishop of Edinburgh, is an old man – 'My departure has been long delayed. I'll be eighty-seven in two weeks' time. Ridiculous . . .' – who has retained the urgent forward momentum of youth. Strikingly tall and slender, he gives the impression of being italicised, leaning into life. He has that particular air of wisdom which emanates from people who have learned to be satisfied with questions not answers.

It is not so strange that he would refer to *Still* as she – he associates it with Alison Watt, his dear friend, and feels for the painting and for this church a familiar and passionate love. He has been coming here for decades. He first visited while on holiday from Kelham Hall, a seminary in Nottinghamshire. 'I was sixteen years old. During the Easter vacation of 1950, I travelled up on the train with a young man called Aeneas MacIntosh – great name, only a Highlander would have that name. We got off the train at Waverley, we had an hour to wait for connections, and he said, "There's an interesting church up here ..."'

Passing beneath the great arch of the Scotsman bridge, what they would have found on Jeffrey Street is much as one finds now. Old Saint Paul's is a black arrow of soot-dark stone. A sign explains that it is part of the Scottish Episcopal Church: 'Founded in 1689, Old Saint Paul's has been an

18th-century refuge for Jacobites, a 19th-century home for Anglo-Catholic revival, a 20th-century centre of spirituality and action, a 21st-century community of prayer and service.' Hung on the front is a wooden Crucifixion, Christ gazing across the valley of the railway station to St Andrew's House, the art deco seat of the government, and the Balmoral Hotel – the great clock of which is kept three minutes fast, the better to hurry commuters towards their trains.

On either side of the church is a close, the word used in Edinburgh for the steep, narrow passages that run like ribs from the spine of the Royal Mile. North Gray's Close is strewn with rubbish, jungled with buddleia, and features the world's least effective blue plaque: a tribute to Albert Ernest Laurie, who was rector of the church between 1897 and 1937. The plaque is more or less hidden from public view and Laurie's name has been obscured with black spray paint. Carruber's Close, on the other side of the church, is gaudy with graffiti and smells like a toilet. One day, no doubt, the passageways will be cleaned up and restored, but for the moment Old Saint Paul's sits in the midst of squalor, a contrast Richard Holloway enjoys. When he first visited the church, seventy years before, he came in through the side entrance off Carruber's Close, and, even now, remembers the experience vividly: 'You open this inauspicious little door and you walk into mystery.'

On that day in 1950, he had arrived in time for morning Mass, which was being held in the Lady Chapel. He had never been in Old Saint Paul's before, but, 'It felt like a strange kind of homecoming. Especially going into the chapel, which sits like a wee lifeboat above the nave. I can't explain it. I've always had a kind of mystical feeling for place. Some places are sacred, powerful, giving places, and this was immediately one of them.'

# PAINT

Old Saint Paul's is a dark space. More than that, it feels dark and full of shadows. Photos show the gold of the reredos, the colours of the stained glass, but the impression when you are inside is of a palette of grey and black. I have never known a church with a greater weight of melancholy. If it is an unburdening place to visit then that is not because you leave feeling cheered up. It's more like when you are sad and listen to sad songs – to sense one's emotions being mirrored by another consciousness, whether an old church or an old crooner, brings comfort.

Those with an instinct for the melancholic, as Richard Holloway has, those who bear into this place their own sadnesses, may find that they fall in love with the church. They may find it a sigh made of stone.

Old Saint Paul's, being so near Edinburgh's rail terminus, is a good place to sit for a while before catching the train home. It acts as an airlock between the day's work and the evening's rest. One needn't be a believer to find consolation here. One need never attend a service. Indeed, the spirit of Old Saint Paul's may be at its most potent when the church is empty and there is nothing going on.

'It seems to me that churches – at least, the kind of churches I like – are not theatres where you go just for an event,' Holloway said when I asked about this. 'Churches that are kept open, especially if they have this kind of mystical Catholic tradition, are places of solace. You see people in corners crying, saying their prayers, or just passing the time.

'This church listens, it discloses, it withholds, it comforts, it challenges. It's a place to bring the complexity of a human life, which is why I'm always sad when places like this have to shut. They are a kind of resource for needy people, and we're all needy in all sorts of ways. And I like that it's dim. Who was the poet that said places that are dark are best for prayer? I think it was John Donne. You come in as if in hiding and you can bring your sorrow, your penitence, all of that.'

We had walked up the Calvary Stair from the street. This is the name given to the thirty-three stone steps – one for every year of the life of Christ. As rector of Old Saint Paul's for twelve years, Holloway led many a funeral procession down those steps and out to the waiting hearse. It has been a privilege and a sorrow to have lived so much of his life with a coffin at his back.

Holloway is an 'unbelieving Christian' – an admirer of Jesus who is not sure about God and heaven and all of that. By the time he became priest at Old Saint Paul's in 1968, his faith was already weak but this Edinburgh church seemed to suit that weakness. It was a building which, in its sadness, seemed to speak more eloquently of doubt than conviction. 'I knew I had an unquiet heart,' Holloway wrote in his memoir, *Leaving Alexandria*, and Old Saint Paul's seems to keep the same broken beat.

We sat in the Memorial Chapel on two wooden chairs, and looked at *Still*. Two figures in dark clothes seated before this pale ghost. Cold light from a side window spilled across the names of the dead.

They are written on the walls, those names. One hundred and forty-six men and one woman: Sybil Lewis, a doctor who served in Serbia and Macedonia during the First World War, spending four months as a prisoner-of-war in Hungary, and dying from an illness in 1918; her ashes are buried in the church. The chapel, which remembers those from the parish who died during the world wars, is a small austere space. It was consecrated in 1926, but, some feel, was not truly complete until *Still* was hung in 2004.

At that time, Alison Watt was an acclaimed and accomplished artist in her late thirties, with a solo exhibition at the Scottish National Gallery of Modern Art behind her. She had long harboured an idea of making a painting for a non-secular space. But where? It was Richard Holloway who introduced her to Old Saint Paul's.

'The first thing I remember was the smell,' she told me. 'I was brought up as a Catholic so I'm very aware of that smell of incense and old wood and candles. All of that immediately hit me. I stood at the back for a while and allowed my eyes to become accustomed. Then, as soon as I walked into the Memorial Chapel, I just knew that I was going to make work for that space. I wanted to describe in some way how I felt.'

And how was that? The answer is complex. She felt safe, she felt embraced, 'But the overwhelming feeling was sadness. I find it impossible to look at those names on the walls and not immediately conjure in my head who those people might have been. Making the painting was a way of articulating something that's hard for me to say in words.'

Watt has no religious faith, but the imagery of her upbringing has stayed with her and infused her work. 'Robert Mapplethorpe said something I love: "If you are brought up as Catholic, everything you make will be an altar."'

She, like most people, refers to the Memorial Chapel. Richard Holloway prefers to use its older name – the Warriors' Chapel: 'To me, these were warriors,' he said, gesturing towards the names. 'I admire soldiers. I rarely admire the men in panelled offices who send them to die, but I admire the men and women who go.'

His preference is shaped, perhaps, by the fact that he has experience of war and its consequences. Born in Glasgow in 1933, he moved to the town of Alexandria, in the Vale of Leven, when he was seven. 'My father took me out into the street one night in March 1941 to look at the red sky above

Clydebank.' This was the industrial town being burned by the Luftwaffe. Of 12,000 homes, 4,000 were completely destroyed; 528 people were killed and 627 seriously injured. The Holloways observed this inferno from ten miles to the west. 'He took me and my wee sister Helen out and told us not to forget.' The following day, Holloway's father, Arthur, encountered a family of bombed-out refugees – a husband, wife and daughter – and brought them home to live with them. Here was an early lesson in good and evil.

Meanwhile, just across the Clyde at Port Glasgow, Stanley Spencer was at work on his shipbuilding paintings – rendering in oil the sanctifying fire of a welder's torch. Art could make war work look noble, and perhaps it was, but there was nothing noble about the aftermath of the Clydebank Blitz. The *Glasgow Herald* of 18 March 1941 reported on the burial of unidentified casualties, children among them, in a common grave: 'The bodies, wrapped in white shrouds covered with Union Jacks, were transported in five large vans to the cemetery, where policemen acted as pall-bearers.'

The chapel in Old Saint Paul's, which is used daily for morning Mass, was built with two purposes in mind: to remember the lost lives of the Great War and to have a place in the church where the dead could rest on the night before the funeral. It is a small and sombre space, the grey walls ensanguined, when I visited just after Remembrance Sunday, with gashes of red – poppies dividing the columns of names. The chapel was the vision of Albert Ernest Laurie, the priest with whom Old Saint Paul's is closely associated. 'He was an extraordinary man,' Holloway said. His Edinburgh parish, which he joined first as a lay reader in the late nineteenth century, was a slum, and he became known for his pragmatic compassion toward the poor and vulnerable. There are stories of him going out in the freezing darkness to light fires and make tea for those on their sick-beds before opening the church in the morning.

When the war broke out in 1914, a great many young men from the parish went off to fight. Laurie, who was in his late forties, volunteered to become a chaplain. He was awarded the Military Cross twice – the first for his actions during the opening day of the Battle of the Somme. 'He worked all day in helping the wounded back from the front line trenches under heavy fire,' the citation reads. 'When his brigade was withdrawn he remained and continued collecting wounded for two days and two nights under heavy fire, showing an utter disregard of personal danger.' His second medal came a year later for similar actions during the Battle of Brood-seinde.

Both citations mention 'gallantry and devotion to duty' but Laurie seems not to have found much gallant about war. In the year before his death, he reflected upon his first experience of the battlefield – 6 July 1915 – when the 1st East Lancashire Regiment attacked the Pilckem Ridge on the Ypres Salient. He wrote in the Old Saint Paul's magazine that he had been emotionally and psychologically unprepared for what he encountered:

> Up to this time ghastly wounds, frightful agonies of death had been alleviated by the kindly humanities possible even in a Field Hospital, but how difficult it was to refrain from tears, how one's whole being quivered with indignation, or sickened with shameful horror as one went from one writhing figure to another, with the consciousness of such feeble helplessness! Words that seemed utterly futile, trivial efforts at relief that mocked the agonies of the torn and battered, muddy and bloody figures, so many of whom I had preached to and

communicated but a few hours before. The tenderness of their dying messages, the heroic endurance of their misery, were almost beyond bearing. I can remember in a tempest of indignant grief, catching the arm of the cool young surgeon who was with me, with the cry, 'How is it possible that such things can be?'

The chapel is a place of public remembrance that feels like an expression of private grief. There is something obsessive and intense about it. One could regard this as a post-traumatic building for a post-faith age; a chapel for those who had known hell and were, as a result, no longer as certain of heaven. 'The story that moves me most is that Laurie used to come along here at night, when the church was shut, and remember the names,' Holloway said. 'I cry thinking about it.' Stifling a sob, he continued. 'He used to swing a little pot of incense and name the names. He would have known them all. There's a real potency to the remembering he did in here. An extraordinary thing to have done.'

During his years as rector of Old Saint Paul's, Holloway lived in Lauder House, Laurie's former home, where in 1937 he had died. He made it his habit to sit at the fireside after evensong, reading his predecessor's library of Trollope novels, each pencilled with Laurie's signature. It is clear that he feels a strong personal identification with the priest, just as Laurie himself identified with the young men of his parish who had fought and died – a chain of empathy linking back through the decades, forged of faith and doubt and pain and love. The chapel, during all those decades, from the 1920s through another world war and into the new century, played its role in the life of the church. There was, though, an air of expectancy, of life lived in ellipses. 'It was almost,' Holloway thought, 'as if it was waiting for something . . .'

Alison Watt spent almost a year making *Still* between 2003 and 2004, painting in Leith in a studio above a funeral parlour. She worked on it in four pieces at first, then as a single composition, which required the use of scaffolding. She went back and forth to Old Saint Paul's several times a week, as if to a well: sitting in the chapel, filling herself with the spirit of the place, and bringing it back to the canvas. She made herself ill through exhaustion and obsession. She is a vocational painter, and there was no sense in which she was doing this work as a detached professional. 'There's an emotional cost to making work as well as a physical one,' she told me. 'The making of a painting is the creation of a private world and you end up inhabiting it.'

*Still* is not an explicitly religious work of art, and has no clear association with war and remembrance, but most who spend time pondering its meaning are likely to think of Christ's shroud, and winding sheets in general. Those bodies of the Clydebank Blitz. It may also bring to mind the word 'cenotaph' – which means 'empty tomb' – and a line from R. S. Thomas: 'this great absence that is like a presence'.

For Watt, the painting had two specific inspirations. First, a small black cross that hangs on the wall of the chapel. Known as the Martyr's Cross, it is thought that from the sixteenth century it hung on a house in the Grassmarket, opposite the gallows. Tradition has it that this iron cross was the last thing seen by the condemned before death; eyes filled with fear rested on it for that final moment and, one feels, left the scorch mark of their gaze. It is, therefore, a powerful and unsettling object. The cruciform umbra formed by the four parts of *Still* is intended as a shadow of this Martyr's Cross.

Watt also had a particular painting in mind: Francisco de Zurbarán's *The Martyrdom Of Saint Serapion*, painted in 1628 for a monastery in Seville. 'His martyrdom, in the twelfth century, was brutal,' Watt said. 'He was tied between two trees and tortured and decapitated. But in the painting the explicit details are not shown, and he seems to be almost suspended between life and death. His body is draped in these incredible white robes, each wrist is bound with rope, his head falls to one side, and he is utterly beautiful and magnificent.

'The painting was made for a room where monks were laid out before burial. It seems that each fold in the robe that St Serapion is wearing has been pared down to the simple elements of light and shade. Initially, when you look at the painting, you are seduced by the apparent simplicity but Zurbarán's genius is that he manages to elevate something humble – this simple white cloth – to an almost divine level. There's this really powerful sense of the transformation of an object into an idea. Zurbarán's fabric is to be touched, it's to be listened to. It's almost like a living Mass.'

In the documentary *Alison Watt: A Painter's Eye*, Watt spoke about her almost obsessional connection with another Zurbarán painting, *Saint Francis in Meditation*, and said that if it had a sound it would be that of the saint's breath. What, I asked her, would be the sound of *Still*?

'Perhaps,' she said, 'a sigh.'

*Still* was not intended as a permanent part of Old Saint Paul's. It was installed as part of the Edinburgh Art Festival in 2004, the idea being that it might be shown for a maximum of three months. 'But then,' Watt recalled, 'an extraordinary thing happened: the congregation asked me if it could stay. It's the only painting I've ever made that has actually been blessed.'

The blessing was by Bishop Brian Smith. The painting was lit by candles as he spoke: 'Light of Christ, shine through this image, and be reflected in the hearts and minds of all who look at it.'

Alison Watt had spoken to the congregation. 'Thank you,' she said, 'because this church has changed my life.'

What did she mean by that, I asked.

'Old Saint Paul's has become part of my life,' she explained. 'It's in my heart. It's a place that I go to seek solace. It's a place that I go to and sit on my own. I've cried there, I've been comforted there. For me it's a real place of reflection and contemplation. It's a space that allows you to just be.'

She does not often attend the services, preferring to visit the church – and her painting – alone.

'It's hard to explain, to try to put a feeling into words, but a few years ago I wanted to go there not long after my mother died. I needed to. I arrived just before an evening service in the middle of the week. Apart from the young woman priest preparing to say Mass, I was the only person in the church. Before she began, she asked me to join her at the altar as it was just the two of us. So I sat next to her, where one of the choristers might sit. It was extraordinary. The meaning of the liturgy seemed to change as we shared the experience. I sat and wept silently throughout. Even now, I find it hard to think of it without crying. It was profoundly moving. When the service was over, the young priest moved towards me and put her arms around me.

'This may sound strange, but I felt completely loved. I'll never forget it.'

*Still* hangs above the altar in the chapel. Something I had never noticed until Watt pointed it out: the painting is suspended by chains from the ceiling rather than being attached to the back wall. 'That's deliberate and important,' she said, 'because I wanted it to have a feeling of looming forwards.'

Often, when she paints a picture, it is bought by a private collector and she never sees it again. There is a sense of loss. Other works make their way into museum and gallery collections; whenever she sees those paintings it is in public view and can feel like a performance: The Artist Contemplating Her Genius. *Still* is different. There is a sense of collective ownership. It is hers, but also belongs to the congregation, and each of them projects on to it – into it – whatever they need in that moment.

The title seems important. *Still* meaning unmoving. *Still* meaning a thing that endures. The focal point of the painting is a teardrop loop of cloth almost black at its deepest point. During the long months of lockdown, when the Scottish capital was eerie in its emptiness, the silent darkness at the centre of the picture seemed to spill out and spread across the city. Edinburgh, enshrouded.

Artists, Richard Holloway believes, are often better than theologians at expressing the intricacies of the human soul. *Still* certainly does so. 'Oh, yes,' he said. 'It expresses longing, hope, doubt – all of the stuff that humans do. I mean, we're thrust into this universe, we don't know where we came from or where we're going. We get, if we're lucky, ninety years and then we're over. And I'm getting close to the exit gate.'

Holloway has a taste for the elegiac – 'It's been one of my lifelong addictions' – and it is no surprise to learn that he has planned his own funeral. It will, of course, take place in Old Saint Paul's, amid that smell of wax and dust and stone, and will be 'Humanist-Christian' in character. There will be hymns and poems; music and, no doubt, some laughter.

After the service, before the cremation, before his ashes are scattered on Scald Law, the highest hill of the Pentlands, his body will be carried down the Calvary Stair and out on to the street. 'Yes,' he said, 'those steps are important to me. Those thirty-three steps, then out under the Scotsman bridge and away . . .'

His coffin will spend the night before in Old Saint Paul's. It will be his final visit. He would love to lie, he told me, in the Warriors' Chapel – on the stone catafalque where so many of the parish have lain before. There, as Alison Watt's painting looms above, his unquiet heart will, at last, be still.

*

TOWARDS THE END of May 1919, Pablo Picasso travelled from France to England, where he spent nine weeks designing scenery and costumes for Sergei Diaghilev's ballet *The Three-Cornered Hat*. He stayed at the Savoy, attended lunches and parties, admired the omnibuses, shopped in Savile Row. He was already famous and fashionable, but even so his visit was imperfectly chronicled. There are gaps.

Early one morning, shortly before leaving London, never to return, Picasso strolled out of his hotel dressed in his blue serge suit and new bowler hat. He caught a train south to Caterham, and walked the last couple of miles through the countryside to the village of Chaldon. The church was unlocked and empty, and it did not take him long to find what he had come to see. He could hardly miss it. That large red mural on the west wall; it was like staring into the mouth of an oven. Standing there, looking up at the images of torment and resurrection, the Spaniard felt a kinship with the artist – no celebrity, utterly unknown – who had painted here some seven hundred or so years before. His hands gave a yearning twitch as he imagined how he himself might have shaped those demons, how he would have formed their blank eyes and rank snouts. As he turned and left St Peter and St Paul's, taking care to close the door behind him, he was content that he had at last encountered a painting more powerful than anything the great galleries of the English capital could offer. Having seen purgatory in Surrey, he could go back home to the heaven of Paris. In *Guernica*, a few years later, he would paint his own vision of hell.

This is, of course, pure imagination. Though Picasso was in London in 1919, he did not visit Chaldon and may never have known that the mural, *The Ladder of Salvation of the Human Soul, and the Road to Heaven*, even existed. But anyone contemplating the painting now must surely be struck by the way it seems both ancient and queer *and* radical and modernist. At least, so I found on a visit one spring morning.

It was a bright day, thick with an impasto of birdsong. The churchyard was a pointillist canvas of violets, forget-me-nots and lesser celandine. The trees, and the rusting iron railings of a particular tomb, were strung with ribbon left over from an Easter trail for local children. St Peter and St Paul's feels set apart from the village, surrounded by fields and reached by a narrow rising lane. It is a classic English country church: flint walls, red tiles, spire like a witch's hat. The cockerel on the weathervane gleamed in the sun, gilded dignity compromised just a little by the starling – an iridescent dissenter – perched on top. Another starling, nesting, flew into the spire through a hole in the shingle. The tower and spire are Victorian additions, the body of the church much older: late Saxon, they reckon. 'May Christ Bless This House' had been chalked across the lintel, part of the ceremony of reopening after lockdown, and a sign fixed to the door offered condolences to the royal family on the death of Prince Philip. I went inside.

The mural is on the west wall and best visited in the morning when lit by the east window. It is just over seventeen feet long by eleven high. To see it properly, you have to walk backwards, between box pews, towards the altar, stepping on

the seventeenth-century grave slabs set into the floor. 'Here lyeth the body' they proclaim, and on another day, in another church, you might stop and look who lyeth, but it is hard here to focus on anything but the painting.

It is thought to date from around 1170. It depicts purgatory, where the souls of the dead would suffer until their sins were expiated. The picture is divided into four by a ladder and a horizontal band of cloud that form a cross in the centre. The bottom half is the province of demons busy at their labours. Two stir a cauldron full of murderers; their colleagues force sinners along a bridge of spikes. A hell-hound chews a woman's arm; devils press forks to the head of a money-lender until white-hot coins spill from his mouth. In the upper half of the picture, St Michael weighs the souls of those who seek escape to heaven, but a demon, some miserly Screwtape, places a claw on the scales, tipping them in his favour. Christ, meanwhile, is shown spearing Satan, who lies blocking the jaws of hell. The narrative is complex, based on Biblical apocrypha, and ideas – some quite new at the time of painting – of what the afterlife might be like. But if the content is intellectual, the total effect is visceral. It must have been a fearful experience for medieval church-goers to stand facing the altar with this horror show behind them. I bet they smelled the sulphur. I bet they felt the heat on the back of their necks.

'The whole picture, which includes the seven deadly sins, can be viewed as a stark illustration of the struggle of good over evil,' Professor Edward Howard explained. Ted, who is eighty-five, is a worshipper in the church and a member of the choir. He is fascinated by the picture and has made it his business, over the last twenty or so years he has lived in the area, to study it carefully. 'If you took this off the wall and remounted it in a museum, as I've seen done on the continent, people would realise that it is absolutely priceless and unique.'

Medieval churches were richly painted, but of the roughly 10,000 in England, fewer than 10 per cent retain any significant survivals of the original scheme. Much of it was whitewashed at the time of the Reformation when such imagery was decried as idolatrous. Later, in the nineteenth century, more was lost in the Victorian enthusiasm for removing ancient plaster from interior walls, known as the Great Scrape.

'Whatever its condition almost every painting demands a long-jump of imagination,' writes Roger Rosewell in *Medieval Wall Paintings*:

> We have to visualise complete salvos of coppery greens, ocean blues, and bold reds blazing across walls lit by flickering candles and tapestries of coloured glass . . .

Today, when many can only be seen as patches amidst otherwise plain and sparsely decorated walls, they can appear without meaning or context. But five hundred years ago, when windows shone with colour, polished silver chalices gleamed on altars, and polychromed statues wore velvet cloaks and gold rings, wall paintings provided an enclosed artistic setting for the church's sacred rituals and public ceremonies.

Much of what remains is faded and fragmentary. But some is large and dramatic, in particular the Last Judgements which show Christ separating the saved and the damned, the former ascending to heaven, the latter often being devoured by the fanged mouth of hell. These Dooms, as they are also known, were usually painted above the chancel arch, a spot of such prominence that no one could possibly miss the grim message. Famous examples can be seen at St Peter's, Wenhaston and St Thomas's, Salisbury. Stanley Spencer had long intended to paint a Last Judgement, but died without ever having done so.

Among what remains in churches of medieval wall painting there is nothing else quite like *The Ladder* at Chaldon. The primitive style and the simplicity of the colours – red and yellow ochre – are like a child's recollection of a nightmare, and at the heart of the picture's power is an invisible element: time. When we look at it, we are looking into the far past. Yet it also has the immediacy of all art: an individual's thought fixed in paint. The demons, the bridge of spikes, the killers on a rolling boil – these were in a man's mind once, flickering images behind his eyes, and he set them down on a wall before returning to his workshop, job done, picking ochre from his fingernails, having conjured fear from a handful of dust. The painting is a ladder between the twelfth century and the twenty-first. We descend, rung by rung, into a place of fire and faith. When we ascend again we are a little changed. Those broken images flicker behind our eyes now, too.

As Ted Howard was showing me his favourite details of the mural, a local couple wandered over. They were Ted's neighbours, knew he was an expert, and had questions. 'Now,' asked the man, 'where's Adam and Eve?'

'They were supposed to be up here,' Ted replied, pointing to an empty patch of the adjoining north wall. 'But they were chiselled off.'

The mural was covered with lime-wash during the Reformation and forgotten about until 1870 when the Reverend Henry Shepherd, overseeing renovation works, noticed colour peeping through and ordered his workmen not to remove any more of the plaster. Sadly, figures thought to have been Adam and Eve had already been destroyed. The picture was then properly uncovered and restored, and its meaning decoded, by the artist and antiquary John Green Waller.

What must it have been like to gaze upon these scenes of damnation and salvation for the first time in centuries? Waller, in his short book on the mural, does not confide his feelings. Yet it was surely thrilling, perhaps even unsettling, to come so close, in that dim church, to the hand and mind and eye of an artist long dead.

The excitement of discovering a lost medieval wall painting is captured by J. L. Carr in his novel *A Month in the Country*. In the summer of 1920, Tom Birkin, a veteran of the Great War – 'nerves shot to pieces, wife gone, dead broke' – is engaged to find and conserve a fourteenth-century mural hidden beneath lime-wash in a Yorkshire church. It is a Doom painting, a Last Judgement, and before long he finds the face of the Judge:

'For my money, the Italian masters could have learned a thing or two from that head. This was no catalogue Christ, insufferably ethereal. This was a wintry hard-liner. Justice, yes, there would be justice. But not mercy . . . Here I was, face to face with a nameless painter reaching from the dark to show me what he could do, saying to me as clear as any words, "If any part of me survives from time's corruption, let it be this. For this was the sort of man I was."'

What sort of man was the painter of the Chaldon mural? A monk, it is believed, perhaps from Merton Priory. An intellectual, Ted Howard thought, and not too young. Someone who had read widely and thought deeply about the religious ideas of the time. Not that the painting has no relevance to our own age. 'To understand that picture I think you have to be a pessimist about human behaviour,' Ted said. 'If you pick up any of the popular newspapers you will see examples every day of almost everything in this picture. Killing people, charging exorbitant rents, not paying taxes – it's all there.'

Ted is a retired surgeon; the picture speaks to his years of observing humanity at moments of crisis. 'I'm not a morbid person,' he said. 'I try to be a realist, but if you're in medicine you have an amazing chance to see how people really behave. I think about times when patients have died and families would come to hospital and they fight over the bed about inheritance. Can you imagine that selfishness? It used to drive me spare.'

He shook his head slightly, as if to clear bad memories. 'My wife says I shouldn't think about these things.'

The vicar of Chaldon church is the Reverend Helen Burnett. We sat out in the morning sun and talked about the end of days. It was April and there was a chill in the air. She wore a long red coat – a brighter shade than the mural – over a black clerical shirt and dog collar. Pinned to her left lapel was a large badge bearing the hourglass insignia of Extinction Rebellion. Helen, who is in her early sixties, is a member of that group as well as the related Christian Climate Action. She sees the climate emergency as a spiritual as well as environmental crisis, a crucifying of creation.

She and another activist priest had recently been found guilty of obstructing the highway during a sit-in protest in London. 'What kind of a mad world is it,' she had asked the court, 'that has two vicars who can see and understand the catastrophic harm to human, animal and plant life that is the climate catastrophe standing in a dock before you for telling the truth about an existential threat? We have looked into the abyss, seen the despair, and our hope is to find agency in whatever way we can through action and contemplation; to do something before we die for a world that is dying.'

A vicar who looks unblinking into the abyss is, it seems to me, the right person to have custodianship of a wall painting in which damnation and salvation hang in the balance. What I see in the mural, I told her, is not the burning pit where my soul will go if I am lustful or insufficiently charitable, but something of the fate – the fires and floods – that we are creating through our treatment of the planet. In that sense, the picture is absolutely contemporary and visionary and the monk who made this was right to accuse us of a kind of sin, although not the sort he meant.

'Yes,' she nodded. That interpretation has grown on her during the few years she has been at this church. The painting, she feels, speaks of 'the personal hells that we build for ourselves'.

That central image of the ladder, though – it offered hope to a pre-industrial people. In the twenty-first century, in the age of ecocide, can we realistically feel that hope? Is there a ladder for us? Or are we already sunk deep in the cauldron?

'It's very hard when a system is so broken,' Helen replied. 'We're so far down the line of constant growth and capitalism that it's hard to see how we pull back from that, especially in a moment when the political trajectory is more and more to the right. So, looking around the world at the moment, it doesn't feel very hopeful. But in small acts of kindness and the capacity that people have, that's where the hope is for me. As a woman of faith, I have to talk about hope, but that's not a fake optimism. The deep hope is in the human spirit.'

Our conversation made me think of the writer Paul Kingsnorth. A few years before, I had visited him at his home in Ireland and he had put me up for the night in the cabin where he writes. He was planning a novel, *Alexandria*, and the walls were covered with notes toward that. Kingsnorth is a founder of the Dark Mountain project, a movement of artists united by a belief that environmental collapse cannot now be stopped, and a desire to respond to this accepted fate with works that are honest and beautiful. When we met, he had called himself a Zen Buddhist. Since then, to his surprise and initial reluctance, he had become a Christian, baptised in the River Shannon. 'I don't believe now that a human culture can last for any length of time unless it has a spiritual core: unless it is built around some path to God,' he explained in an interview. 'That's one of the themes of *Alexandria*: if you don't worship what is greater than you, you'll end up worshipping yourself. The result of our self-worship – of our rebellion – is climate change and the death of the seas. We'll have to find a truer path, because this way of living is driving us mad and destroying the ground it stands on. But there's a fire to be walked through first.'

This walking through fire is what the Chaldon mural seems to me to show.

Helen Burnett does not like the picture. Her God is the God of love not the God of fear. She does not believe in original sin or hell as a place. She is wary of a faith that seeks to frighten and repress. Once, while holding up the wafer during Communion, the sun shone through the east window, casting the shadow of a churchyard tree on to the image of Crucifixion pressed into the disc. That love of creation, that mingling of ecology and theology, is where her ministry lies. Painted demons have no place in it. 'But I'm very grateful to the mural,' she said, 'because I think, if it wasn't there, the church would probably have been closed down.'

St Peter and St Paul's, like many rural churches, has long had a precarious existence. An average Sunday congregation of around thirty-five to forty-five doesn't sound half bad considering that this is such a small and out-of-the-way place, but still it's not many. 'I think if we threatened to close there'd be uproar,' Helen said. 'But mostly people don't come.'

The church does, however, receive a huge number of visitors: amblers and ramblers and many drawn by the wall painting. The writer Andy Miller grew up a few miles away from Chaldon, and from early childhood was a regular visitor during Sunday afternoon strolls with his family. The mural left a deep impression. 'It was the most ancient, interesting and complex thing available to you if you grew up on the outskirts of Croydon in the 1970s,' he had recalled when we spoke on the phone. 'There aren't many intimations of the eternal in Surrey, but that painting is like peering down into the deep.'

Why such a large and sophisticated work of art should have been made for, as the vicar put it, 'a funny little church

down the end of a lane' is something of a mystery. John
Green Waller, in his 1885 report on the painting's discovery,
wrote that it had been 'addressed to the sight and understanding of the inhabitants of a small and obscure parish,
even now quite secluded from the busy world, but which in
the twelfth and thirteenth centuries, must have been a wild
district in the midst of the chalk downs'. Well, yes and no.
Although no proper roads led to Chaldon until 1870, the year
of the mural's discovery, the Pilgrims' Way, the medieval
route between Winchester and Canterbury, passed along
the southern edge of the village. It may have been that the
church was a rest stop for those on their way to the shrine
of Thomas Becket. He was murdered in 1170, around the
same time as the mural is thought to have been painted, and
canonised in 1173. It has been estimated that around 100,000
pilgrims visited Canterbury annually towards the end of the
1100s and in the early years of the new century. Even now,
with pilgrimage increasingly popular and fashionable, those
on their way to Canterbury Cathedral by foot often call in
at Chaldon, where Helen Burnett is happy to stamp their
pilgrim passports with the small demon logo that proves they
have visited the church.

So much for the tourists. What about the locals? I asked
Helen how her congregation feel about the mural.

'I suppose they think of it a bit like an elderly relative,'
she replied. 'In fact, it tends to be referred to as "Muriel".
And for all of us, it lies heavy on our minds in terms of the
sheer financial weight of keeping it maintained and looking
after it. We get no extra funding for it, and we find ourselves,
by virtue of living in this parish, having responsibility for
a unique work of art.' Recently, there had been essential
conservation work; the west wall had become damp and this
seeped through to the plaster, damaging the picture.

If *The Ladder of Salvation* ever was to be, as Ted Howard had imagined, taken down from the wall where it has been for so long, and put into, say, the British Museum, it would likely be regarded as a highlight of the collection. It would be protected by sophisticated security systems. It would appear on fridge magnets and T-shirts. It would be safe forever. But think what would be lost. Objects acquire their potency from the place and purpose for which they were made, and it is both a strength and a vulnerability of old churches that they have such treasures within them.

The mural is powerful because, just as the flint wall at its back has been exposed to a thousand years of English rain, so the picture itself has absorbed centuries of prayer. Think, too, of the eyes that have regarded it, by candle glow and electric light, in terror and wonder. Medieval eyes. Victorian eyes. Twenty-first-century eyes. Many generations of villagers. That, ultimately, is what makes this painting resonant and meaningful: it has been part of the inner land-scape of all those who have worshipped here or simply lived in the neighbourhood.

'It is,' as Helen Burnett put it, 'an inheritance.'

# BONE

SISTER PATRICIA HARRISS led the way up the aisle, limping a little as anyone might at eighty-seven, and bowed at the altar. She wore ordinary clothes; a denim skirt and cerise blouse. Only the silver cross around her neck, carved with the letters CJ for Congregation of Jesus, indicated that she is a nun. Like the building we were in, there was much more to her than could be taken in at a glance.

'This chapel was built in 1769,' she said. 'Secretly,' she added.

Secrets within secrets within secrets – that's the Bar Convent, York. The chapel, which is on the first floor, resembles an elegant Georgian drawing room, all gold and white and pistachio green. Look closer, though, and its true nature is revealed. This is a place in which unusual emotions swirl: not only hope and love, but fear, courage and defiance. The clue is in the doors. There are eight of them. 'Never mind about entrances,' Sister Patricia explained, 'it was getting out that mattered.'

Worshippers had to be able to scatter, should Mass be raided by the authorities. A narrow brick tunnel beneath the floor provided the priest with an escape route. Even the dome is invisible from the street, concealed by the pitch of the surrounding roofs. There was no threat from the air in the eighteenth century. That came later. In the small hours of 29 April 1942, a Luftwaffe bomb fell on the convent, killing five nuns – all of whom are buried in a small private cemetery within the grounds.

Sister Patricia took a few steps to the left of the altar and pulled a cord, raising a green blind, and revealing a pane of glass. 'So,' she said, 'there we go.'

We were looking into a shallow alcove. It contained a glass dome, rather like the bell jars you see in collections of old medical specimens, except richly decorated with Christian symbolism. Palm fronds of silver gilt clasped the sides and sprouted from the top, concealing for a moment the precise shape of what lay within, so that one had to bend and peer.

It was a hand. A small hand. A right hand. Perhaps a child's hand? No. There had likely been a reduction in size as a result of decomposition and whatever embalming or mummification process had taken place. Also, the top of the pinky was missing, adding to the impression of smallness. That portion had been sliced off as a gift for the wealthy Catholic family who, in 1874, had contributed the reliquary.

I knew of similar relics in England and elsewhere. The right hand of St Edmund Arrowsmith, a priest executed in Lancaster in 1628, is present on the altar and used in the blessing following Mass at a church in Ashton-in-Makerfield, near Wigan; it is said, over the centuries, to have cured many illnesses, including, in 1961, lung cancer.

The remains of St John Southworth, a priest who had been a friend and fellow prisoner of Father Arrowsmith, were discovered in 1927 during the digging of foundations for a shop on the site of the English College, a former seminary in Douai, northern France. He had been martyred for his faith at the Tyburn gallows on a day of summer storms in 1654 – hanged, drawn and quartered. The surviving parts of his body, purchased from the hangman for forty guineas by the Spanish ambassador, were stitched back together, embalmed, and smuggled out of Oliver Cromwell's England. In France, the lead coffin was displayed and honoured until the Revolution, at which point it was buried for safekeeping and, over time, lost. In the plague year of 1636, Southworth had worked in London, tending to the sick, distressed and dying, and it was to London that his relics, exhumed and examined, were returned – by rail to Calais, passenger-boat to Dover, and, in 1930, by catafalque into Westminster Cathedral.

He is now one of two saints whose shrines bookend Victoria Street, the other being Edward the Confessor in Westminster Abbey. The king's enshrinement was chronicled in the Bayeux Tapestry, the priest's by Pathé News, and although Edward is by far the better known, visitors to the Catholic cathedral will find that John does not lack for impact. He lies in a glass casket, wearing vestments and a black cap; head resting on a red pillow, severed hands replaced by silver, his face covered by a gleaming mask. During the annual ordination rite, new priests lie face down in a line along the nave, like jets readying for take-off, while Father Southworth, their predecessor and example, lies on his back among them. 'It's a powerful thing,' one man who had been ordained there told me, 'to go through that experience with your local martyred saint.'

The Spanish nun and mystic Teresa of Ávila died from a haemorrhage of the lungs in the convent at Alba de Tormes on 4 October 1582. Her coffin was placed into the walls of the church, but nine months later she was exhumed and found not to have decayed. This was a sign of sainthood, and so her left hand was removed as a relic. 'This hand could do many things,' wrote Vita Sackville-West. 'It could destroy all other scents, however powerful; even the scent of musk smeared on it with the tip of a knife. It could cure indigestion of twenty years' standing by merely being laid upon the stomach; it could cure the murderous jealousy of an injured husband by being laid upon the heart.'

Sackville-West went on, in *The Eagle and the Dove*, to describe what, over many decades, was done to the saint's body by those seeking miracles. Here was the scene in the convent by 1750:

> They had taken the right foot, and some fingers from the hand that was still raised in benediction; some ribs had been torn away from the side; pieces of flesh had been torn off for distribution among the crowd . . . The head itself, which now lay on a cushion of crimson satin embroidered with silver, was in a pitiable condition. Part of the jaw had been taken, and the left eye was now an empty socket. But the other eye was intact even to its lashes and its pupil, as though it could still observe with glassy amusement the antics of the devout.

In the course of the Spanish Civil War, St Teresa's left hand came into the possession of Francisco Franco, who regarded it as an object of great importance to him personally and to the fascist cause. He kept it on his bedside table at night, and took it with him when he travelled. One government minister visiting the palace in Madrid found the dictator passing a cheerful afternoon signing death sentences while dipping dry toast into hot chocolate. The hand, of course, was there. And even in the ordeal of his dying, in 1975, Franco and the relic were not parted. Archbishop Pedro Cantero Cuadrado brought it to La Paz hospital, laying it with due reverence at El Caudillo's feet.

I had read about such things in newspapers and books, considering their oddness from a distance. Now here, before me, was the hand of St Margaret Clitherow, 'the Pearl of York', or so tradition says. It was brown and waxy, fingers curling inward. It is believed to have been in the Bar Convent since its foundation in 1686, although the woman from whom it was severed had been executed a century before that. It had been within these walls when an anti-Catholic mob roared at the gates and when Nazi fire rained from the sky. 'We are enthusiastic custodians,' Sister Patricia said. 'We feel it's an honour to have it. For me, it's a connection with a very holy and brave woman. I look back to her as I look to the others of the English martyrs: with great devotion.'

Margaret Middleton was born in 1556, married John Clitherow, a prosperous butcher, in 1571, and went to live in the Shambles, the butchery district of York, where, according to one biography, 'she was constantly obliged to pick her way through sawdust and blood'. At around the age of eighteen, she converted to Catholicism, and would have been in no doubt that this, in the reign of Elizabeth, was a dangerous step. In the year following her marriage, Thomas Percy, the Earl of Northumberland, was executed in a marketplace close by the Clitherow home and his head mounted on a nearby gate in the city walls. Had he recanted his Catholicism, his life would have been spared. However, his last words from the scaffold were a refusal to acknowledge the Church of England. Margaret may well have witnessed and been inspired by his death, just as Guy Fawkes – a teenager in York at the time of her execution – may have been influenced by hers. Martyrs beget martyrs; bloodstains spread and seep.

The house where she lived is still there. I walked to it from the convent, passing over the Ouse Bridge, on which a plaque informed me that 'Near to this place' – in fact, about fifty to a hundred yards downstream from the present crossing – Margaret Clitherow 'was martyred for her Christian Faith' in 1586. Her former home is now a shrine. The Shambles, a narrow throat of a street, is always choked with tourists, and it feels strange that a set of rooms so quiet and serious should exist there. It is always a pleasure to get away from the noise and crowds for a few moments, but there is something uncanny about it, too – as if one has stepped out of the present century entirely – so that going back out into the air is also, in a way, a relief. 'In a world of indifference, people are seldom indifferent to the story of Margaret Clitherow,' the young priest who looks after the shrine told me. 'It is a powerful, shocking story. A pregnant woman crushed to death.'

Margaret Clitherow's rebellion began with her refusal to attend church, for which she was fined and imprisoned in York Castle. There she learned to read and write, and, while in the company of other recusant prisoners, became what we might now call radicalised. Certainly, she emerged hardened in her position and intent on participating in the rituals of her faith, regardless of the consequences. 'English Catholics were now living at an unparalleled intensity of spiritual experience,' writes Katherine Longley in her biography of the saint. 'The Protestant attack on the Mass had called forth a much greater devotion to, and understanding of, it among Catholics, and when the saying or hearing of Mass became penal offences, those who took part in it became deeply aware of their share in the redemptive suffering and sacrifice of Christ.'

Clitherow made arrangements for Mass to be celebrated in her house, for herself and other furtive worshippers. This involved providing the priest with a secret chamber in a neighbouring house, and the construction of a hidden passageway leading to it from her own home. Legislation passed in 1585 made such harbouring a felony punishable by death, but priests relied upon the ingenuity and courage of those who would give them shelter. Between 1582 and 1583, five known to Margaret Clitherow had been captured and executed, and she herself was now at great risk. 'Then you must prepare your neck for the rope,' Father John Mush warned her. He was her confessor. In his account of her life

and death, written in the weeks following her execution, he
refers to himself as her 'ghostly father'.

On 10 March 1586, the house was searched and the priest's
chamber, though not the priest, found. Clitherow was taken
into custody and, four days later, her trial began.

She was treated with little delicacy. 'It is not for religion
that thou harbours priests, but for whoredom,' one of her
accusers sneered. Despite such provocations, she made no
formal plea, refusing to agree to be tried by jury. This meant
that she would be executed anyway, and she knew this.
'I thank God,' she said, 'I may suffer any death for this good
cause.'

The hope of the authorities seems to have been to
frighten Clitherow into apostasy – a renunciation of her
Catholicism – rather than to end her life. One of the two
judges told her that the evidence against her was not strong
and that she could expect mercy. It seems at least possible
that she could have saved herself. What, then, to make of
her fatal refusal to engage with the formal procedures? This
has been interpreted as a mother's sacrifice; she explained
that she sought to spare her children – her eldest daughter
Anne being then about twelve years old – from having to give
evidence against her.

Yet, was there something more? She often felt drawn to
the Knavesmire, the marshy area outside the city walls where
priests she knew had been killed; she would walk there barefoot and kneel beneath the gallows. Was she seduced by the
idea of such bodily oblation? The modern reader may detect,
in Father Mush's account of the events leading to her death,
an unsettling eagerness for execution, as if it was a bridal or
maternal urge. 'I confess death is fearful, and flesh is frail,'
she said, 'yet I mind by God's assistance to spend my blood
in this faith, as willing as ever I put my paps to my children's

mouths, neither desire I to have my death deferred.' She was described during the trial as smiling, cheerful, joyful. Some who saw her declared that the holy spirit must be bringing her comfort. 'Some said it was not so, but that she was possessed with a merry devil . . .'

Margaret Clitherow was killed on the morning of the Feast of the Annunciation, Friday 25 March, in the tollbooth on the Ouse Bridge. The means of execution was *peine forte et dure*, also known as pressing – being crushed beneath heavy weights. It was thought that she may have been with child, which, if proven, would have at least delayed her end until after the birth, but on this point she was uncertain.

She lay on the ground with arms outstretched and bound, a handkerchief over her face. A heavy door was laid upon her body and a sharp stone, the size of a man's fist, was put under her back. Upon the door were placed weights so large that she died within a quarter of an hour. Ribs burst through the skin, like wings from a pupa. The metamorphosis into martyr was complete.

Denied a churchyard grave, she was buried at midnight in 'an obscure and filthy corner of the city' beside a dunghill, its location kept secret so that her broken body could not become a trophy. The authorities, according to an anonymous writer thought likely to have been Father Mush:

> use singular diligence and wariness in martyring us, that no part of blood, or flesh, or garment, or anything belonging to the martyr be either unburnt or escape their hands. The sacred blood they consulate and cast into the fire. The apparel the murderers take and disperse, the pins, points, buttons, and all, lest Catholics get them and use them for relics. They boil also the quarters in some filthy mixture, and the heads they bedaub with

some black matter, to cause them to seem more loath-
some and grizzly.

Nevertheless, after six weeks, Margaret Clitherow's
corpse was discovered by Father Mush and unnamed others
– it was bloodstained but said not to have decomposed – and
taken far from York, to a place unknown, for proper burial. It
is at this point that the priest is thought to have removed her
right hand. How it came to be at the Bar Convent is specula-
tion, but Mush was later confessor to Mary Ward, founder of
the order that established the convent, so it may have passed
from him to her, and thus into the care of the sisterhood.

There is a kinship of secrecy between the building and
the relic. This is England's oldest living convent, founded in
1686 at a time when to be Catholic was still illegal and dangerous. It was established as a school for girls, but had this
deeper covert identity. The nuns, ghostly sisters, wore slate-
grey gowns so that they appeared to be teachers and nothing
more. The chapel was built later, when the convent was being
remodelled in the Georgian style, the work concealed within
the larger construction project. So: a forbidden relic in a
hidden chapel in a secret convent.

These days, the Bar Convent could hardly be more open
to the world. There is an exhibition, a cafe, a website, even
a B&B. Eight sisters live and work in the active convent, and
another nine in neighbouring quarters for those who require
nursing care. These seventeen women are aged between fifty
and 101, and each is a story in herself.

Sister Agatha, about to turn ninety at the time of my visit,
was born Shirley Leach in 1931 and grew up in a manor house
in the North Downs of Kent, a *Tatler* world of chauffeurs,
stable boys and spinster governesses. One afternoon in 1940,
a Messerschmitt pilot bailed out over their grounds and was

brought into the house for cake and tea. One evening in 1947, a debutante among four hundred others, Shirley was presented to George VI. One morning in 1952, she entered a convent, driven there by her former fiancé, Jeremy, who had insisted: 'I am giving you to God, no one else is going to do this.'

Sister Patricia has been at the Bar Convent, off and on she told me, since 1962. She has also lived and worked in Slovakia, Russia and in Rome. Had she been a man, she would like to have become a Jesuit priest, but as the Catholic Church does not ordain women – 'You might live to see it; I won't' – she joined a religious community that seemed outward-looking and engaged with society. 'Maybe I entered Mary Ward's institute because of her walk across the Alps,' she said. Mary Ward, founder of the Congregation of Jesus, is sometimes regarded as an early feminist. Between October and December 1621, she had gone on foot from Liège to Rome, to ask the pope to approve her vision of an order in which nuns could lead active lives of ministry, as the Jesuits did, and not have to spend their days in cloisters. 'It sounded so exciting and adventurous, and she was the very first person to have seen something that women could do other than be locked away behind enclosed walls.'

It was hard to know how to react when Sister Patricia showed me Margaret Clitherow's hand. Some visitors get down on their knees and pray. Conversely, there is always a risk that such objects can appear kitsch, or simply horrible, though the nuns do their best to deter gawpers and ghouls. 'The relic is something that we try to explain carefully and reasonably to the people who come,' she said. 'It isn't there for every passer-by to look at. But for people who seem genuinely interested, if you're showing the chapel you'll raise the cover and reveal it. It's not about sensation. It's about holiness and reverence and prayer.'

# BONE

There were, I noticed, fingerprints on the screen. Such a human desire: to touch another's hand, fingers to fingers, palm to palm, especially in the time we had been going through when touch was taboo. That cluster of yearning smudges seemed eloquent on the subject of loneliness.

By the time I left the chapel, the blind had been lowered and the relic concealed once more. It would wait there, dimly cocooned in glass and time, beckoning the next curious pilgrim.

\*

THE FRAGMENT IS KEPT in a plastic case, in a metal box, in a locked cupboard, in a Belfast house of Georgian brick. One enters through a golden door pocked by bullets, and the shrapnel of German and Irish bombs.

It lies in the dark, this scrap of a man. It is brought out once a year, on the anniversary of his death – 17 March – to bless the faithful who gather for St Patrick's Day.

'Let me just gently, gently show you,' said Father Eugene O'Neill, lifting the edge of the case the slightest crack so that we could squint within.

The bone, a tiny yellowish thing, lay on a piece of purple cloth. Neither of us touched it. You wouldn't want to even breathe upon it. For here was a relic of Ireland's patron saint, the missionary credited with bringing the island to the faith. On this slice of bone, in a sense, has been built 1,600 years of devotion and authority, the beauty and horror and shame and love of Christianity's cultural dominance; not to mention the soft power of the diaspora, American presidents supping Guinness, the Chicago River dyed green.

'Now,' said the priest, 'this is the reliquary. I believe insured for several million. See how splendid it is. It can only be touched with white gloves.'

He put them on and lifted it from its security box. It was a forearm and hand of silver gilt, just a little smaller than life-size; dainty, you might say. The pinky and ring finger were crooked in toward the palm, the other fingers raised in a gesture of benediction. The middle finger wore a ring set with a stud of light purple glass.

Known as the arm-shrine of St Patrick, the reliquary is thought to date from the fourteenth or fifteenth century, and to have been made for Down Cathedral. I had last seen it on a visit to the Ulster Museum, where it had a display cabinet to itself, in keeping with its significance, but shared a room with other objects from medieval Ireland. A Sheela-na-gig, I remember, looked down from a wall, set high above eye level as if it was hoped that no one would pay her any mind.

'We keep the reliquary at the museum, as we can't really afford to insure it,' the priest explained. 'Also, we were afraid of it being stolen.'

Until the 1980s it was kept at the church – St Patrick's on Donegall Street. 'One of my chums was an altar boy here. He remembers that they'd put it up their sleeves and tickle each other. And they would throw it like a rugby ball.' Father Eugene, who is in his mid fifties, looked a little pale at the thought. 'Oh my goodness, I handle it with trepidation.'

He took the small case containing the relic and placed it inside the hollow sleeve of the reliquary: precious bone and precious metal reunited for morning Mass.

Having first changed into a white chasuble embroidered with shamrocks, he walked into the church, carrying the reliquary before him. He placed it on a stand, and spoke to the people in the pews: 'Today, friends, we celebrate the life and contribution of St Patrick.'

The saint, he explained, was kidnapped from his native Britain when he was almost sixteen, around the turn of the

400s, and brought, enslaved, to Ireland. He was put to work as a shepherd, during which time he found God. His labours often required him to stay overnight in the woods and hills, but he would get up before the sun had risen and say his prayers, kneeling in snow and ice and rain.

We know this because Patrick – or Patricius, as he called himself in Latin – wrote about his life in two letters, which exist in ninth- and tenth-century copies. But much remains uncertain. For example, Patrick's home, the Romano-British town, which he calls *Bannavem Taburniae*, must have been on the west coast, accessible to Irish slavers on a lightning raid. But where? That every part of the present day island – Scotland, England and Wales – has claimed him as a native son is indicative of the status that comes from association with an important saint. And where did Patrick the slave boy look after the sheep? Because of references in the letters to distance and topography, it is often said to have been County Mayo in the west of Ireland. However, according to a tradition that dates back to at least the seventh century, the mountain of Slemish is the true place of Patrick's captivity and religious conversion.

'I know that landscape well,' Father Eugene told his congregation. 'I used to be a priest there. And yesterday I had the great privilege of climbing Slemish.'

I had gone with him. We drove north from Belfast, a journey of less than an hour. Slemish was still several miles away when it came into sight: a dark peak rising from flat Antrim farmland. 'Look at how it looms,' the priest said. 'I find it rather beautiful. But what you see is not what Patrick saw. Ireland was a country of forests. He would have looked out on woodland.'

We talked, as the hill neared, about the relic. The tradition is that the remains of Patrick – along with those of two other saints, Brigid and Columba – were discovered in or beside Down Cathedral in the late twelfth century, and that parts of their bodies were taken first to St Mark's in Rome and later to the Vatican. In 1870, a small piece of bone, said to be from the arm of Patrick, was sent back from Italy to Ireland, where it has remained. Father Eugene is its latest custodian. It is a role that he seems to approach with appropriate seriousness, but no mysticism, theatrics or naivety. He's read his Chaucer and knows all about 'pigges bones' being used to part fools from their money.

'Priests are the most sceptical people about relics,' he said. 'I am prepared to believe this is a bone of St Patrick, but I know it can only be a matter of conjecture. However, what makes me believe it is more than possible is that relics were more important than jewels and gold in the early church. They were considered precious and kept very carefully.'

'So,' I asked, 'you're choosing to believe?'

'I'm choosing to believe on the balance of probabilities. And with all the caveats about historicity and fraud, I feel comfortable enough to be able to carry it through the church.'

The word 'relics' comes from the Latin *reliquiae* – meaning remains or remnants. The open veneration of relics was made possible by the Roman Emperor Constantine's edict of 313 that Christians were at liberty to follow their religion. Thus began centuries of a practice that existed at the nexus of faith, commerce and power. The idea was that saints were somehow present, spiritually, where even the smallest parts of their bodies were enshrined, and therefore available to intercede on behalf of those who visited and prayed to them – and of course left an offering of money. It was like having an influential ally in heaven. A church had a saint's finger, but that saint had God's ear.

Little wonder that relics became generators of wealth. In 1220, the year in which Thomas Becket's remains were moved – or translated, to use the proper phrase – from the crypt to a new shrine, revenues from pilgrims accounted for two-thirds of Canterbury Cathedral's income. In 1239, King Louis IX paid 135,000 livres for the Crown of Thorns at a time when the annual budget of the French monarchy was 250,000 livres. On 15 April 2019, the Crown was among the treasures saved by Parisian fire-fighters and their chaplain Father Jean-Marc Fournier from the flames of Notre Dame.

Louis IX himself, upon his death while on crusade in 1290, was treated as if he were already a saint, which is to say he was taken apart with greedy love. The flesh was boiled from his corpse in wine. His heart and guts were enshrined in Palermo. His skull went to Paris, the rest of his bones to Saint-Denis. France's great relic-hunter had become a feast of relics, broken like a fowl at a banquet.

'A desire to possess some fragment of holy remains was of course so strong and so common as to over-ride all human queasiness or even a natural aversion to the idea of dismembering a once loved and revered person,' Vita Sackville-West has written. 'An excessive example of ardour may be found in the case of the Portuguese lady who, on being allowed to kiss the foot of St. Francis Xavier, bit off a toe and carried it away in her mouth.'

We had arrived at Slemish. The path led up between two wind-bent hawthorns. A pair of crows contested – in the high court of beak and claw – the title deeds to the sky. They tumbled and cawed through the blue.

'There is something about the landscape holding memory,' Father Eugene said. 'In this locality, for over a thousand years, there has been a memory of Patrick and something spiritual happening here.'

The way was steep, boggy for stretches, but a quick climb. On St Patrick's Day itself, thousands would be out on the hill and the place would become, in Father Eugene's phrase, 'a glaur-pit' of churned mud. Much better to go up the day before, when you have it to yourself, or nearly.

Slemish is a dolerite plug, the ghost of a volcano. It isn't especially high, just 437 metres, but the flatness of the land all around gives an impression of great height. The dyked fields, as we looked down at them, were a gallery of green paintings, hung so close together that the frames touched. To the south-west, an expanse of water shone silver. 'Lough Neagh,' said the priest. In his writing, Patrick refers to the Western Sea. Father Eugene thought it possible that he mistook the lough, which is enormous, for the Atlantic. After all, he was just a wee lost boy. 'Think of him kidnapped and taken from his mates and family and trafficked here with the possibility of never ever getting back home.'

After six years of servitude, Patrick tells us in one of his letters, he ran away. He was encouraged to do so by God, who spoke to him in his dreams. He found a ship crewed by pagan sailors, and travelled back to Britain, where he was reunited with his family, who begged him to never leave them again. These days, we would expect someone with Patrick's experiences of abduction, forced labour and flight to have post-traumatic stress disorder, to suffer flashbacks. The young man sleeping in the childhood bedroom was no longer the child once plucked from the bed. Patrick writes that he had a series of visions, which he interpreted as a divine call that he should return to the land of his captors, capturing and enrapturing its people with the story of Jesus Christ. He answered that call. He went back. 'I travelled everywhere among great dangers,' he wrote, as an old man, a priest and bishop, recollecting his years of mission. 'I even went to the most remote parts of the island – places at the very edge of the world, places no one had ever been before – to baptise and obtain clergy, and confirm people in the faith.'

He missed Britain, but wanted to die in Ireland, and did – in the year 461, so they say.

We had reached the top. The Scottish coast came into view: the Mull of Kintyre, Sanda Island, and there, as if reflecting Slemish in a mirror, the hazy volcanic hump of Ailsa Craig. A wooden cross, much weathered, stood dark and dramatic against the bright sky. 'Somebody's even put the shamrock on it, look,' called a woman sitting on a nearby rock, drawing our attention to the little pot of three-leafed plants placed at the base of the cross.

Patricia was here with her two sisters, celebrating her sixtieth. They were from Antrim, but now lived in Scotland. 'Back to the land of the birth for the birthday,' Patricia laughed. She was named for St Patrick, having been born close to his feast day, and so it had felt appropriate to climb Slemish and mark the occasion. The year before her birth, 1961, had been the 1500th anniversary of Patrick's death, celebrated at the mountain with a great open-air Mass attended by thousands. 'But this would be a very Protestant part of the world,' Father Eugene had told me earlier. 'There would be very few Catholics living here. And everything was done by the locals to make it difficult. Trees and telegraph poles being cut down and put on the roads. People having to park miles away. I knew the priest, now dead, who was the organiser of it. He said he was sick with anxiety until the whole thing was safely over without anyone being killed.'

The way back down was quick, and before long we were in the car, heading for the city.

We talked about what it's like to be a priest in an increasingly secular society. 'Ireland is extraordinary because we've moved so swiftly not just to neutrality but a real hostility to religion,' Father Eugene said. 'I think people are bored of religion. They've had too much of it, and it became too controlling.

'When I was ordained twenty-five years ago, I was going to save the world. Once people heard faith explained cogently to them, that would be it. But I've realised that just ain't how it is. So that creates a sense of instability, uncertainty. We priests have kind of lost our role. We're just not relevant any more, and we're the focus of ire. But we're also, at the same time, expected to be at every funeral, wedding and baptism. It makes me feel that I need to attend very carefully to the purpose of my life. I'm at present trying to think all that through.'

'St Patrick was at the beginning of the story of Christianity in Ireland,' I said. 'Do you feel you're at the end of it?'

'No,' he replied. 'I see myself as being part of a story that I don't fully understand.'

The mountain was gone from the rear-view, but it would be a while till Belfast, so I told him a story in turn.

'About a month ago,' I began, 'I was walking in a cemetery in Glasgow . . .'

It had been a stormy day, the dregs of winter; the sun, breaking through at last, gave the Victorian tombs a freshly washed look. It was late in the afternoon, and I was on the point of heading home, when I got talking to a woman. Arlene had come up from the coast to remember her father. He had no grave there, his ashes were at home, but she felt close to him in that place. He'd had dementia, she explained. The cemetery, so calm and accepting, was where she used to come and spend time in an attempt to bear the sorrow of losing him, bit by bit, to that illness.

He went into care at the start of the first lockdown and

the family were unable to see him for five weeks. 'We watched him die on a WhatsApp call,' she said.

After his passing, Arlene painted a forget-me-not on a stone and carried it to the cemetery, placing it deep in among the roots of an old tree, by the spot where she had so often found comfort. It makes her smile to think of it – and, by extension, her dad – hidden there. The landscape holds his memory. The birds sing. The leaves bud and fall.

She took me to the tree. She crouched, and reached an arm into the roots.

She brought out an object lying within, and turned it over in her hand. The painted flower was a bright blue.

'Hiya, pal.' She addressed the stone – so much more than a stone – in her palm.

'He will be here forever,' Arlene said.

That tree was a reliquary, it seems to me now; the stone a relic. Not a relic of his body, but of the love between a daughter and father. It was a way of remembering the time of his forgetting, and perhaps, in time, a means of forgetting the pain.

# BATS

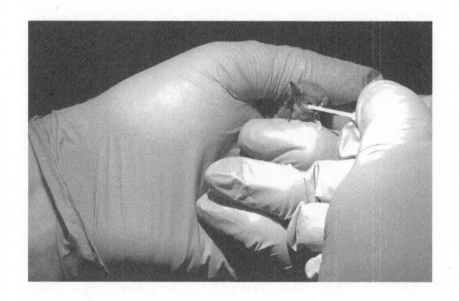

WHAT IS IT LIKE to be a bat?

So asked the philosopher Thomas Nagel, in 1974, in an essay of that title. It is a good question, difficult to answer. The way those mammals experience and perceive their environment is so different from human consciousness that we cannot easily extrapolate from our own perception of, say, an old dark church and think our way into the mind of a bat flying through the nave at midnight. 'Even without the benefit of a philosophical reflection,' Nagel wrote, 'anyone who has spent some time in an enclosed space with an excited bat knows what it is to encounter a fundamentally alien form of life.'

I thought of this, one sultry evening in July, when I joined the ecologist Philip Parker and his team for a bat survey at the church of St Margaret, Saxlingham, a few miles inland from Norfolk's northern coast.

It was getting on for sundown and they were setting up for the night. Four women and Phil and all their kit: lights, cameras, bat detectors, camping chairs, bug spray, flasks of tea. The hiss of running water that I took for an unseen river turned out to be a fountain in the garden of the Elizabethan manor house next door. Lisa, who was wearing a T-shirt with the counterintuitive slogan 'Crazy Cat Lady' – counterintuitive, because cats kill huge numbers of bats – said that when passers-by notice them working they often mistake them for ghost-hunters. That is the sort of trade the English would be disappointed not to find being practised in a churchyard after dark.

St Margaret's is a square-towered fifteenth-century construction, much remodelled by the Victorians. Above the door, carved into stone, are the words, 'Let Everything That Hath Breath Praise The Lord'. A good motto for a church full of bats. 'Yes,' said Kate, another of the surveyors. 'They are part of the church. Part of the congregation.'

Not everyone feels that way. The romantic idea of bats in churches is often contradicted by the unromantic reality. Bat shit on the Bible and in the vicar's hair, bat piss on the keys of the organ and in the communion wine; dead bats on pews and in loos; live bats flying out of the manger during the nativity play – these are the horror stories you hear.

A heavy bat presence smells a bit like a seabird colony, but not as strong. Bad enough, though, to put couples off getting married in an affected church, with the resultant loss of income. Churches have even had to close because elderly parishioners can't keep on top of the cleaning. 'We have some hardy volunteers, but it's demoralising when you clean the church and the next day it's dirty again,' the warden at St Mary's in the village of Gayton Thorpe had told me. 'It gives the false impression that the church isn't cared for and looked after.' The droppings, though unsightly, can be swept up, but urine is a real problem. It eats into the fabric of the building, sparing nothing, not even rare and valuable brass. Many a crusader knight has been burned and scarred by the pee of an infidel bat.

'If you wanted to design the perfect bat roost, you would probably end up with an English medieval church,' Rose Riddell, an engagement officer with the Bats in Churches project had explained before my visit. Most churches are built with the altar in the east, meaning that they have a long south side, the roof of which catches the sun and is nice and warm in summer for maternity roosts. Churchyards are rich in insect life, an easy food source without flying far. The walls of old churches, especially those, as in Norfolk, built from uneven pieces of flint mortared together, often develop small holes where stones fall out, allowing entry and exit. In winter, when bats need stable cold and humidity to maintain a torpor state similar to hibernation, they will doze away the bleakest months in the church's tower or crypt. The only part of a church that bats don't usually much like, contrary to the popular saying, is the belfry. Far too windy and noisy; bats and bells don't mix.

Not that these animals are quiet. It's just that we can't usually hear their racket. The soprano pipistrelle, a highly regular churchgoer, may weigh as little as four grammes and have a wingspan of just twenty centimetres, but its echolocation shriek has been measured at 120 decibels and likened to the experience of holding a smoke alarm to your ear. The pip – as bat fanciers call this species – performs its signature cry at around 55 khz, a frequency too high for human hearing. Bats are a choir inaudible.

It is likely that there have been bats in churches for as long as there have been churches, and therefore for as long as there have been clergy. The Hampshire parson and naturalist Gilbert White knew the pipistrelle and was the first person to describe the noctule, Britain's biggest bat, which he observed in 1769 feeding high in the air. Two years later, he procured two males of the species, writing that, 'Nothing could be more sleek and soft than their fur, which was of a bright chestnut colour . . . They weighed each, when entire, full one ounce and one drachm. Within the ear there was somewhat of a peculiar structure that I did not understand perfectly; but refer it to the observation of the curious anatomist. These creatures send forth a very rancid and offensive smell.'

The peculiar structure inside the ear would have been its tragus – a fleshy projection, mushroom-shaped in the case of the noctule, which is now known to act as a kind of receiver.

Echolocation, the means by which bats navigate and hunt in the dark, was not identified until the years of the Second World War. How does it work? A bat emits many high frequency cries of extremely short duration which then bounce back to it from its environment. Multiple echoes allow it to build a picture of large things that are static – a pulpit, a barn, a tree – and to be avoided, as well as very small objects that are moving and might therefore be eaten. It is thought that bats can distinguish between different types of insect by interpreting how fast they beat their wings, and thus make a decision about whether they are suitable prey. Bats can tell in which direction an insect is moving and at what speed. It takes less than one second between first becoming aware of an insect and eating it. In this way, a pipistrelle catches 3,000 midges a night.

Inside St Margaret's, sitting on a pew near the door, Phil Parker had almost finished setting up his monitors. He is in his late fifties and a great man for bats.

'How do you feel about them?' I asked.

'What,' he laughed, 'apart from love them?'

Vespertine shadows obscured the chancel. We would soon be able to see the bats leaving their roost, made visible on screen by infrared and thermal-imaging cameras. Phil spends his summers engaged in this work. From mid May to September he is out five or six times a week. The idea is not just to count the bats, but to identify where they exit a church and where, a few hours later, they come back in. This means being there at dusk and still there at dawn. It is a job of gloamings and cockcrows. 'I sleep better in a church than I do at home,' he said. Except, that is, here at Saxlingham, the only church in which he will not spend the night. It is quite small, with lots of bats and nowhere to get under cover; his camp-bed would end up soaked. So he dozes in his car, and considers it worth the discomfort. 'If you're an ecologist and you see it as a job then you're not a proper ecologist,' he said. 'It's a vocation. It's not about money, it's about interest and love for the things you're trying to protect.'

Having experienced a significant decline in numbers dating back to at least the start of the twentieth century, bats have been protected by law since 1981. It is a criminal offence to kill or injure them, and to damage, disturb or obstruct a roost. This means that churches have to live with their bats. Indeed, the whole point of the Bats in Churches project – a partnership between the Church of England, the Bat Conservation Trust and others – is not to exclude the animals, but to manage the way they use the building in a way that is compatible with how people want to use it. A few congregations have gone beyond mere toleration and have found ways to rebalance and even monetise the relationship: selling bat merchandise, for example, or running bat-walks. Others rather like the idea of providing a home for bats, to the point that they are competitive about numbers. St Mary's in Gayton Thorpe has the second-largest known bat roost in a Norfolk church – around 550 pipistrelles – and one of the committee members has her eye on the number one spot.

Bats do not always find safety in a church. Most of the worst cruelties are many years in the past, thankfully, but the animals do at times suffer for trying to share space with humans. 'Recently,' said Phil, 'we had a report of someone who had picked up a baby bat from a pew and went outside and stamped on him. We got the police involved because that's just abhorrent, isn't it? We know in the past that roosts have been gassed. One church used to have "bat-whacking night" – catching them as they were coming in and killing them. Another church we worked on, plastic and carpets had been nailed over the door to stop the bats coming in. We've found churches with spotlights shining up at the roost. We've frequently come across people using powerful ultrasonic devices to try and deter bats. Other places have put stuffed owls in the church. Another got someone with a motorbike to run up and down the nave to try to kill them with carbon monoxide. Two churches, they used cyanide.'

It was half past nine and quite dark. The church smelled of citronella and ammonia. Phil's radio crackled: 'Oop, there's the first bat out,' said Emily, one of the team. She was outside, keeping watch by the south transept, the bats' favoured exit. 'A Natterer's – over.'

The Natterer's is a medium-sized bat with large ears. It eats moths and spiders. Bats, like birds, have a characteristic way of flying that helps with identification. The flight of the Natterer's is often described as a lollop or slow undulation, but it flies at 4.5 metres per second so can hardly be considered a dawdler. It is a woodland bat. The roof beams of a church must seem to it a kind of forest. A newborn Natterer's, furless, resembles Dobby the House Elf from *Harry Potter*.

In St Margaret's, the bats roost in the chancel, above the altar. They usually come in through the north transept, in a tiny gap at the top of the wall. We switched on our head-torches and Phil led the way through the church. A copy of the *Telegraph* had been laid upon a brass memorial set into the floor, protecting it from urine. I had no such defence. I could feel, but not see, a spritz of wee against my anorak. 'There you go,' said Phil, 'you've been christened.'

He showed me what he was doing to mitigate the bat issue. The idea is to contain them in the north transept by putting in a false ceiling and creating a void in which they can roost. Already, some of the joinery work had been done, but with bats it is a case of little-by-little, allowing them time to get used to changed circumstances, so progress is necessarily slow. Eventually, though, the bats will have their own small enclave and will be unable to fly around within – and therefore damage – the main body of the church.

There is justice in this surrender of a little territory. It is, after all, as a consequence of human behaviour that bats are increasingly coming into churches. The clearing of dead trees and the conversion of agricultural buildings such as barns and tumbledown cottages into holiday accommodation forces them to seek shelter elsewhere. Add to this the fact that rural churches are likely to be not as well attended, and may not be in as good repair as even ten years ago, and you have a set of circumstances that makes an old church seem pretty attractive. The bats are, in a sense, refugees fleeing urban encroachment and agricultural intensification. To allow them sanctuary seems the least we can do. This is not to minimise the problems their presence creates, but perhaps there is an opportunity. One could argue that churches with bat populations ought to qualify for public funding, similar to that offered to farmers who promote wildlife diversity and restore natural habitats. A roost for the bats, a boost for the churches – winners all round.

I went outside to see how the survey was coming along. To supplement the special cameras, lamps had been directed to the side of one of the known exits, so that surveyors could count the bats that flew out. Red filters were used so as not to disturb the bats with white light and deter them from emerging. This practical measure had an atmospheric effect: the church appeared lit for a vampire movie; the walls were bloody, the churchyard, too. I sat against a gravestone to enjoy the show.

'There it goes!' said Kate. 'Over the top of your head, a Natterer's. Did you see?'

I did, sort of, though it was more as if I sensed it: a small dark shape, very fast, a couple of feet above me; a tatter of shadow tossed by the wind. Kate's bat detector was picking up its echolocation. The sound is commonly likened to the crackle of burning stubble, she explained, but it seemed to me more like dice rattling in a cup. 'Can you see it circling around?' she asked. 'What a fascinating creature. It feels good to do this work, progressive. It makes me feel like I'm protecting the church *and* the bats.'

Bats are the only mammals that can fly. This allows them to avoid ground predators and to cover some distance in their own predations. But it puts a strain on their bodies. Pipistrelles, the other type of bat in St Margaret's, have a heart rate of between 200–450 beats a minute at rest, rising to between 800–1,000 while flying. In its torpor state, hanging in some dank cave, a bat's heart may beat once every six seconds, and it may take as little as one breath per hour; statistics that I would interpret as a well-earned rest. In flight, they breathe in on the downstroke, out on the upstroke. Bats have certain characteristics that may make people, if they can get past the shudders, regard them with something approaching empathy. They live for much longer than mammals of comparable size – seven years, on average, for the Natterer's, four or five for the pip – and they usually give birth to just one pup per year. Female bats suckle their young.

Although they show up in the fossil record around 52 million years ago, bats are thought to have evolved millions of years before that. They may have witnessed the fall of the dinosaurs. Certainly they saw the rise of humans. They were here first. We are the Johnny-come-latelys with our fire and false light.

There are eighteen species of bat in the UK, although one – the greater mouse-eared – exists as a solitary example, wintering in a disused railway tunnel in an undisclosed location in West Sussex, its wings, half a metre in span, kept furled until spring, when it leaves for who knows where. This creature out of time is as anachronistic as the locomotives that used to speed through the sooty tunnel and which now are cherished by nostalgic steam enthusiasts. And so it is, in a way, with all bats – there is something elegiac about them, some lament in their flight, if only we could read those cur-licued swoops.

Or maybe we should just get over ourselves and admire bats as they are. 'For it is not his impression on the mind of man,' wrote the naturalist Russell Peterson, 'but the bat's own identity which holds the true fascination; this delicately balanced flying machine is one of the most highly specialised mammals next to man himself. The weird tales of horror and the repugnance that have enveloped him are tamely unimaginative compared with the fantastic intricacies of his true nature.'

The night wore on. The bats kept coming. At five past eleven, Phil called time. There were still a few flying around in the church; he judged that these were juveniles trying out their wings but not yet ready for the big wide world. The sur-veyors packed up and went home. Soon, Phil would snatch a few hours in the car, but there was another job first.

He opened the boot of his vehicle. Time to feed the foundlings.

'Have you got a mask?' he asked. 'There's a big fear of spreading Covid back to bats.'

We masked up. He put on gloves and opened a small box that had been made to carry cremation ashes. Three tiny bats were clinging to a pair of socks. 'Soprano pipistrelles of various sizes,' he said. Two or three weeks old, they were still flightless, but had their fur. Lost or abandoned by their mothers, Phil had discovered them on the floor of the local crematorium, which he monitors regularly, and was trying to keep them alive. He cradled them one at a time, their heads the size of fingertip, and fed them warm puppy formula from a dropper. The biggest of the three, he thought, was about old enough to move on to solid food: 'Mealworms. You pull the head off and squeeze its insides out.' A fourth bat, a common pipistrelle with a black face, had been recovered from the church at Gayton Thorpe. It looked up at us with affronted eyes from an empty tub of Cadbury's Heroes.

*

It was 2.45 a.m. and still dark. 'Sleep okay?' Phil asked. He was fiddling with the cameras, setting them up outside to catch the bats coming back in. We'd be starting again before long.

Moths flickered in the beam of my head-torch. Birds called in anticipation of the dawn. Phil named them as soon as he heard them. I'm not sure he knew he was doing it.

'Moorhen.'

'Young tawny owls.'

'Oystercatcher.'

'Heron.'

He pointed out where the bats would re-enter the church: beside a drainpipe, behind some guttering. 'That'll be where they swarm.'

The first went in at just before half past three, and after that they came fast. They didn't head for the roost straight away, preferring to circle and swoosh a while. The bat detector, tuned to their frequency, made a noise like heavy rain on a roof. They were still catching insects, too, a last snack before bed. We could hear it happening. The interval between echolocation pulses decreased as a bat zeroed in on its prey, so that just before it caught a fly the noise had a rapid-fire chitter that recalled a machine gun or electronic music of the most uncompromising sort. I wonder what it's like for a bat, that moment of attention and focus, curiosity and hunger satisfied with each intercepted bug? There is an idea that such hunting can't be the result of conscious thought, that it is too quick and involves too many coordinated processes. But I don't know. A bat seems to me a great rationalist. It asks straight questions and acts upon the replies.

'They're a darn sight cleverer than we are,' said Phil.

Bede writes, in his *Ecclesiastical History of the English People*, of King Edwin, who, in the seventh century, was considering whether to convert his people to Christianity. He gathered his wise councillors to ask their views. One offered his opinion in the form of a parable. Picture a sparrow flying through the royal banqueting hall on a winter's evening – in one door and out the other. While passing above the feast, amid the rising smell of meat and mead, the bird is safe for a moment, but back outside must endure the bleak cold rain once more. So it is, the councillor said, with man. The flight through the hall is our life on earth, however long we are granted. But what comes before that life, or after? On that matter, all is darkness. Let us turn to Christ, therefore, for illumination.

It is a lovely story, likely Bede's own invention, and I never hear it without thinking, yes, but what if it was a bat? Imagine for a moment that this particular creature had delayed its journey to the hibernation roost and instead found itself flying through the court of the Northumbrian king. The parable doesn't work for a bat. It would appreciate the firelit hall, the kindred shadows on the wooden walls, but would have no fear of the dark. It would find no mystery there, no silence. It would call out and receive, in the echo, answers. Bede's sparrow is all very well, and perhaps a good metaphor for our transience and ignorance, but give me a bat – its splendid awareness of its surroundings, its eldritch dart and flit.

The final tally at Saxlingham? Seventy-four. The Natterer's were in by just after four. The pips straggled on for almost an hour longer. The sun rose over flat fields as I drove away, and I felt uplifted by my night in the company of these animals. A bat in a church is no small thing.

# FEN

IN 1974, A THIRTY-YEAR-OLD university lecturer called Max Sebald wrote a travel story for a German newspaper titled '*Die hölzernen Engel von East Anglia: Eine individuelle Bummeltour durch Norfolk und Suffolk*.' As W. G. Sebald, he would, by his fifties, be regarded as one of Europe's great writers, the author of *The Emigrants, Austerlitz* and *The Rings of Saturn*. He died at fifty-seven and was buried in the churchyard of St Andrew's, Framingham Earl, following an accident while driving on the A140 near Norwich. Suffering a heart attack at the wheel, he veered into the opposite lane and collided with a lorry. This was eleven days before Christmas. He was buried in the new year with notebook and pencil in his shirt pocket. Pilgrims to the grave leave pebbles upon the headstone, devotional offerings made in gratitude for the sombre grace of his writing and in regret for the books he did not live to write.

The article for *Die Zeit*, aimed at those of his fellow Germans contemplating an English holiday, contains a few recognisably Sebaldian flourishes such as the recommendation that they 'study the emptiness of transience' at Sutton Hoo, and look out for Elizabethan ghosts. Mostly, though, it is a functional piece of work in which the young academic proposes an unhurried itinerary of inns, antique shops, historic buildings and strolls in the melancholic twilight, all of it intended to make the traveller feel that they are taking a holiday not only in another country but another century. 'How many days you need to reckon for such an East Anglian journey,' he writes, 'depends on how often you want to lose yourself in contemplating the many wooden angels who, with seeming ease, carry on their backs the hammer-beam roofs of many of the region's countless churches.'

Those angel roofs were what had drawn me to the area. I had wondered at them, and about them, from afar, leafing through pages and clicking on pics until page and screen were no longer sufficient, and the time came to do as Sebald suggested and lose myself in them for a while. That meant a journey. Of the 170 examples of these roofs that survive in the UK, nearly 70 per cent are in Norfolk, Suffolk and Cambridgeshire, with most of the rest in neighbouring counties. I like that these angels, as characteristic of eastern England as salt air and eels, are at once ornate and obscure, creatures of light hidden in the dark. 'Such sculptures are the works of absolute masters and deserve comparison with the best medieval carvings in any museum in the world,' Michael Rimmer says in his book *The Angel Roofs of East Anglia*, 'but because they are distant, inaccessible and fixed, they remain little known.'

That they are hard to see and harder to reach saved them from destruction. 'Such medieval figurative art as remains today in English churches is the minutest tip of a lost iceberg of sculpture, painting and stained glass,' Rimmer writes. 'The English Reformation was not just a religious revolution. It was an artistic holocaust.' The angels are survivors. They looked on as the glass was smashed, the walls whitewashed, the statues decapitated, the roods torn down. Destruction was nothing new to them, of course; they were born of it. Acorn to oak to angel, these were trees once. They had roots and branches, drank from the earth, knew the thistledown touch of the sky. Birds landed and nested in them, the wings of crows foreshadowing their own coming form. In time, they felt the kiss of the axe, the teeth of the saw, and they began to take shape, to become angelic.

When, as a boy, William Blake walked from his home in Golden Square to the fields of Peckham Rye, he saw angels in the trees, 'bright angelic wings bespangling every bough like stars'. When a medieval carpenter considered a tree growing in a wood, he too saw an angel; not as a revelation, but as a form waiting to be revealed. The churches of these parts are sylvan with the products of that visionary labour, so that when you look up at them, up at the beams of a Fenland church, you are looking at a forest.

\*

'Welcome to our angels!' said the Reverend Nigel Whitehouse. 'You get your eye in, you start seeing them everywhere.'

The rector of St Peter's in the Norfolk village of Upwell had unlocked the church and invited me inside. Now, he was introducing me to its residents. Staring down at us from the roof, they were impressive, even formidable, with a solemn gaze and six-foot wingspan. The rector was still getting to know them himself, having moved to the parish not quite a year before and the church having been closed, as a result of the pandemic, for much of that time.

This, though, was Freedom Day, so-called. All legal restrictions on social contact in England were now lifted. It felt a long while since I had made my previous visit to an angel – that steel giant by Gateshead – when there was snow on the ground and fear in the air. The breakfast news, before I set off for Upwell, had shown young people queueing for entry to nightclubs and then, as midnight arrived, rushing into the music and heat and lights. For many, clearly, today represented a release. Yet, as I travelled around Fenland towns and villages, there was little sense of freedom and none at all of victory. Cases were still rising. People were still dying. We didn't know quite how to feel. And this uncertainty had a visible symbol: the mask. It was no longer a requirement of law to wear one in public indoor spaces, which meant that continuing to do so became a statement, whether the wearer sought to make one or not. A mask said that you were vulnerable or frightened or cautious or courteous, perhaps mistrustful of the government, or some mixture of those things. It was strange to go masked into a Post Office to borrow the key for the local church and find the young woman behind the counter with an uncovered face. She smiled with her mouth; I didn't have to read it in her eyes, and that mundane skill of parsing a stranger's expression felt like a nostalgic pleasure – as if whistling along to an old song.

It was a pleasure, too, to spend the day within cool quiet churches. The Met Office had issued its first ever extreme heat warning. The sky was huge and blue, piled with cotton bales. Light danced on long straight roads. Dragonflies hovered over the Nene.

'The stillness of the Fens,' begins a church pamphlet I picked up, 'anciently recognised as the Holy Land of the English, still lingers in those vast reaches where, in times gone by, the sun and moon reflected from water spilling from lake to lake, overwhelming the marsh in winter, completely surrounding the islands where early missionaries made their homes.'

Even now, after centuries of drainage, the Fens have the unsteady feeling of land that was once water and looks forward to the day when it will be again. Daytrippers to Upwell sometimes come by boat, mooring outside St Peter's and writing the names of their vessels – *Sundance* was one that I noticed – in the visitors' book. The earliest parts of the church were built in the thirteenth century, but it was much enlarged in the early fourteenth, from which period the angels are said to date. The building and its carvings are thought to have inspired the fictional Fenchurch St Paul in *The Nine Tailors*, a 1934 novel by Dorothy L. Sayers. 'Incredibly aloof,' she writes, 'flinging back the light in a dusky shimmer of bright hair and gilded out-spread wings, soared the ranked angels, cherubim and seraphim, choir over choir, from corbel and hammer-beam floating face to face uplifted.'

Hammer-beams project horizontally from a church wall, supporting curved braces, and are connected to the roof rafters by vertical posts. They make possible a wider span, create the illusion of greater height, and allow angels a place to perch. 'The hammer-beam roofs of Norfolk and Suffolk,' writes Alec Clifton-Taylor, 'are indeed the greatest glory of English medieval woodwork.' For the likely origin of the form, however, it is necessary to look to London. Westminster Hall, built at the end of the fourteenth century, has the earliest surviving large-scale hammer-beam roof, and the first known angel roof. King Richard II, for whom it was built, had a taste for angels. At a public pageant on the day before his coronation in 1377, a gleaming mechanical angel built by the Worshipful Company of Goldsmiths bowed to the ten-year-old and offered him a crown.

The angel-roof tradition that began with a monarch ended with one, too. Following Henry VIII's break with Rome in 1534, such imagery was regarded by the authorities with – at best – suspicion, and even outright hostility. Parliament, in 1644, decreed that all representations of angels in churches should be 'taken away, defaced, and utterly demolished; and that no such hereafter be set up'. The angels of St Mary's in Earl Stonham, Suffolk, bear the marks of this destruction. They have all had their heads sawn off.

That so many have survived in East Anglia is, as I have said, very likely to be because they are so high and hard to reach. But this also makes them difficult to examine properly, and Sebald should perhaps have advised his readers to pack binoculars. The great delight of St Peter's in Upwell, however, is a pair of nineteenth-century galleries that allow visitors to get nearer to the angels than is possible in any other church.

Climbing the stairs to the gallery at the west end, I lay on the floor in front of one of the pews. Above me was an angel. It brought to mind the red kites I had seen all that summer, circling above motorways. The angel's primary feathers were long and curved, ticking up at the tips; closer to its body, its secondaries clustered like shingles on a roof. It wore a gown, falling in carved folds; a hexagonal peg had been driven through its thorax, fixing it to a beam. Its hands were held out and open in what was likely intended as a gesture of blessing, but which seemed, now, a kind of warning, as if to say 'Keep back!'

I went closer.

The angel, when I stood, was near enough to touch. It was genderless, its hair a densely looped mass, like honeycomb tripe. The eyes, too large for the face, had chiseled irises; the pupils were deep dark holes. The grain of the wood swept down across the forehead and brow, over the nose and slightly downturned lips.

I reached up my right hand and stroked its left cheek. Because of its great age and because it had been more than a year since I had touched anyone outside of my immediate family, to touch a face, even a wooden face, felt transgressive. It was smooth. Many hands over many years must have experienced this same strange intimacy.

The head was tilted a little to the left, as if expressing pity. *Malach*, the word for angel in Hebrew, means messenger. Their role, most notably at the Annunciation, when Mary learned she was to carry Christ, has been to bring the word of God to humanity. This angel, however, perhaps because of

its long proximity to the congregation of St Peter's, seemed to have taken something from humanity back to the heavens: the sadness of our little lives. It had caught that from us, sickened with it, and now looked down upon us with wooden eyes from which no tears, only dust, could ever fall.

*

The roof angels of St Agnes's in the village of Cawston are very different from those at Upwell; indeed, they are unique in that they stand upright at the edge of their hammer-beams. Some have hands clasped in prayer, Olympic divers going for gold, others hold up their open palms in the orans position, but all are impressive – six feet tall and clad in suits of wooden feathers modelled, it is speculated, on the costumes worn by actors playing angels in mystery plays. It is difficult to make out from the brick floor so far below, but their suits retain traces of medieval paint in patterns of sunset red and forest green, an afterglow of how this place must have looked in the late fifteenth century. 'A riot of colour, a blast, a visual assault,' reckoned Andrew Whitehead, the priest whose church this is.

St Agnes's was rebuilt at the end of the fourteenth century, he explained, with the wealth of the de la Pole family, the earls of Suffolk, and had always been much larger and more ostentatious than was necessary for its village location. That is even more the case now. The church can seat seven hundred. 'We routinely get between twenty-five and thirty-five people on a Sunday, so you rattle around a bit,' the priest said. 'But one of the things about these village churches is that when it comes to the festivals, certainly Christmas and Remembrance, we fill the place. Christingle, every pew is taken.' St Agnes's, he said, is 'a completely unmanageable and ridiculous building' and yet it was clear that he loves it.

Two years previously, in order to facilitate repairs, a scaffolding platform had been erected inside the church, allowing workers – and paying members of the public – to get close to the angels. 'That was a phenomenal privilege,' Whitehead recalled. 'You went up through the trapdoor and your head came out somewhere near the feet of the Angel Gabriel. It was like stepping into another world, so quiet and still. We were up there, isolated from the rest of the church, but it felt like we were in communion with these angels all around.'

He had given much thought to the meaning of the figures. 'There's a real sense that you're witnessing an escalation from the earthly to the heavenly as you look up to the roof. I suppose that, for many people, is what the angels represent. And then there's the idea of the guardian angel looking over us and interceding for us. A lot of that thinking persists, and that fascinates me: the folk culture of angels.'

I mentioned my visit to the Angel of the North, and the shrine I had found there, the offerings and tokens and tinsel. The priest nodded. He had noticed something similar – an intensely felt identification between people and place. 'One of the chaps who rings the bells,' he said, 'he doesn't come to church; he rings the bells because his family have always rung the bells. He has a love for the church, and knows it better than most, and yet he's not a believer.

'People are invested in this building. We've got a parishioner in her eighties who remembers when there was a visible blush on the cheeks of all the angels, before the paint degraded. She holds that living memory. And there's another woman, Roman Catholic, very much lapsed, who has started volunteering to clean here. She doesn't come to church on a Sunday and probably never will, but has a real sense of being watched over, a real sense of peace and calm, and that is communicated by the angels. She finds that compelling.

'So there's a deep and persisting connection with the physical properties of this space. I'm sure that back at the time of the Reformation, people felt the same: "This is important to us, this is part of who we are, and we're not going to see it destroyed."'

This is ours, and it is us. Whitehead believes that this feeling of mutual possession is a reason why so much from the medieval period has survived at St Agnes's. The church is known, in particular, for a rood screen, separating the nave from the chancel, which dates from the late fifteenth century and depicts saints on colourful panels. St Matthew, the most photographed of the figures, appears a little comical now; he holds a pair of spectacles in his right hand and looks up from the Bible, as if displeased at being interrupted in the middle of a good book.

The screen is an important artefact and an internationally

significant work of art. It's also emblematic of the challenges many old churches face with regard to their inherited fabric. 'We have been told we can't clean the screen,' Whitehead explained. 'It's so delicate and in such a precarious state that even running over it with a duster will take off medieval paint irreparably. So we now have to wait until we can attract some major funding to have it cleaned in a painstaking way by a specialist. There's a problem with sustainability. We can find people to run around with a duster, but we can't find fifty grand to have somebody pore over it for weeks. Anywhere else in the world, this would be in a museum. It would be in a temperature-controlled, dust-controlled environment and it would just sit there with people marvelling at it. But here it's in a working building where we have toddlers, and we have cake.'

It isn't so long since the church spent £360,000 on window repairs, drainage and some internal reordering, most of that funding coming from the National Lottery. It is hoped to raise a further million pounds, to be spent on the roof and other works. That is a lot of money for thirty people to come and sing hymns on a Sunday. Another way to look at it, though, is that churches are akin to museums and art galleries in which the building itself is the star exhibit. Almost half of all Grade I listed buildings in England are parish churches. A case could be made that the repairs and maintenance of such buildings ought to be paid for by the state, rather than as it is in the current situation: responsibility lying with an ever-smaller congregation to raise funds through grant applications and bake sales and the collection plate. In France, all churches built before 1905 are in public ownership, with cathedrals being the particular responsibility of the government, although that does not mean, in practice, that adequate money is spent on their upkeep. Should the UK introduce a similar funding model? If we all benefit from the existence of historic churches, as repositories of historic treasures and cultural memory, then why should the financial load press down solely upon those locals who use them for worship?

The truth is that old churches, like St Agnes's, are places where the ritualised past and the messy secular, or secularish, present rub up against each other. 'I'll tell you a story,' said Whitehead. Not long ago, the church was visited by a museum curator who gasped at the sight of the priest holding a fifteenth-century chalice in his bare hands.

'We would wear gloves,' she said.

'We use it every week,' he replied. 'It's a cup.'

And that, he said now, 'is my experience of living with the heritage. Yes, it's wonderful, it's amazing, it's beautiful, but it's a church. If we didn't have visitors and toddler groups and craft fairs and all the things we do these days, it wouldn't be a church. It would just be a closed building with some interesting stuff in it.'

*

Towards the end of my day among the angels, I walked into a church. I won't say which church. And I spoke with a man. I won't say his name.

He was in a wheelchair. He was concerned about the virus, so I sat at a distance that seemed to reassure him, and together, apart, we looked up.

There were – what? More than a hundred angels. More than I could easily count. The collective noun for angels is 'host', from the Hebrew word 'sabaoth', which also means armies. But that didn't seem right for this roof full of lift and light. I thought instead of birds and bats. A flock of angels; a roost. I thought of fighter jets: a squadron.

Wings spread, they gave the impression of gliding above the nave. Those lower down, attached to wall-posts, held musical instruments – rebec, lute and shawm – and appeared to carry, on their shoulders, saints holding the instruments of their martyrdom. St Lawrence gripped the grid-iron on which, by tradition, he was roasted.

What we were looking at, the man said, was timber felled in the forests of Suffolk. It was first worked and then brought to the church, which at that time was on an island in the malarial Fenland, by barge, and horse and cart, and assembled in the grounds.

This church was named for a saint skilled in healing the sick. The beautiful roof was made to honour that gift. The angels were carved at benches, by carpenters sitting across from one another, and it would be inevitable, the man thought, that they served as each other's models. 'These,' he said, 'are undoubtedly the faces of the men who carved them five hundred years ago.'

He had pleasure in his voice. He seemed moved by this idea that the angels had been made in the image of their creators, and this caused me to be curious about his own beliefs. Is he, I wondered, a religious person? Had I asked him that question a few years ago, he replied, the answer would have been no. Funerals and weddings were the extent of his church-going. But something changed. Mobility problems, damage to his spinal cord, meant that he had come to rely on crutches; it got to the point where he was having difficulty even standing, and he felt himself falling into despair. One day, a visiting priest came to the church. 'I can't ask for a miracle that I walk again,' the man said to him, 'but will you pray for me that I can stand up for a bit longer?' This was done, and, a couple of days later, he felt a wave come over him: 'I got the holy spirit.' He was much better, regained his confidence, too, and took to giving talks and tours in an effort to repay the church for the place it now held in his life. Only very recently has he had to start using the wheelchair. He believes he was granted three good years.

Again, we looked up. A defect in its construction had meant that, over time, the roof developed a serious structural fault; an ingenious system of rods had, in recent years, been put in place near the apex to hold it together. The old wood was made strong by new steel, the man observed, and I could not help but think that his bones, too, had found support and strength – though in faith not forged metal.

Whether or not you believe in God, and, if you do, whether you believe that God would and could heal someone's body – well, that doesn't matter really. The point is that this man believes that happened in his life. Little wonder, then, that these angels, these symbols of God's desire to communicate with us and intervene in our lives, had become so important to him.

'Oh, yeah,' he said, quietly. 'They're not just bits of oak.'

\*

IN HOLY TRINITY, Stow Bardolph, a few miles south of King's Lynn, there is a side-chapel, and in that side-chapel there is a wonderful, terrible thing.

Enter the small church. You are likely to be the only visitor. No sign will tell you what you are about to see. It is as if they would rather you didn't know. Pass up the nave and into the chancel and turn left through an arched doorway. Walk to the north-west corner and you will find a cabinet of dark wood. You will find that you are able to open it, and then you will find that you are opening it, and then it will be too late and there she will be: Sarah Hare.

Or rather, a wax effigy of Sarah Hare, a member of the local gentry who died on 9 April 1744 – poisoning her blood with the prick of a needle. She was fifty-five and resident in

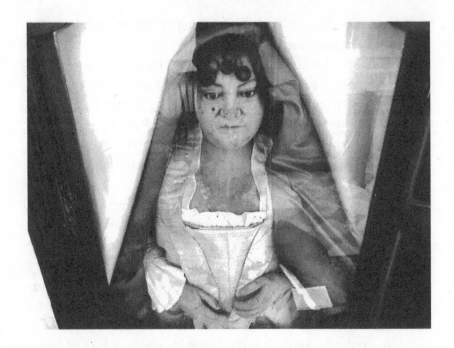

Essex at the time of her death. It was her wish that she should be memorialised here in this way.

'I desire to have my face and hands made in wax,' she declared in her will, 'with a piece of crimson satin thrown like a garment in a picture, hair upon my head, and put in a case of mahogany with a glass before and fix'd up so near the place where my corps lyes as it can be . . .'

The waxwork is life-size and life-like, probably made from a life- or death-mask, and is in no way a flattering portrait. Beneath the red cloak, almost pressed against the glass, is a face: plump and over-ripe; ingrained dirt gives the impression that it is veined like cheese. The eyes are blue. Dark curls fall upon the forehead. The effigy has grown grubby and worn. The neck and décolletage are filthier than the face, and her hands are filthiest of all. Her left index finger is coming away at the knuckle. She wears a damask robe. She wears a neutral expression. She brings to mind Dorian Gray, Miss Havisham, the ending of *Don't Look Now*. It would be the most natural thing in the world, the most dreadful thing in the world, if she smiled.

Where is Sarah Hare's body? Buried beneath the flagstones, most likely, at the foot of the cabinet. One thinks of her lying there, a trapdoor spider feasting on the shock and revulsion of visitors. This is church as fairground booth, as freakshow. It is an odd kind of eternal life.

'I'm rather fond of her, actually,' said Lady Rose Hare, over tea and biscuits, when we met at her nearby home. 'She's part of our family. Reading bits and pieces about her life is like reading a Jane Austen novel. The person comes alive. I think she was a strong lady with strong opinions and a strong family feeling. She wanted to come back to Stow to be buried. I would have liked to have known her.'

Lady Rose was eighty-five when we met. 'I'm her guardian,' she said of the effigy. What relation is Sarah Hare to her? 'Well, I don't quite know. She's my husband's ancestor. The Hare family have lived here since – oh golly – the 1500s, so there's always been Hares about. And she's one of them. But she's amazing, isn't she? She's got her own clothes on. And the V&A told us that the wig is her own hair. She's so precious, almost unique.'

*Almost* unique because the only other wax funeral effigies in Britain are those exhibited in the Queen's Diamond Jubilee Galleries, Westminster Abbey. The royal tradition of placing a replica of the deceased on the coffin as it was paraded and lay in state was first known in England in 1327; Edward II's coffin, while on public view in Gloucester, bore a wooden likeness of the king wearing a copper crown and dressed in armour. The earliest of Westminster's wooden effigies is that of Edward III, made in 1377. With the death of Charles II in

1685 came a new practice among royals and nobles of wax effigies being placed upright by their own tombs. Frances Stuart, the Duchess of Richmond, a noted beauty, left instructions in her will that she should be modelled by Maria Goldsmith, who ran a celebrated waxwork museum, and dressed in the robes she had worn to the coronation of Queen Anne, a few months before. She died in 1702 and her effigy can still be seen, alongside her stuffed pet parrot, a favourite that did not long survive without its mistress. The abbey collection of effigies numbers twenty, including that of Robert Sheffield, the Marquess of Normanby, who died at the age of three in 1715; his likeness is three feet three inches tall and wears the boy's own clothes – a silk gown and velvet robe, in the back of which are slits to accommodate baby reins.

If the modern visitor finds these effigies unsettling then that is not necessarily because our sensibilities are so different from those of the age in which they were made. They have long had a disquieting power. The German novelist Sophie von la Roche visited Westminster Abbey in 1786 and felt the strangeness of the dead who seem to live. 'The custom of exhibiting wax figures of important personages, clad in the costume of their day, struck me as very queer,' she wrote. 'A beautiful Duchess of Richmond seems to come towards one, when the doors of her cupboard have been opened, fan in hand, in her court-dress of green velvet embroidered in gold, as seen a hundred years ago . . .'

There was a fashion for waxwork shows in eighteenth-century England, and it is possible that Sarah Hare's decision to have herself remembered in wax, though unusual and remarkable, was not without some sort of precedent. Hers may be the only effigy outside Westminster Abbey to have survived, but others were made. When the playwright William Congreve died in 1729, his lover Henrietta Godolphin, the Duchess of Marlborough, commissioned – according to gossipy reporting of the time – a life-size copy. This figure joined her at the table for meals and was taken into her bedroom at night; however, after two years it broke into pieces when a servant dropped it coming down the stairs.

Whenever I have gone to see Sarah Hare in Stow Bardolph, I have thought of W. G. Sebald's words in *The Emigrants* – 'And so they are ever returning to us, the dead.' On the occasion of my most recent visit, there was an additional touch of the otherworldly: a white peacock ambled through the village and cried out as I passed on my way to church.

Holy Trinity is Norman with a mostly Victorian interior. The mausoleum chapel was built in 1624 and has provided a resting place for many generations of Hares. Members of the family are no longer laid to rest inside the chapel, but the tradition continues in the form of memorial plaques mounted upon the wall. Lady Rose's late husband, Sir Thomas, died in 1993 and is remembered thus; his plaque is close by Sarah Hare's cabinet.

To experience the full power of an encounter with the effigy, it is best to visit the church by oneself. As Sarah Hare is at once presence and absence, there is a shivery sensation of being both alone and not-alone. Many have felt this over the years. D. P. Mortlock, in his *Popular Guide to Norfolk Churches*, published in 1985, observed that the impact of the waxwork on the visitor is 'totally shattering'. The conservationist Lady Wilhelmine 'Billa' Harrod, who campaigned to save many of the area's medieval churches from demolition, is sometimes said to have been the first to rediscover and write about the effigy. She chanced upon it one evening in 1955, just before dusk, opening the cabinet with no idea of what lay within:

'Peering at me, her eyes glistening, the hands and bosom appearing to move in the shadows, sad, distraught, with a mottled face, dressed in a white tucked silk gown, with a red cape and hood over her ringlets, upright in a box, stood a young lady dead for over two hundred years. I was frightened, really frightened. I was alone in the church; outside the rain was beating down and leaves were being blown against the windows . . .'

The effigy would, she felt, have provided a fruitful subject for the ghost story writer M. R. James. Indeed, there is something about the flat expanses of this part of England that seem halfway to the page already. A fairy-tale place, Graham Swift calls it in his novel *Waterland*:

> And it is strange – or perhaps not strange at all, only logical – how the bare and empty Fens yield so readily to the imaginary – and the supernatural. How the villages along the Leem were peopled with ghosts and earnestly recounted legends. The Singing Swans of Wash Fen Mere; the Monk of Sudchurch; the Headless Ferryman of Staithe – not to mention the Brewer's Daughter of Gildsey.

It is a landscape of transformation: water becomes land; rivers become dykes; a teenage girl, in Daisy Johnson's story 'Starver', ceases eating and becomes an eel. It is quite proper, in such a place, that flesh should become, not dust, but wax.

Stow Hall, the Elizabethan manor house where Sarah Hare grew up, was demolished towards the end of the eighteenth century. The Georgian mansion that replaced it was replaced in turn in the 1870s by a neo-Elizabethan house which was knocked down and cleared in the mid 1990s. The outline of the hall can be discerned in the hedges that mark where its walls once stood. Another transformation: brick becoming yew. This is the place to which Sarah wanted to return.

Lady Rose laid a copy of the will on the table as we spoke. Sarah Hare had asked for her body to be wrapped in one of her own blankets, forbidding the use of a shroud; her coffin, which was to be 'of the best Elm', should bear her coat of arms and a quotation from the Bible: 'They that humble themselves shall be exalted.' She asked that her body should be brought to the mausoleum from Essex, 'in the cheapest method possible' – by cart, she thought, though she did not mind so long as she was not conveyed by water. That preference is not explained. She may have had some sort of horror of water, which is curious in a Fenlander. Did someone she loved drown?

'I desire six of the poor men in the parish of Stow or Wimbotsham may put me in the ground,' the will continued, 'they having five shillings a piece for the same.' She bequeathed two shillings and sixpence to each of the poor people who lived in the local almshouses, specifying that it should be given to them at the graveside. Her best clothes she left to 'any unfortunate person not too proud to wear them . . .'

It is a strange document: such emphasis on humility, and yet she asks to be made into a waxwork, like one of the great ladies of the London court. If this was not self-regard then what was it? A clue may be found in that line she chose for her coffin plate. It is from the same verse of Matthew in which Christ likens the scribes and Pharisees to 'whited sepulchres' – tombs – 'which indeed appear beautiful outward, but are within full of dead men's bones, and of all uncleanness'. Not for Sarah Hare, then, a grandiloquent marble memorial of the sort erected by her mother Elizabeth for her father Sir Thomas. He lies just a few steps from his daughter beneath a white altar tomb on which he is represented as a reclining figure, dressed in a wig and Roman armour. He died at the age of thirty-six, when Sarah was just three years old, so she would have known this grave for much of her childhood. Perhaps she took from it a suspicion of false appearances and vanity, a desire to present things as they really are. Here I am, her effigy seems to say, as I was. Here I was, as I am.

'Just have a look at this,' said Lady Rose, passing me a bundle of photographs. 'This is the condition she was in.'

The pictures were taken in the winter of 1984 and show the waxwork in the mausoleum, having been removed from the box for conservation work. Her red hood is up and she has been placed on a table in good light, all the better to see her with. 'When we lifted her out of her cabinet with great care, it was the first time, we think, that she had been out since 1744,' Lady Rose said. 'It was quite a moment for all of us. We weren't quite sure what we would find.'

They found that the effigy was damp and rotting. Mice had eaten through the clothes and made nests in the hay with which the body – a wooden frame – was stuffed. Had she been left much longer, she might have been beyond repair. 'It took my husband more than a year to find somebody to do the work,' Lady Rose recalled. 'He was advised to go to a deaf nun in Germany who did waxworks, but we thought that might be tricky.'

The wax elements were, in the end, conserved by Jean Fraser, former chief sculptor of Madame Tussaud's, and the clothes by Judith Doré, who had been senior conservation officer with the Victoria and Albert Museum. Centuries of spiderwebs were removed; moth cocoons were picked off with tweezers; the whalebone in the corset, gnawed to bits by rodents, was strengthened. The face and hands were dirty but relatively undamaged; they were cleaned and the wig shampooed. 'Her hair was about twenty years behind the times in style because she was a country lady,' said Lady Rose fondly. 'It wasn't up to London standards.' She keeps in the attic – she mentioned – the hay with which Sarah was once stuffed.

'It would have been very wrong to let her collapse,' she continued. 'We've got to do everything we can to preserve her. We're custodians, aren't we?'

The cabinet is left unlocked, she explained, on the grounds that it might otherwise be damaged by some opportunist thief trying to break in. Also, it honours the dead woman's wish that she should be seen. Whenever Lady Rose had noticed someone looking in the cabinet, she introduced herself as a relation lest they say something unkind about the effigy, but most visitors were simply fascinated. She remembered one man, an orthopaedic surgeon, who, after careful examination of the wax hands, observed that, 'She had quite bad arthritis, didn't she?'

Maybe this is what happens when you stare into the face of Sarah Hare: your own experiences and interests are reflected back. Lady Rose saw a member of the family. The surgeon saw a woman in pain. I see a fairy-tale creature because I am drawn to stories.

Do you think that Sarah would be pleased, I asked, that getting on for three hundred years after her death, she is still looking out through the glass with those bright blue eyes?

'I would have thought she'd be absolutely delighted,' Lady Rose replied. 'There she sits in splendour, just as she's always been.'*

\*

---

* Lady Rose died on 26 April 2022, less than a year after we had met. A service of thanksgiving for her life was held at Holy Trinity, Stow Bardolph. Sarah Hare was, of course, present.

JOHN VIGAR, I AM CERTAIN, has visited more churches in England and Wales than anyone now living; more, probably, than anyone who has ever lived; and more, there is a fair chance, than anyone ever will. He carries in his mind an index of churches he has known and loved over half a century, and on his body a tribute to that love affair. His left arm is bright with saints; Patrick, bearded and haloed, stares out from his shoulder. These are tattoos, based on favourite stained glass windows, but it would be little surprise to learn that they had burst spontaneously from his skin, the psychedelic stigmata of a man with churches in his blood.

'My life,' he told me, 'has been about showing things to people that they wouldn't otherwise see.'

John, who is in his early sixties, is an ecclesiologist, an expert on church buildings. He has written several books, takes tours, and gives entertaining lectures. I had attended one – 'Murder, Sex and Mayhem in the English Church' – that more than lived up to its title. He has visited approximately 12,000 churches in the UK, gets to around 700 each year, and can manage somewhere in the region of twelve to fifteen in a day. He grew up in Kent, but he and his husband have settled in East Anglia, lured by the quality and number of medieval churches, there being more per head of population than anywhere else in Europe. The German original of Sebald's *The Rings of Saturn* had the subtitle *Eine englische Wallfahrt* – which translates as *An English Pilgrimage* – and this is how I had come to think of John Vigar's life and work. Not a pilgrimage in the strict religious sense (he is no longer a believer) but certainly an expression of his devotion to beauty and craft and the faith-filled people of the past. There could, in short, be no one better with whom to spend a day in the Norfolk countryside.

'What would you like to see?' he had asked. Mostly, I wanted to see churches as he saw them. I wanted to be carried along in the slipstream of his attention.

He drove, I followed. The road shimmered and the land was supine with heat. The radio played Happy Mondays and Alice Coltrane: *Hallelujah, Hallelujah. Krishna, Krishna.* We passed the shrine at Walsingham, England's Nazareth. Union flags hung from a garden wall. A muntjac lolloped between stalks of corn. Metal detectorists walked the fields, lost in the whine.

We stopped at the church of St Lawrence in the village of Harpley. 'This place is amazing to me,' John said. He pointed out the fifteenth-century door – 'One of the best church doors in England' – which is carved with figures including a rather eerie St Jerome, identifiable by his hat.

Standing in the porch, about to try the door, is always a nervous moment. Will the church be open, which is a rush? Or will it be locked, a deflating snub? Most Norfolk churches are open every day, another good reason to live there, but not everywhere is so blessed. Too often there will be the troublesome business of phoning up the vicar for the key. Certain parishes, even entire counties ('Nottinghamshire,' John tutted) are notorious for poor access, but only one site in the whole of England is considered impossible: the Bedford Chapel, private mausoleum of the Dukes of Bedford, which is part of St Michael's in the village of Chenies, Buckingham-shire. 'That,' John had said, 'is the holy grail.'

Now, in the porch of St Lawrence's, he tried the handle. It turned with a satisfying clank and we stepped inside.

\*

Over the last few months I had spoken with several church-crawlers, many of whom had delighted in recollecting the sensuous pleasure of that moment when the door gives. 'I get excited just thinking about it,' a young priest in London confessed. 'The joy you feel when you find that the door is unlocked is even more joyful when the cobwebs break as you open it.'

The expression 'church-crawling' appears to have been coined by either John Betjeman or his friend and colleague, the artist John Piper. Certainly, Betjeman used it in a 1948 radio broadcast, and then expanded upon this in an article of that name the following year. 'The instruments you need for church-crawling,' he informed his readers, 'are (1) a notebook in which you can sketch and write remarks; (2) opera or field glasses for viewing roofs and stained glass; (3) a one-inch map; (4) most important, an unprejudiced eye.'

At times, a pair of wheels could also be useful. The buildings selected by the poet for the *Collins Guide to English Parish Churches* should include, he insisted, 'one object which, regardless of date, was aesthetically worth bicycling twelve miles against the wind to see'.

One needn't be a church-goer, as Betjeman was, to be a church-crawler. Indeed, among those I have met, atheism is common. Ask them why they do this and religion doesn't much come into it.

'I needed beauty in my life and I found it inside churches,' one told me.

'I've never felt the presence of God in any of these places,' said another.

A third told me that she always feels slightly embarrassed when they are visiting a church and her husband sits down to pray.

Perhaps most Christians are happy in their own parish church and feel no need to look elsewhere. Church-crawlers, by contrast, are unfaithful, their heads easily turned by a fancy spandrel. This desire for new thrills has been intensified, in recent years, by social media, where a community of crawlers post photographs of their latest conquests, prompted by hashtags such as #FontsOnFriday, #AugustAngels and #SeptemberSaints. One woman told me that, while she had always had an eye for churches, Twitter had turned a flirtation into an obsession. An entirely positive one. When visiting churches now, she was really looking at and engaging with them in a way she hadn't before. The hobby, for her, was no longer a solitary pursuit; it was about photographing treasures and sharing them online with others who are just as magpie-eyed.

It isn't just about what you can see, though. Church-crawling engages the other senses. The smell often hits first, that odour of damp stone, mouldering prayer books, beeswax and bat so closely aligned with the overall feel of a church – that impalpable somethingness – because both are created by the long passage of time. One crawler told me that he enjoys walking into a country church on a very hot day, after cycling for miles through the lanes, as the cold damp air offers a sudden smack of relief. Another spoke of the experience of being inside during a storm; the creaking timbers and gush of water in gutters, 'almost like the church is hunkering down against the weather'. There is, too, the exhilaration of those summer evenings when swifts come screaming out from the eaves.

*

Inside St Lawrence's, John Vigar drew my attention to the north-west window. What he wanted me to see was low down in the right-hand corner, but I still had to stand on a stone bench to get high enough. A clear glass diamond pane appeared to have something scratched into it.

'Can you make out what it says?'

Not at first, but then, yes, I could. A name – Joseph, perhaps? – and a word that, even on such a warm day, provoked a shiver: 'Hanged.' This man, being a criminal, wouldn't have merited a memorial, but someone who cared for him, perhaps a friend or brother or lover, had scratched his name into the glass with the jewel in a ring as an act of remembrance and, for hundreds of years, the sun had shone through it into the church. This graffiti is not mentioned in any guidebook, but the ecclesiologist had found it according to his unvarying method – careful loving patience – and thus someone's tragic fate was brought once more into the light.

'The more you look,' he said, 'the more you see.'

That philosophy was apparent again and again as we visited churches. The itinerary was themed around medieval stained glass, Norfolk having far more surviving than many other counties. In a window of All Saints, Bale, a barefoot angel wearing a suit of feathers brought to mind those magnificent figures on the hammer-beams at Cawston. Norwich was a major school of stained glass production in the fifteenth century. 'There would have been a street with lots of different glaziers,' John said, 'each with their own little kiln.'

Norwich glass, typically, is clear with black and yellow colouring. The black was made using iron oxide mixed with powdered glass and wine or urine, the yellow through the application of a silver compound which was then fired. Of course, the Reformation and its long aftermath resulted in the smashing of huge amounts of glass. William Dowsing, a Puritan appointed by Parliament to carry out the destruction of religious images, visited a great many East Anglian churches. On 9 January 1643, he and his men reached St Gregory's in Sudbury, where his journal records the breaking of 'mighty great angels in glass, in all, 80'. As a result of such iconoclasm, a significant amount of the medieval glass we now see in East Anglia has been assembled from fragments, often in a church other than the one for which they were created. This gives some windows a jumbled jigsaw feel – here a head, there a hand – that has a certain weird charm. One such figure, I noticed, is like something from Hieronymous Bosch: a woman's breasts, a demon's talons, a face of grass and leaves.

That window is in the church of St Mary Magdalene, Warham, a couple of miles east of Wells-next-the-Sea. 'This is my favourite church for stained glass,' John said. 'Some of these faces appear in the Betjeman film.'

John Betjeman's *A Passion for Churches* was broadcast by the BBC a little before Christmas, 1974, the same year in which W. G. Sebald was writing about roof angels. John Vigar saw it when he was fourteen, and it made him realise that churches aren't just about architecture and fittings, they're about people. This lyrical television essay, in praise of the diocese of Norwich, seems, now, a portrait of an almost vanished England. Sunday-school kids with 1970s haircuts bash toy drums and tambourines. The Norfolk accent of an elderly bellringer is strong as cider. The rector of St Mary the Virgin, Martham, oils his model locomotive as choirboys, in cassocks and ruffs, rehearse in the room below. 'A place to think of when the world seems mad with too much speed and noise,' Betjeman observes. He is talking about the convent of All Hallows, Ditchingham, but the sentiment is true of old churches in general. The film is a celebration but has a strange sad power, the poet in straw boater and shiny mac, ambling ursine from tower to tower. Anglican traditions are presented as enduring and important, even in the face of growing public indifference. 'It doesn't matter when there's no one there,' says Betjeman, in voiceover, as the vicar of Flordon says matins to empty pews. 'It doesn't matter when they do not come.'

John Vigar wrote to the poet and was invited to visit him at home in London. 'I didn't realise at the time what a famous and important person he was. I went to his house in Chelsea and had tea and cakes and we talked and talked. He was sitting at a table piled with books and papers, and although I was a shy boy, quite intimidated by grown-ups, he was warm and empathetic and made me feel at home straight away.' They kept in touch for around eight years, until Betjeman's health began to fail. It was an important formative relationship. 'Without him, I wouldn't be here today. There's no question.'

It was around this time, somewhere between his first meeting with Betjeman and the Poet Laureate's death in 1984, that John Vigar lost his faith. He had been very religious as a child, but in his late teens, early twenties that changed. 'It didn't help that I was gay,' he said. 'That was an issue at my church. I'd given everything to that place. I had been in the choir, then I was a bellringer, then sacristan. The clergy were fantastic, really supportive, but the people in the church were not.'

'You experienced bigotry?' I asked.

He nodded.

'People who I had grown up with, who I thought were my friends, turned out not to be.'

Happily, John has found a way to love churches without loving God. Since 1974 he has sought to do for others what Betjeman did for him: help them to see and understand the beauty and fascination of these places. His whole life has been about passing on that gift.

I felt his enjoyment in sharing as we stood and looked at a window in the church at Warham. John first visited this place in 1984 and has been hundreds of times since. 'These really are old friends to me,' he said of the faces. He meant, in particular, two square fragments of fifteenth-century glass, about the size of a man's palm, set low down in the window. Each shows an angel playing the lute, their wings and instruments and wavy hair yellow with silver stain. A musician might be able to tell from the position of their fingers what chords they are playing, but I found it difficult to focus on anything other than their features. Angels, as with the one whose cheek I had stroked at Upwell, were often portrayed by medieval artists as generic messengers of God, ageless and unsexed. These angels in the glass, though, were surely based on real people. They are teenage boys, gawky and gallus, with the rascally look of street urchins. 'They could easily have been apprentices in the workshop,' John thought, 'or maybe the sons of the chap who made them, or people he saw going past the shop every day. They could have been buskers. They probably didn't even know that they were being replicated in glass.'

He was moved, in particular, by the angel on the left – lips parted, perhaps in song, revealing crooked teeth. 'In the middle ages, it was thought that if you opened your mouth an evil spirit could get in. That's why figures in stained glass very rarely had open mouths.' The lute-player was, therefore, in danger, and yet seemed blithe. I envied his lack of concern. Like most people, I had in recent times grown used to regarding the nose and mouth as both vulnerable and threatening. My breath could hurt others, and theirs could hurt me. That was why we wore masks: as small acts of reciprocal mercy.

'You can't get more personal than this,' John continued. 'This is the artistic expression of people just like us, who were going through the same things that we are; who had their own plagues and shortages of money. But the people who made this glass have put the best of themselves into it.'

Bodily suffering and loneliness are points of connection between our time and theirs. An empty stomach is an empty stomach, an empty house an empty house, regardless of the century. I had spent the last year or so taking food to strangers, shopping for those whose 'underlying health issues', as the bland phrase ran, meant that catching the virus would be especially serious. A number of these people, those referred by social work, had additional financial problems and so relied on donated groceries. They lived in small blocks of flats, stairways littered with fag ends. Very often – whether out of fear or shame, I don't know – they wouldn't answer the buzzer or door. When I looked up at the windows, I could see light and movement behind the panes, sometimes I could hear music (once, I remember, it was Simon and Garfunkel's 'Scarborough Fair') but, in the end, I would have to leave the box of tins, teabags and pasta on the mat, trusting that it would be brought inside before it was stolen by someone even more desperate.

There was one woman I did get to know a little. She lived alone. I would lay the heavy shopping at her door, step well back, and we would spend a couple of minutes in conversation. I'd ask after her grandchildren. She'd ask after my boys. She had never, in all those months, seen the lower part of my face, and I do not think she would recognise me in the street. This was one of the vicious peculiarities of the virus, the way it inverted the norms of human connection, so that keeping your distance became a kindness and covering up was not about hiding but rather seeking to protect others from pain. Yet, for all that this was understood, the long months of masks had a strange choking sadness. That was why spending those Fenland days exposed to so many faces, in wood and wax and now in beautiful windows, felt like a greedy inhalation, like sucking in deep lungfuls of air after having lived behind glass for too long.

We walked out to look at the churchyard. Billa Harrod, who had that frightening encounter with Sarah Hare in 1955, died sixty years later and is buried here in the shadow of St Mary Magdalene, Warham, one of the churches she saved. We stood at the grave, amid an arcadian scene: butterflies and wild flowers; the croon of wood pigeons and squeak of a gate; farms and fields and the river beyond.

'Oh,' I said, 'it's so English!' But John Vigar, English pilgrim, corrected me.

'So *Norfolk*,' he said.

# WELL

I HAD TURNED ON TO Well House Lane and was walking up the hill when I noticed a druid struggling to open the boot of his Nissan. He held an elaborate staff in one hand, and the wind – blowing hard and cold – fretted the hem of his robe.

'Good morning,' I said.

He turned and smiled. 'Morning!'

His hood was up. A grey beard spilled out like water from a cave.

'Are you Nik Greenheart?' I asked. 'I'm looking for Nik Greenheart.'

'No,' he replied. 'I'm Merlin.'

'Oh,' I said. 'Have you been up the Tor?'

'No,' said Merlin. 'I'm just here to collect the light and then I'm off to Stonehenge.'

I wished him well and carried on up the lane. This was a big day for pagans. It was the first of February, which meant that it was Imbolc, an important festival marking the start of spring, the return of heat and light; the seeds in the earth, on this day, begin to think green thoughts about the world above. Here in Glastonbury, Imbolc would be celebrated with rituals at two sacred springs, but there was a little time before those began, and so I had decided to climb the Tor.

The Tor is the five-hundred-foot conical hill that dominates the Somerset town and the flatlands all around. Driving over from Wells the previous day, it had suddenly come into view, sunlight angling down through the clouds and gilding the summit tower. It was easy to see why it has been for so long regarded as a sacred place, the focus of the area's mythic as well as physical landscape. Some say that the Tor was a prehistoric labyrinth, others that it is the entrance to a supernatural realm; still others point to associations with King Arthur.

As I climbed the ridge, I kept my eyes down, saving the view as a treat. The wind grew so strong that staying upright took effort. I felt I was surfing the crest of some great wave – Hokusai's Tor – as it crashed across the countryside. Spindrift sheep flecked the lower slopes. It was a dull day, yet from the top it was still possible to see for many miles in all directions. At the faraway horizon, the sky grew pale and indistinct, a soft nacreous light.

The stone tower at the peak is all that remains of a fourteenth-century church. Richard Whiting, the last abbot of Glastonbury, was hanged, disembowelled, beheaded and quartered here in 1539. Of that execution there is, of course, no sign, but it is possible to see what the condemned man may have seen in his last moments: a carving above the western doorway of St Brigid milking a cow.

That carving was what I had come to look at, for – as well as being Imbolc – this was St Brigid's Day. She is one of the national saints of Ireland, but there is a tradition that in the fifth century she spent a number of years living in a religious community in Glastonbury in an area now known as Bride's Mound. Was she even a real person, though? She is often interpreted as a Christianised version of the goddess of the same name, associated with fire and the coming of spring. In Glastonbury, where Christianity and pre-Christian faiths co-exist and sometimes seem to overlap, the goddess and the saint are hard to tell apart, and she is referred to with fond familiarity as Bridie, as if she is a neighbour from along the road.

Back down on Well House Lane, a crowd had gathered, around fifty or sixty, with more arriving all the time. Tie-dye trousers, woollen caps, ragbag headscarves, hippy skirts; these were the Glastafarians, people who had moved to the town, or arrived to hang out for a while, drawn by the come-all-ye air of spiritual-seeking. I saw Merlin sharing a joke with a young woman wearing faux-fur over a pink corset. There was a lot of hugging. People wished one another a happy Imbolc and compared thermal underwear strategies: 'Layers! That's the secret!'

We were standing outside a windowless stone building set into the hillside. Within a dark doorway a few dim figures stooped to light candles. The sound of running water came from inside, and more gushed from a tap low down on an exterior wall, from which people filled bottles or cupped hands and drank. The White Spring is a Victorian reservoir and pump house that had been repurposed as a water temple. The Imbolc ritual due to take place here should really have started by now. Impatience is a not-very-Glastonbury emotion, but a woman from Brighton was getting antsy. 'What time is it?' she asked, and when I told her she rolled her eyes: 'We're on Pagan Standard Time, ain't we?'

That was a new one, though I had heard of Avalonian Mean Time and Glastonbury Maybe Time, and they all meant the same thing: that this was the sort of place where things happened when they happened and so maybe you should just, like, chill, man. Time is watery here. The Iron Age and the Middle Ages and the 1920s and the 1970s and the right-now seem to sluice together. So nobody bothers much with keeping to a schedule. Still, the delay was an opportunity to gather my thoughts about the town.

You can learn a lot about a place from the books in charity shop windows. The Oxfam in Glastonbury, I had noticed, paired a Mary Berry cookbook with Geoffrey Ashe's *The Quest For Arthur's Britain* – the literary equivalent of the arrangement a few doors down in which an Italian restaurant is on the ground floor, a Tibetan healer upstairs. The esoteric and mundane rub along just fine in this corner of England. Shop for Hunter wellies and Barbour gilets on one side of the High Street and then cross over to the Sons of Asgard Witchcraft Emporium. 'Mummy's going to pop in here,' I had heard a young woman tell her toddler, 'to see if they have chakra spray.' Yet Glastonbury resists the labels quaint and twee. It has an edge. Signs by the doors of little pantiled houses offer past-life journeys, yes, but also addiction recovery. A cat cleans its paws on the sill of a chocolate-box cottage below a window sticker lamenting ecosystem collapse. For all the dope-haze bonhomie, this town, one senses, is well acquainted with darkness both personal and global – and so people look for the light where they can.

'Good morning!' A man addressed the crowd outside the White Spring. 'Blessed be!' He wore a torc around his neck, and a cloak the colour of moss. He had a kingly profile; unearth an old coin from a fallow field and you might find such a face. This, it turned out, was Nik Greenheart. He would be leading today's ceremony. People of all faiths were welcome, he said. It didn't matter whether you considered Brigid to be a goddess or a saint. 'In these times of anger and fear amongst the populace,' he added, 'we're going to rise above and go with a coming-together kind of vibe.'

There were whoops at that, the Glastafarians being great whoopers, and before long we went inside.

A chamber of domed brick was lit by candles and whatever light trickled in through small skylights. Cold water cascaded from a pipe at the back, filling a series of pools in which people can and do bathe, sometimes unclothed. A sign at the door – I had noticed on a previous visit – forbade photography and phones, and urged caution in various matters: 'Naked flames, deep water, faerie portals, uneven floor.'

Water enters here from beneath the Tor, passing through limestone. When the reservoir was built in 1872 it was intended to provide drinking water as the town had suffered cholera outbreaks. However, there was controversy in that construction meant the destruction of an attractive grove. Water had flowed from a cave in the hillside, and through a series of small mossy caverns into a natural basin, all the while leaving behind calcite deposits on stone and leaf and wood, so that the whole area appeared rimed with frost. Building upon this beauty spot was done with good intentions, but the benefit was short-lived. Calcite clogged the pipes, and by the end of the nineteenth century the reservoir had fallen out of use. Over time, the building has been turned to various commercial purposes, including a cafe, though none seemed to stick. Vicki Steward, who writes the Normal For Glastonbury blog, recalled attending a hot-tub party some time in the 1990s: 'I was there for thirty-six hours. There were loads of naked people. I remember swimming around and thinking this is probably what my mum imagines I do in Glastonbury all the time.'

It has now been a temple for almost twenty years. There is a strong sense that the space yearns to return to the cave and grove it once was, as ice carries a memory of water. It is dark and cavernous, loud with splash and echo.

The White Spring seems to me a good example of Glastonbury's facility for the kindling of enchantment; people study the stories of the past until they find some likely ember and blow it into life. So: a spring becomes a reservoir becomes a temple. I could see now, as my eyes grew used to the murk, that shrines had been set up in different parts of the chamber. One, within a bower of bent willow, contained a statue of Brigid as a young woman holding a swan. Beside her, someone had left a cross made of straw, the four arms extending from a woven square. I had last seen this design on a chasuble worn by Father Rafal at St Bride's. It was strange, but did not feel inappropriate, to find it in this very different context. Elsewhere, in a stone arch by one of the upper pools, was a small effigy of a Black Madonna known here as Our Lady of Avalon. In a far corner, in deep shadow, was a statue of a horned god. This was the King of the World of Faerie, a psychopomp said to ride out on Hallowe'en from his home beneath the Tor and shepherd the souls of the deceased to the underworld.

What to make of such beliefs? I enjoy visiting Glastonbury, but whenever I am there I feel I am struggling to keep my footing on the leaf litter of myth and legend. The steadiest approach is to make no attempt at separating the Christian elements from the pagan, but rather to understand the town's people as seekers after truth and meaning wherever they think they can find it. Lisa Goodwin, one of the founders of the White Spring, puts it thus: 'I basically like to hang out where God hangs out. Be that a church, a cave under the Tor, a crazy old water reservoir, or out in nature in the woods, I like to experience the divine.'

\*

May Day a few years ago was the last time I had been to Glastonbury. It is celebrated as Beltane, the beginning of summer, a much noisier and more spectacular occasion than Imbolc. I had been in town for about five minutes when someone handed me a horn full of mead and invited me to drink, saying – in a Wurzels accent – 'May you never thirst.'

Later, I joined a procession through town. Among the crowd was the Reverend Diana Greenfield, known as 'the goth vicar', whose clerical collar peeped over an elaborate mantle of leather and fur. She was strolling alongside Tracy, a woman in full paganish fig – an antlered headdress wound around with ivy. Tracy was walking Oakley, a wirehaired vizsla, and the goth vicar had brought her own pet, Cara the collie. The bonds of dog ownership were clearly more important than differences in belief, which is kind of how it has to be in a town with an estimated seventy different faith groups from mainstream Anglicanism to the small and obscure. You will see a priest in a Beltane parade; you will hear pagan poetry in a church; that's Glastonbury. I had read an essay by Greenfield in which she discussed her role as 'Avalon Pioneer Minister' – building relationships with followers of other paths. 'There is a twisting and twining of the spiritual influences in this town that goes back to within sixty years of Christ's death and resurrection,' she had written. 'It would be impossible to untangle the myth from the legend, from the Christian or the pagan, but somehow the gospel message still belongs.'

The town's religious history is most obvious in the form of Glastonbury Abbey, a ruin of such size that the visitor has no doubt of its former majesty. In 1191, monks claimed to have discovered the bones of Arthur and Guinevere on the south side of the Lady Chapel, which was handy as they were at the time badly in need of pilgrims' money to fund rebuilding following a fire. The remains were later moved to a black marble tomb, a ceremony carried out in the presence of King Edward I. The tomb did not survive the dissolution of the abbey in 1539, but its site is marked by boundary stones in the grass.

Whatever the truth of King Arthur's bones, whether or not the find was a fraud, the incident demonstrates Glastonbury's compulsive weaving of its own stories. The town is a tapestry forever reworked. One can see that same compulsion in action at St Margaret's Chapel, a pretty little medieval building half-hidden by houses and tucked away down a lane. The chapel is named for Queen Margaret of Scotland, who had paid for the construction of a hospital on the site, but is referred to throughout Glastonbury as the Magdalene Chapel. Mary Magdalene's associations with sexuality and the divine feminine mean she is the sort of saint that the town's non-Christians can get behind. An icon placed in front of the altar was inspired by the legend that she visited Glastonbury after Christ's death – she is portrayed standing at the foot of the Tor, wearing a red robe. Thus Margaret is picked out of Glastonbury's story and Mary threaded in. Even the local crows are ruthless editors, having lately pecked away the head of a statue of the queen at the top of the bellcote.

The place where Glastonbury's streams of legend meet is the second of the town's two famous springs: the Chalice Well. Just as the White Spring, rising on the side of the Tor, leaves a white deposit, so the water that emerges from Chalice Hill leaves a rusty stain where it flows – and this is why it is called the Red Spring. Rich in iron, it tastes a little of blood; every sip is a heartbeat.

This water can be sampled as it spills from a drinking fountain in the shape of a lion's head, part of the twelve-acre complex of gardens, fields and buildings that form the Chalice Well grounds. The site is run as a trust, founded by Wellesley Tudor Pole – writer, businessman and mystic – in 1959. It is thought that the water comes from beneath the Tor, but nobody knows for sure. Some 25,000 gallons a day pass through a series of landscaped falls and pools. The Chalice Well links two of the most significant Glastonbury traditions – Christian and Arthurian – through the legend of the Holy Grail. There is a story that Joseph of Arimathea brought the young Jesus to England – as told in William Blake's 'Jerusalem' – and that after the Crucifixion he returned to Glastonbury with the cup used at the Last Supper. Joseph is said to have buried this, together with cruets containing fluids from Christ's wounds, on Chalice Hill, hence the tang of blood in the water.

The well itself is near the top of the garden, within a small sunken amphitheatre of stone seats. The shaft was built in the twelfth century. On Imbolc, the oak lid was raised, revealing an elaborate wrought-iron design, known as the *vesica piscis*, representing the piercing of Christ's side with the spear. The well-head had been festooned with leaves and pink flowers, and would later be the focus of a meditative ritual attended by many from the White Spring. Typical Glastonbury: a holy well with a long Christian association, at the centre of a pagan gathering, in a garden cared for by a Buddhist.

Ark Redwood is the Buddhist. He has been head gardener at Chalice Well for twenty or so years. Call upon him there and he will tell you: 'I've watched trees grow. I've grown them from seed and now they're thirty feet tall. That's a great satisfaction.' Ark is in his sixties: long hair under a brown wool hat; red fleece, orange scarf, orange trousers. He loves February because it is the season of the snowdrop, which means renewal. He recommends bowing to shrubs before pruning. When he turns a compost heap, he feels he is stirring a cauldron. Chalice Well presents itself as a meditation garden, and it is the gardener's task to help visitors maintain this feeling of serenity. He plants flowers in cool colours – blues and purples and pinks and whites – seeking always to maintain what he calls 'hushness'. That feeling you get in old churches is what he wants for the Chalice Well. And he is ever mindful of symbolism and storytelling. He has put into the garden the delphinium varieties King Arthur and

Guinevere, placing between them the cultivar known as Lancelot. He regards himself as part of a story, too, part of a long line of people who have tended and defended this sacred space: 'We all see ourselves as being in service to what the well has to offer. The trustees and staff work to keep this place fulfilling its purpose, which is to offer sanctuary and refuge. The last two years have been trying times. We know that people have been suffering. But they can come here and reflect and contemplate.' So many come to Glastonbury hoping to find peace within themselves and the world. That is the true grail quest.

In the eighteenth century, the Chalice Well became popular with the sort of health tourists who made Bath and Bristol fashionable spa towns; you could be cured of ailments, it was said, if you took the waters for seven successive Sundays. In the nineteenth century, a Roman Catholic seminary was established upon the site. But it was in the early twentieth century when the place became associated with a loose grouping of well-to-do bohemians and intellectuals, known as the Avalonians, whose interest in spirituality and the arts has shaped the atmosphere and image of Glastonbury ever since. In 1913, the seminary buildings and grounds were bought by Alice Buckton – poet, playwright, feminist and educational reformer. She set up a hostel for visitors, and a women's college, offering 'Home Management, Gardening, Bee-keeping, Book-binding, Weaving, Needlework and Embroidery, Missal-painting, and Banner-making; combined with the study of Heraldry, Elocution and Legendary Drama'. In 1922, she wrote and oversaw the making of a film, *Glastonbury, Past and Present*, in which locals re-enacted key events in the town's long story, beginning with the arrival of Joseph of Arimathea. She established the Chalice Well as a place of pilgrimage, and did much to intensify that sense of Glastonbury as a place where time is in spate and history slips by unmoored. She died in 1944, but it would seem quite natural to come upon her in the gardens, in the cool shade of a yew, wearing the faded black cloak that had once belonged to Lord Tennyson. There are no ghosts in Glastonbury, I don't think, but old faces do come drifting out the dark.

*

Once we were all inside the White Spring, the doors were closed, skylights covered, candles snuffed. From the blackness came the voices of the keepers, calling for silence.

In normal times, this is observed, but the ceremony hadn't taken place in the previous year, the virus making it unsafe to crowd into a small enclosed space, and it seemed that those now gathered felt the need for some kind of release. For ten minutes or so there was a steady drone as people chanted 'om'. Someone started to ululate and was shushed. No hushness here. Eventually, the keepers of the spring tried again – 'Silence! Silence, please!' – and this time they were heeded.

Total darkness. Total quiet. Then: three loud knocks at the door. A girl stood in a rectangle of daylight.

Nik Greenheart greeted her. 'Welcome, Bridie!'

She wore a white shawl and a white dress and had snowdrops in her hair. This was Lyla, Lisa Goodwin's eleven-year-old granddaughter. This was her third and final time embodying Bridie. Another child would take the role next year.

She held up a lantern within which burned a thick white candle. The Bridie flame would be used to light the White Spring for the next twelve months. Outside, earlier, we had watched as Lyla sparked it into life, kneeling to light tinder with flint and steel.

Now Bridie walked into the temple. We fell back to let her pass. She walked, unspeaking, to the edge of the largest pool and turned to face the expectant darkness. The keepers lit candles from the lantern and went about the crowd, putting their flames to the tea-lights that we all held in our hands. A song began – 'Air my breath and fire my spirit, earth my body, water my blood' – and soon the White Spring was aglow.

'Happy Imbolc!' called Nik, and we went back out, whooping, into the morning.

\*

It was St David's Day. The daffodils, rising to the occasion, had bloomed in the farmyard. A cockerel crowed. A cat slunk past. A small brown goat – druidic beard, redacted eyes – peered through the gate at the visitor.

Why had I come back to Wales? I wanted to see a hidden place.

Glanllyn Farm is a ribbon of river valley, a little south of the city of St Asaph in Denbighshire. Almost a third of its 160 acres is steep woodland; much of the rest is pasture for livestock. The Elwy flows through for one and a half miles. Sam Kenyon had farmed here, she explained, for the past five years, but it's been in her husband Alex's family for generations. She keeps sheep, a small herd of goats, and forty or so hens. She also has the care of Ffynnon Fair, a holy well, ancient and strange. 'I've felt privileged and very protective of it, like a guardian, since we came here,' she had told me ahead of my journey. Now, the animals fed and the day being fine, she suggested we walk over and have a look.

# WELL

We set out from the farmhouse. Her sheepdogs, a mother-and-daughter team of border collies called Floss and Nell, shot ahead – energy and pure delight.

Pregnant ewes, nebulous with twins, made a cloud-field of the meadows. It would soon be lambing season, Sam's favourite time of year: 'Six weeks of pure mindfulness,' she smiled.

Sam is thirty-nine. Her red hair was tucked under a wool cap. Her sweatshirt had a picture of Snoopy lolling across the globe, and the slogan: Save Our Planet. She is deeply engaged with environmental issues and follows farming practices – among them planting trees and hedgerows, and sowing grasses instead of crops that leach strength from the soil – intended to make the land resilient.

'We're in a biodiversity crisis,' she told me. 'One in six species in Wales is threatened with extinction, and I want to make a difference. I want my farm to be a little island for all the biodiversity that we can't see, as well as what we can. Everything I do, I do with nature as a partner. If we were to have a boardroom meeting, nature would be at the head of the table.'

We walked along the river. Ducks rose from bright water. Fording a small stream on stepping stones, we turned into a field, and there, enclosed by rusting railings and half-lost in trees, was an abandoned chapel. Built and extended between the thirteenth and fifteenth centuries, it had fallen out of use and into disrepair towards the end of the seventeenth. It is a roofless shell – enchanting and just a little eerie; I should like to see it by moonlight when, no doubt, those qualities are reversed. The most striking of the walls still standing is the south-west gable with its large unglazed window and door-less door. To pass through the arch into what was once the

interior, we crossed a stone slab laid over a narrow channel of flowing water. There was a sense that we had entered a fluid realm; that stone's grey dominion had been usurped. The church that occupied this land had been overthrown by a green insurgency.

The damp ground was thick with butterbur, a carpet of heart-shaped leaves. Ivy, heavy with dark berries, draped the tops of the ruin. The farm goats, in summer, scale the walls and crop new growth. It has been known for visitors to notice a goat looking down at them, chewing ivy with great serenity, from the heights of the chapel. 'Heritage grazers,' Sam calls them.

For all that the green chapel is picturesque, the well was what I had come to see. Ffynnon Fair, Welsh for Mary's Well, is set within a star-shaped basin, eight feet or so across at its widest point. The spring appeared clear, and just a few feet deep, but a brown mush of fallen leaves made it hard to see within. 'It never freezes and it never dries out,' Sam had said, before leaving to check on the dogs.

I stripped to a pair of trunks, and, feeling vulnerable and self-conscious, lowered myself into the water. The drop in temperature made me gasp. My feet pushed through a soft layer of silt and found balance on some loose rocks below.

Cold water.

Wild garlic.

Rattle of magpies.

Prattle of doves.

The world narrowed to that which could be sensed. What else? A feeling of taking part in a ritual that had drawn worshippers, antiquarians and the simply curious to this place for centuries.

Wales has a great number of holy wells, many of them associated with healing. There is little doubt that the Welsh well cult, so-called, predates Christianity and was assimilated by it. Perhaps it will outlive it. 'Rooted in paganism, "converted" to Christian usage, condemned by Protestantism, "explained" by folklorists, rationalised by modern education, the cult has survived and still wields an influence over the human mind.' So wrote the historian Francis Jones in 1954, adding – 'The old gods did not die: they were not allowed to.' During the years of the First World War, pilgrims to the well in Llandeilo Llwydarth, Pembrokeshire, drank water from the skull of St Teilo in the belief that it could bring peace to Europe.

Gerard Manley Hopkins, the poet-priest, came here to Ffynnon Fair with a friend on 10 September 1874. 'We said a prayer and drank the water,' he informed his journal. He also sketched the star-shaped basin. A month later, on a fine day with snow visible on the mountains, he visited the famous shrine to St Winefride, a few miles east in the Flintshire town of Holywell, bathing in the sacred water and reflecting on the stories of those who had been healed by it. 'The strong unfailing flow of the water and the chain of cures from year to year . . . took hold of my mind with wonder at the bounty of God in one of his saints,' he wrote.

\*

I had been to St Winefride's Well Shrine the day before Ffynnon Fair. While the well on the farm feels as if it is returning to nature, the complex in the town of Holywell is in a remarkable state of preservation. It attracts 35,000 visitors a year and is known as the Lourdes of Wales. In truth, Lourdes is the Holywell of France – the Welsh shrine is far older. Get past reception and the gift shop and you are immediately plunged back in time. 'The Well has been a place of continuous pilgrimage for over 1,300 years,' says a sign at the entrance, but the present buildings are more recent, dating from the late fifteenth century. Their construction is supposed to have been paid for by Lady Margaret Beaufort, mother of Henry VII, in thanks for her son's victory at the Battle of Bosworth Field. If so, this association with the ascension of the Tudors may be why this shrine survived Henry VIII's Reformation.

St Winefride, also known by her Welsh name Gwenfrewi, is said to have lived in the seventh century. She was the daughter of a prince; her uncle Beuno was an abbot who became a saint. The story goes that around the year 630 she was approached by Caradoc, a chieftain from Hawarden. Some accounts say that he tried to seduce her, others have interpreted the incident as an attempted rape. When she fled to her uncle's church, Caradoc pursued and struck her head from her shoulders. It rolled down the hill and, where it came

to rest, a spring burst forth and flowed from the earth. Beuno picked up the head and placed it back on his niece's body, restoring her to life. The earth opened up and swallowed Caradoc.

The most prominent building in the shrine complex is the well chamber. It is highly decorated with rib vaulting, sculptural corbels and bosses, but what seems to draw the eye, and certainly stimulates the imagination, is the graffiti carved into the stone, testifying to the historic attraction of these waters: 'TM Carew, Esq. Meath west, cured here October 1831'; 'T Smith, Manchester, 1808'. Often, all that's left are scratched initials – TS, EB, EM – and scratched years – 1748, 1604, 1595.

In an exhibition area there is a collection of old wooden crutches left behind by pilgrims who claimed to have overcome their lameness thanks to the intercession of St Winefride. Until the 1960s, these were displayed around the well itself. The long tradition that this is a healing well does not belong entirely to what one might consider the credulous past. I was told during my visit of a couple who had been trying for some years, without success, to have children; within six weeks of bathing and petitioning the saint, the woman became pregnant and they now have an infant daughter. In this, whether they knew it or not, they were following the example of James II, who visited with his second wife, Mary, on 29 August 1686, praying that their marriage would be blessed with a son.

St Winefride's well has attracted many royal and noble visitors, as well as notable writers. Richard the Lionheart came in 1189; Henry V in 1416 to give thanks for his victory at Agincourt. In 1605, a number of the gunpowder plotters visited the well; part of their conspiracy, it has been claimed, to murder the king. The fourteenth-century poem, 'Sir Gawain and the Green Knight', in which beheading is a chivalric ordeal, sees the hero ride out from Camelot and pass through Holywell ('Holy Hede' in the text) on his quest. The pioneering traveller and writer Celia Fiennes, on visiting the shrine in 1698, observed an 'abundance of the devout papists on their knees'; she did not bathe, put off by the lack of privacy, but did drink: 'the taste to me was but like good spring water which with wine and sugar and leamons might make a pleasant draught.'

Even now, all these years later, it is common to see visitors filling water bottles at the shrine tap. If they added wine, sugar and lemons, I did not notice. Too busy marvelling at the well itself. The basin is in the shape of a five-pointed star, as at Ffynnon Fair. Rings disturb the surface where the spring rises, and it flows through to an outer pool which, three times a day, the public are allowed to enter. The water is always the same temperature, around fifty degrees Fahrenheit, which feels very cold, but seems to vary in colour and clarity depending on the weather and time of year. On the day of my visit, it was a pale opaque green. It took me a moment to identity the shade: the same as the fizzing wake left by a gannet as it dives in the sea after fish.

Two young women had gone into the pool fully clothed. They had stashed their bags and boots – big and black with silver spikes and high-heels – in the gatehouse chapel and were now wading in circles, hands held up and out, praying the rosary with long pink nails. At the conclusion of this ritual, they stood on a large stone which lies on the bottom of the pool, reputed to be the one on which St Beuno sat with Winefride after she had been restored to life. The women ducked their heads beneath the surface three times, then kissed a cross carved into the stone poolside. They were in the cold water for half an hour. They had driven a hundred miles to be here.

'Why have you come?' I asked.

'For the healing of the sick,' one replied. 'There's miracles in the water.'

*

Were there miracles in the water at Ffynnon Fair? I do not know, but was glad to have felt its shiver on my skin. Afterwards, dried and dressed, I caught up with Sam and the dogs, and we walked back toward the farmhouse.

I wanted to learn more about her feelings for the well and chapel on her land. She is happy to welcome those members of the public whose interest is heartfelt and respectful, but less keen on anyone treating it as a beauty spot to picnic and booze and play football. She has had problems with rubbish being left behind and gates left open, and asks that visitors do not bring candles or dogs. In this, she is concerned for her livestock, but also for the dignity of the site itself.

'I care that it isn't made into some tourist attraction to make money,' she said. 'We've had people say we should do weddings or blessings, but no. It's part of the landscape. It's not a kiss-me-quick kind of place. To me, it's part of the woodland edge and it's to be looked after for the next generation. It's part of the farm. It's beautiful, but it's no more special than the oak trees. The river holds as much mystery to me.'

The Elwy is prone to flooding. Sam has come to dread winter for the heavy rains and destructive power of the river. There was hurt in her voice when she spoke of this. 'It takes the land away. It eats away at the edges of the bank. It washes away trees and fences. We have lost fourteen metres of field edge in four years. We had a flood the other day, and I just can't go and look at it yet. I'm not feeling strong enough. I'm doing my absolute best. I'm going above and beyond what most landowners are doing. But you've still got this huge force of water coming straight down and taking away a lot of our hard work and money. It's soul-destroying.'

Soul-destroying. Like all clichés, it has deep roots in truth. 'No use in talking about getting enlightened or saving your soul,' the farmer and writer Wendell Berry once wrote to a poet friend, 'if you can't keep the topsoil from washing away.' But what if saving the soil is saving the soul?

Sam and Alex have considered selling up, moving on. That they have not is thanks to a certain stubborn morality: 'If I don't set an example of what farmers can do, and what a difference they can make, then no other bugger will.' They are trying, instead, to crowd-fund the creation of a flood-basin – a well of sorts, I suppose – in their largest field, into which floodwater will be channelled and held back, slowing the flow downstream. This sacrifice of a portion of the farm would benefit not only them but their neighbours and the wider community, which has also suffered. Ten years ago, St Asaph flooded, resulting in damage to hundreds of properties and the death of an elderly woman who drowned in her own home.

'Do you feel that the Elwy is your enemy?' I asked Sam.

Her reply was instant. 'No. It brings life. It brings fertility. It's not the river I get angry at. It's land-management. It's those who are not looking after our soils and are messing up our water systems. We live in river valleys all over Wales, and yet we overstock the land. We don't rest it enough. And so our soils are just getting more and more compacted and depleted. That's what I get angry at. It's unsustainable. The river? I feel she needs looking after.'

Note that use of 'she'. As if the Elwy is sentient, a wounded consciousness, a holder of grudges. Pilgrims may offer prayers at wells for blessings and good fortune, but ever-rising water can be a curse; a sign not of abundance, but imbalance. And so perhaps this is what farming in an age of extreme weather will come to be: a series of votive gestures intended to placate an earth angered by the exploitations of the past.

We arrived back at the farmhouse. A steel kingfisher on the wind vane pointed east. Many miles in that direction, a nation of wheat and sunflowers was in the early days of a war.

'I'm listening to the land,' Sam told me, and went off on her rounds to deliver eggs.

*

ASCENSION DAY in Tissington. Two mallards strolled companionably up a shallow channel of water running down one side of the main street. It was a cold morning toward the end of spring, and blossom had fallen from the candles of a horse chestnut, so the pair, as they waddled, found their feet pinked with petals. It suited them. These, after all, were Tissington ducks, given to flamboyance. Every flower in the village is an opportunity for spectacle.

I followed the birds as they followed the flow, and soon we came, the three of us, to a well. This was the Hall Well, named after the Jacobean manor house across the way, and for most of the year it has a plain appearance – a large half-dome, lined with brick, from which a spring runs into two small circular pools and then into the channel down the street. Now, though, it was transformed. Boards had been erected to a height of around twelve feet, and covered with an elegant floral display, the centrepiece of which was a silhouette of the Queen's crowned head in carnations and chrysanthemums, lilac, iris, wild garlic, roses, thistles, heather, daisies, corn-flowers and more. It resembled some great phantasmagoric stamp and had been created in honour of Elizabeth's seventy years on the throne. One of the mallards – the drab brown female – stepped into the largest pool and began to glide, perhaps imagining herself in that moment a royal bird, a swan. Of course, it is a good enough thing to be a duck, but let her dream.

Tissington is one of the many Derbyshire villages that observe the custom of well-dressing. 'For a landlocked county, we're obsessed with water,' one villager told me. Although the practice is likely to have pre-Christian roots, Tissington is believed to have originated the tradition in its present form: an act of thanksgiving for God's deliverance. Ask anyone here how well-dressing got started, and they will mention two things. First, the Black Death of 1348–9, which killed up to half the population of England, but spared Tiss-ington. The cause of the plague was not understood, and so neither was the reason why the people survived; a belief arose that it was thanks to clean water from the wells. Then, in 1615, when the area suffered a drought from March to August, the Tissington springs did not dry up; water, therefore, could be used for drinking and for crops. This second moment of salvation is said to have prompted a grateful revival of the well-dressing that had started after the first.

However and whenever it began, the Ascension Day rite has taken place here for a long time. There are written references to it from the mid 1700s, and by the following century it had become a visitor attraction. An 1817 report observed that the 'floral holiday attracts immense numbers to the otherwise quiet village on the day in question, and is looked forward to with anxiety by all Derbyshire folks; as it is one of the old customs of England that, unlike others, seems to strengthen rather than decline by age – a circumstance highly creditable to the taste of people, and gratifying to every lover of pastoral beauty, which in this instance shines forth superior to any other country custom, the Maypole itself excluded.'

Tissington feels set apart from the world. The main entrance, off the A515, is between a pair of stone gateposts and down a long tree-lined avenue across which, as when I visited, cattle sometimes wander with an enviable lack of haste. The village is dominated by Tissington Hall, built in 1609 for the FitzHerberts, a family that had come to England with William the Conqueror and made good in the centuries since. They still live there. The churchyard is full of past baronets and the village seems full of the present one, a tall man in wellies and hi-viz who has that knack, common in people of great energy, of appearing to be in several places at once: putting out the bins, putting out the cat, giving a speech, singing a hymn, picking up any litter that desecrates the Tissington street, and greeting Japanese tourists who have come to see the well-dressings – 'How do you do? I'm Sir Richard FitzHerbert. I own the village.'

Sir Richard inherited Tissington Hall from an uncle in 1989 at the age of twenty-four. He had been working as a wine broker but now found himself responsible for a country house, a 2,000-acre estate, and a centuries-old tradition. He sees himself as a custodian of historical heritage and it is a sore point that he receives no help from the government: 'They rather think that because he's a nob in a big house with a title he'll be fine. Well, yes, but you've still got to work at it.'

Money-generating innovations include converting the coach house into a tearoom, renting out holiday cottages, and offering the hall as a wedding venue. The well-dressings attract 30,000 visitors over the course of a week, and are therefore crucial to the viability of the village, but of course if nobody came to see them then they would still happen year upon year. They are by Tissington for Tissington. This is what makes them folk art.

I expect the financial side is quite a burden in its way, but Sir Richard did not seem weighed down; he is one of those people who appear to be amused by the universe. Whenever I encountered him during my time in Tissington, I came away with the impression that he had heard a great joke just a moment before, but felt that it would be more delightful if he kept it to himself. He is a practical man, I think, with a sideline in whimsy. He names his dogs after Old Masters whose works he has sold to help fund the upkeep of the Hall. Vossie, he said, had been named after Cornelis de Vos, and Gaulli for Giovanni Gaulli, and I was fortunate enough to meet Zoffany, a friendly golden labrador that shares a name with an eighteenth-century German painter who was shipwrecked in the Indian Ocean and had to resort to cannibalism. The family cat, Mrs Hudson, is named for the English portraitist

Thomas Hudson who painted many society figures of the 1700s, including Sir William FitzHerbert, the first baronet. Mrs Hudson was thought to be Mr Hudson until she was taken to the vet to be neutered, a closer examination prompting the change.

Something like one hundred to one hundred and fifty people live in Tissington. Nobody seems sure of the exact number. The visitor has the feeling of walking around a Ye Olde England stage set. It is a place of stone cottages and tended gardens; fresh eggs for sale, honesty boxes for coins. One house, I noticed, had a floral wreath on the door, while its near neighbour bore a pentagram of willow – a common enough sight in Glastonbury, but surprising here. As a consequence of its famous custom, the village has been photographed and filmed since the earliest days of photography and film. Look at the old footage; nothing has changed except cars and the style of clothing. Tissington places a high value on both the evanescent – the flower petals with which they construct their dressings – and the evergreen: the annual ritual itself. None of the participants are able to quite put their finger upon why they do it, or why it must continue. 'It's tradition,' they say. 'It wouldn't be right if it wasn't done.' Think of the well-dressings as a garland connecting past to present to future. Nobody wants to be the daisy that breaks the chain.

There are six wells in Tissington: Hall Well, Hands Well, Town Well, Yew Tree Well, Coffin Well and Children's Well. They would once have been simple springs in the earth, but most have been built up over time with formal stone surrounds. The exception is Coffin Well, which is in the back garden of a house on Chapel Lane, and might at first be mistaken for a small pond with steep sides. The resemblance to a coffin – in both size and shape – is thought to be natural, or at least the accidental result of someone long ago chipping away some of the rock to provide better access to the water. When I visited, a cat was peering over the edge, fixated upon its own reflection staring back from the darkness.

The well-dressings are revealed to the public on the feast of the Ascension: the day on which, according to the Bible, Christ rose to heaven. I had arrived a couple of days early, in order to get a feel for preparations. 'Outside Derbyshire, well-dressing is a mystery,' ran the opening words of a book I had read on the subject. 'Even inside the county it is a mystery in the Shakespearean sense of a skilled craft practised only by a privileged few initiates.'

I wanted to meet those initiates, and in a small marquee by the stable-block of Tissington Hall, I found some. Here were gathered half a dozen or so women, sitting or standing at trestle tables, pressing petals into soft moist clay. One, wearing a blue apron and holding a bag of greenery, introduced herself as Diana Houghton.

'We've had a classic well-dressing crisis,' she explained, 'and I've just been into town to buy more parsley.'

'Did you blag it?' someone asked.

No, she replied. First, she had bought all the parsley in the greengrocer in Ashbourne. Then she tried the Co-op but they had none. Aldi? No joy. Sainsbury's? Three little bags, hardly worth the trouble. 'I finally went to Marks & Spencer and took everything they had. So it's probably the most expensive piece on the whole board in terms of pounds per square inch.'

Diana is in charge of dressing the Hall Well. She's a relative newcomer, having moved to Tissington eleven years ago. Her twin sister Gill Heppell designs the well each year, and Diana – whose background is in engineering – keeps spreadsheets that help her calculate how many flowers and other types of plant will be needed to cover the space. But it isn't an exact science, hence the parsley crisis. Well-dressers buy some of their materials from florists, while others are picked from gardens and the surrounding countryside. The trick is to use flowers that will last for as long as the displays are left up – a week – plus the few days it takes to make them. Ascension was late this year, and some spring blooms were already past their best. The bluebells were hopeless.

Ascension takes place forty days after Easter Sunday and is therefore a moveable feast, which means that well-dressing coincides to a greater or lesser extent with nesting season. This matters because the displays are built in and around old farm buildings where birds are busy with their own construction projects. The Town Well, for instance, is created in a stone barn open on side; on the morning I visited, it was difficult to hold a conversation over the squawk of jackdaw chicks. The well-dressers were using pampas grass to represent the fur of a polar bear, their design emphasising the need to care for nature, but had been forced to fix it with hairspray to prevent birds robbing it to line their nests. The Children's Well, which was being built in another barn just a few steps away, was kept covered when it was not being worked upon lest swallows, careless of their droppings, make unwelcome contributions to the design.

How are well-dressings made? The foundation is a framework of heavy boards with a great many nails hammered into them, the heads protruding a little so as to hold a thick layer of clay. These boards have been soaked in the village pond for a week, so that the wood does not draw moisture from the clay. This will have been dug locally, mixed with water and salt, 'puddled' – worked with the feet, like treading grapes for wine – and then spread smoothly on the boards. A full-size drawing of the design is laid on top, and the well-dresser pricks through the paper using an awl or some other sharp tool, following pencil lines. The paper is lifted and the dots joined. This outline is then made clearer by pressing in coffee beans or, following tradition, alder cones – known locally as 'black knobs'. Now, comes the 'flowering': colouring and shading with whatever petals and other materials will look good and not wilt too soon. The ideal is that everything used in the designs should be natural, but there are strongly held opinions about what 'natural' means. Does coal dust count? Does sand? Purists harrumph at the use of grit.

The flowering is a delicate operation that has to be done just so. 'These have big flexible petals that behave themselves,' Gill had said as she folded white hydrangeas and pressed them into clay with a small stick. The idea behind folding is that rainwater will run off the petal rather than gather within. For the same reason, work begins from the bottom of the board and proceeds upwards – just as if one were laying slates on a roof. All of this labour stiffens the back and reddens the eyes. Watching the well-dressers hard at their task, I thought of monks bent over vellum in the scriptorium. The difference, of course, is that the treasures created in the barns of Tissington will last for no more than a week, and will never be preserved and displayed in national collections. Yet this transience is part of their beauty. They have their brief season, their blaze beneath the English sky, and then the water flows on as before.

Tissington's well-dressings have, in recent times, become increasingly secular. 'In the old days it always had to be a religious theme,' Sir Richard had told me. 'The Good Samaritan, The Plague of Flies, stuff like that, although we've never done The Last Supper as that's probably a bit depressing. Now, we've all moved on, and it's not quite as prescriptive. I do get letters from stalwarts, though: "Oh dear, Sir Richard, we really didn't like the Dalek on the Children's Well. We thought that lowered the tone. They should all be from Biblical texts." But we're trying to attract the youngsters. They're not going to be interested in the Sermon on the Mount, are they?'

Of the six wells, the only two that now seem to maintain the scriptural convention are Hands Well and Hall Well. This year, though, the latter was marking the platinum jubilee with that floral portrait of the Queen. The team reckoned this still counted as religious, given Elizabeth II's role as defender of the faith, but it meant that only the Hands Well was explicitly Christian. 'I always do a Biblical theme,' Wendy Greatorex had told me when I popped in to see her at work in a barn just along the road from the Hall. 'I feel strongly that we shouldn't move away from that tradition, because we're losing our identity.'

The theme of the Hands Well was the Ascension. Taped to a wall was the drawing on brown paper from which Wendy was working: Christ with his arms raised. Laid on the table was the central panel of the dressing, that holy image recreated in flowers. 'His gown is white carnations,' she explained. 'The halo is lemon carnations. Eggshells for the skin, horse's tail for the hair, and I think that's sheep's wool for the beard – or dog hair, I'm not sure.' She squinted at her efforts. 'I'm not happy with his face, but it's too late now.'

Wendy has designed the well for thirty-five years. 'I did my first in 1987 when I was nineteen,' she recalled. But she has been involved in the dressings since she was a little girl. There were four generations in the barn, helping out. Everywhere you looked there was an aunty. Well-dressing is a sort of heirloom within Wendy's family. Her father Ken Unwin, who is eighty, was in a corner of the room, making a cross of purple hydrangeas. He wore a blue boiler suit and was too busy to spend much time in talk. He first dressed the Hands Well as a boy.

The Unwins have been in Tissington since the 1800s, but Ken's mother's side, the Smiths, have been villagers since the seventeenth century, meaning that this family may have been placing flowers on wells since the drought of 1615. When I spoke with Sir Richard, he told me that he sometimes looks at the portraits of his ancestors and wishes he could ask them about their lives in Tissington over the centuries. Ken and Wendy would have no need for questions. Their people, no doubt, were pressing petals into clay and praising God in that act.

Ascension Day in Tissington begins with church. The bells tolled in the Norman tower and the people filed in.

St Mary's is small, enclosed by a steep churchyard, and notable for a seventeenth-century memorial depicting Francis

FitzHerbert in ruff and armour, kneeling in prayer. It was he who had the hall built. Across from him, also at prayer, are effigies of his two wives, Elizabeth and Jane.

The organist played Vivaldi as villagers found places in the pews. The church was busy, buzzy, chatty. Sir Richard had swapped his wellies and hi-viz for a shirt and tie. He was holding what appeared to be a cricket umpire's hat, somewhat dented, which he put down on the family pew, marking his place while he nipped outside to deal with whatever needed doing – picking up some last-minute litter, probably, or naming a dog Velázquez. Anyway, he was back in time for the start. The vicar climbed into the pulpit. 'I've been warned not to sit down, because of the woodworm,' he said. 'So I shall stand.'

A homily. A few hymns. Then back out into the village for the Blessing of the Wells. We followed the golden cross held aloft by the verger, past the ice-cream van and the cake stall and the portable loos and the duck pond – in the centre of which a coot, skull-faced, made a fine memento mori on a brittle nest of sticks. We stopped at each well for prayer and song. 'God Save The Queen' was sung quietly, with care, as if it was a fragile thing, a fading petal soon to be pressed between the pages of a book. The dressings looked very fine. There was general agreement – and not a little Derbyshire pride – that the Hall Well's depiction of the Queen was superior to anything the Chelsea Flower Show had to offer.

The Hands Well was bright and cheery amid the grey stone of the village. I had watched, on the evening before, as its five heavy pieces were lifted into place by a tractor. This is always a nervous moment; many well-dressers feel sick as they watch the boards brought together and assembled. Will they fall apart? Will the clay and petals hold? But all was grand. Above the main panel with its image of Christ was an arch on which was written, in rhododendrons, 'He Ascended Into Heaven'.

Well-dressing began as an act of thanksgiving. What is it now? Not so different, perhaps. Still a kind of offering: the sacrifice of time and care in order to give something beautiful back to the universe.

I spotted Ken Unwin in the crowd. He looked more relaxed now that the work was finished, and we talked a little of well-dressings past. He had known so many. Indeed, it is thanks in part to his efforts that Tissington still observes the tradition. It had been dormant during the Second World War and was slow to revive. On Ascension Day, 1949, however, eight-year-old Ken and his friend Chris Carr took a notion to place daisies and buttercups around the Hands Well and to try to convince the villagers to revive a tradition that children born during the war had heard about but never seen. They must have been persuasive, these boys, these seedlings, as, the following year, the ritual began once more. There is a fine photograph taken in 1950 of Ken and Chris in caps, blazers and shorts, one on each side of the Hands Well, as an apt quote from Isaiah – 'Grant Us Thy Peace' – arcs above them. They look chuffed with themselves, as well they might, and are still pals now.

Mr Unwin, a lifetime later, seemed to me a man of few words, but spared five to describe his philosophy of well-dressing and, perhaps, of life.

'Really,' he said, 'you just flower on.'

# WEN

CHERRY BLOSSOM CHOKES the gutters. It drifts through the air and settles on the streets in soft pink slush. In the church-yard of St Giles-in-the-Fields, a young man sits cross-legged on a tomb, eating lunch. He does not look up. A couple, arm in arm, window-shop guitars on Denmark Street. They don't look up either, and that's okay. James Preston is used to going about his work unobserved, the wingbeats of startled pigeons his only applause.

He is a steeplejack, an old job in a new world. He is high on the spire of St Giles, just below the golden ball and arrow, tending to wounds in the stone. To get there he ascended a winding staircase and navigated a dusty maze of ladders, platforms and hatches, up through the nest of bells, which gaped like hungry chicks, up and over the workings of the clock, and out on to a cramped gallery surrounded by a balustrade; from there he went by rope, hauling himself heavenward.

'It's a privilege to be up there,' he had said when we first spoke. 'And a strange obsession. You can't get enough. You want to climb as many as you can, so you'll travel the country far and wide.'

The experience of being on a church spire is at times like scaling a ship's mast. Freak weather can catch you out, force you to huddle in the lee and wait for it to pass. Worst of all is the way a spire can suddenly move in the wind. Your stomach drops. You feel the stone sway. It's hard to explain to some-one who has never been there, but sailors might understand. Now though, up here on the steeple of St Giles, the weather is settled and there's only the odd gust. It is possible in such circumstances to take a moment to admire the view, to look out over the city of spires. London's weathervanes gleam in the sun: the dragon of St Mary-le-Bow; the comet of St Mary-le-Strand; the cockerel of All Hallows-by-the-Tower, beneath which, on the morning of 5 September 1666, Samuel Pepys watched the city burn – 'the saddest sight of desolation that I ever saw'.

What is London? Its river and ancient churches, some say. The Thames is the city's soul, and the churches, for centuries, have worked to save those of the citizens. Perhaps more often now they salve souls, offering the balm of rest to the weary, tired and afraid; not only the homeless men and women, one or two of whom are often to be found sitting inside, but any one of us drawn by simple curiosity or a need for shelter from the storm.

'The first thing that is bound to strike any one on entering a City church is the extreme quiet. It has been remarked that there is no place so quiet on the planet. After the hurried life of the street the immediate quiet almost hits you.' Molly Hughes wrote those words in 1932 and, so far as that quality of hush goes, little has changed since. In other ways, much has.

For centuries, London's churches were by far the largest structures in the city. Before the Great Fire, there were more than a hundred close together, a phalanx of spires. Now, though, the experience of walking through central London is that you chance upon churches hidden by much larger buildings constructed since. St Stephen Walbrook is squeezed between a glass and black steel office block and the great Palladian bulk of the Mansion House. St Etheldreda's, the oldest Catholic church in England, is snug in a row of Georgian houses on Ely Place. Even St Paul's struggles to assert its dominance, peering down Queens Head Passage like an eye through the window of a doll's house. There is something pleasant in stumbling upon a church that you did not know was there, something of the treasure hunt, but it is a shame to see them humbled. They were not built for the shadows.

There are forty-eight churches crammed into the Square Mile. Walking around with a paper plan provided by Friends of the City Churches, London appears very different from the gaudy planes of Google Maps. One experiences the streets vertically: staring skywards, spirewards, but also dizzyingly down through time. That clock on the side of St Mary Woolnoth is the one Eliot wrote about in 'The Waste Land', striking nine with 'a dead sound'. The most ancient bell in St Clement Danes – just beyond the City boundary – is old enough to have sounded solemn notes on Shakespeare's ear. In St Bartholomew the Great, London's oldest parish church, a choir is busy at practice, singing John Tavener's 'Funeral Ikos' while Damien Hirst's gilded statue of the flayed martyr, his skin draped over his right arm like a commuter's raincoat, glints in the afternoon gloom.

Around the corner, on Cloth Court, a blue plaque marks the former residence of John Betjeman, that compulsive poet of churches, who wrote of boyhood Sundays spent following the sound of bells to evensong:

> Twas not, I think, a conscious search for God
> That brought me to these dim forgotten fanes.
> Largely, it was a longing for the past,
> With a slight sense of something unfulfilled;

This, surely, is the ideal state of mind for a London steeple chase, the sweet ache of nostalgia mingled with melancholy; tired but not too tired, lost but not too lost. It is pleasant to drift like cherry blossom and see what one can see.

\*

St Bartholomew the Less, hardly visible from the street, is tucked inside the grounds of St Bartholomew's, Britain's oldest hospital, like a flake of bone within a shrine. Both hospital and church were founded in the twelfth century. This district, Smithfield, was for a long time an infamous site of execution, a place to suffer, a sore on London's flesh. Here Richard Roose, a cook, was boiled alive for the crime of poisoning a bishop's soup. Here, in 1555, John Rogers, the vicar of St Sepulchre's, was burned as a heretic, washing his hands in the rising fire as if scrubbing up for supper. In 1849, during excavation work for a new sewer, a mass of ash and blackened bone was discovered, and charred oak stakes.

I approach through the hospital's Henry VIII gate. A sign points to the Centre for Reproductive Medicine; another to the Cancer Centre. This is a place to feed the cradle and starve the grave.

The little church's octagonal interior is full of light. Stained glass shows a woman in a blue and white uniform; she is on her knees, palms upward, head tilted up – a memorial to St Bart's nurses who died in the Second World War. The hospital, which treated civilian casualties of bombing, was itself hit on a number of occasions. One nurse, Kathleen Raven, later recalled going up on to the roof – on 29 December 1940 – and looking out over the city in flames. The smoke cleared for a moment and there was St Paul's and London could take it alright. 'One can never forget the spirit of the country in those dark days,' she wrote.

Shortly before half past twelve, worshippers begin to arrive, and soon the congregation numbers seven. At the last moment, a young nurse enters and sits in a pew near the back. Now we are eight. A bell rings for the start of Mass.

'We pray for those who are in pain of body or mind or spirit . . .' The Hospitaller, as the priest here is known, can

not easily be heard over the sound of banging and grinding, shouting and laughter from the building site outside. Yet it does not seem an intrusion. This is how London has always been: the temporal and spiritual rubbing together, the city built and rebuilt, the gospel told and retold, nails hammered in and in and in. You'll sometimes struggle for quiet in these streets, but stillness can be sought.

The filmmaker Derek Jarman came here when he was dying, a patient in the Colston Ward. He wrote about it in a letter to the *Independent*: 'I escape to the 18th-century court-yard and read in the pavilion to the sound of the fountain, before retiring to the hospital church of Saint Bartholomew, which itself is cool and filled with the peace of time.'

One retired nurse who still attends worship had told me about her experience of the church. 'This is a very comforting space,' she said. 'It wraps its arms around you.' She remembered coming here in the aftermath of the Old Bailey bombing of 1973 and the Moorgate Tube disaster two years later. In the wake of major trauma incidents, St Bart's the Less is a place where medical staff can, if they wish, sit and breathe and gather themselves.

The duties of the Hospitaller, a young Scot called Jonathan Livingstone, combine both the usual functions of a parish priest with chaplaincy at St Bart's and the Royal London. He had come into the job in the midst of the pandemic and found himself ministering to patients and medical staff during a period when London's hospitals were under the most pressure since the Blitz. This work was twofold. Much of it was about befriending patients who did not have Covid but whose physical vulnerability – if they were being treated for cancer, say – meant that they had to shield in a hospital room and did not see family for months.

'There have been huge levels of loneliness and isolation,' he says when we speak after the service.

Then there were those who had the virus. Wearing a surgical gown with his name and 'Chaplain' written upon it so that he was identifiable beneath his protective kit, he attended the bedsides of intubated patients. He offered prayers and, when required, administered the last rites, anointing with oil, his priestly hands gloved.

'Those are scenes that will stay with me for the rest of my life,' he recalls. 'These were people very close to the end of their lives. The beds were a guddle of wires and machines. You couldn't really see any flesh, any person. You could barely see their eyes.'

In that situation, when even ordinary contact was challenging, did God feel present?

Very much, he replies. God's presence was apparent in the love, care and compassion shown by staff to patients and to one another. In that time of masks, something was revealed, he says: human life was 'sacred and beautiful and worth fighting for'.

Near the doorway, an A4 pad lies open, inviting visitors to request prayers. The church is open daily until 10 p.m., allowing patients to slip in before bed, and accommodating the shift patterns of staff. Reading through the pages, it is easy to imagine that many of these messages were written following consultations with doctors or while awaiting test results. These people will have asked questions, listened, nodded, arranged their features into expressions of courageous neutrality. They may have smiled and held the hand of a person they love, and then come to this church and set down the truth in ink. For here was hope and fear in the raw; a data chart of the human heart:

*Hello God, it's me again. Please make my Jimmy strong enough to have his chemo . . .*

*To whom it may concern, I'm writing to ask if you can help my dad recover from his illness. I myself am not a believer but if you could show me that I should believe I will forever be indebted to you . . .*

*Dear God, I pray to you so you can make me and my family's life easy by making my mum healthy again and making my dad able to come back home and give us enough money to live . . .*

*Dear Lord, we are trying for a baby for couple of years but no luck. Could you please help us to make a family of our own . . .*

*Please think of my father. He lost his fight, but I know how much peace he drew from this quiet place . . .*

*For my dearest mum, I am in awe of your strength, grace and beautiful spirit . . .*

*Take the life I have left and give it to my wife so she can live
    on with our son . . .*
*Please let it be good news, we could really do with some . . .*
*Please God, protect everyone from the virus . . .*
*Please God, keep my family and friends safe during the
    pandemic . . .*
*Please pray for our Ward 4C. Give us strength and support in
    this difficult time . . .*
*Please help the doctors and nurses get through this . . .*
*Please make the world go back to normal . . .*
*Dear God, can you make it stop raining?*

\*

HERE THEY COME, the Pearly Kings and Queens, with hearts
on their sleeves and feathers in their caps, processing into
St Mary-le-Bow. As they pass between the pews, we see
– picked out in buttons on the backs of their jackets – the
names of the places over which they reign: Finsbury and
Forest Gate; Thornton Heath; Woolwich, Royal Greenwich,
Welwyn Garden City.

The Pearlies are led into the church by Doreen Golding, a small lady of great dignity whose broad-brimmed hat
is trimmed with large pearl buttons and topped by a white
ostrich feather. She is the Pearly Queen of Old Kent Road,
a title that came with her marriage to Larry Golding, the
Pearly King of Old Kent Road, and which she retained following his passing. However, Doreen – who is in her early
eighties – is also the Pearly Queen of Bow Bells, in some
ways the earthly representative of the most famous bells in
London.

They have gathered, a round dozen, for the annual
Costermongers' Harvest Festival. A huge loaf has been placed
on the altar and the band outside has played 'It's a Long Way

to Tipperary' and we have said farewell, for a while, to Piccadilly and Leicester Square, and have entered the world of the Pearlies – keepers of a proud tradition of grassroots glamour stretching back to the Victorians. 'We give thanks,' prays the rector, George R. Bush, 'for the fruits of the earth, and the charitable work of the Pearly Kings and Queens.' He is a sort of unofficial chaplain to this culture, crowning new Pearly monarchs in his church. 'I've done more coronations than any living cleric,' he had told me, laughing, when we spoke ahead of the service.

The Pearlies were established in 1875 by Henry Croft, a teenage street-sweeper who had been born in the workhouse and grew up in an orphanage. Croft, while sweeping Somers Town market, became acquainted with the street sellers – of fruit and veg and fish – who were known as costermongers; a costard being a very old variety of apple. These Croft

admired for their flamboyant dress, solidarity, and generosity to those in poverty. Inspired by both their flash and
their cash, he created for himself a suit and top hat covered
in mother-of-pearl buttons. Despite being under five feet
tall, this outfit ensured that Croft stood out when collecting
money for those hospitals, which, before the NHS, treated
the poor.

Pearl Binder, in *The Pearlies: A Social Record*, interprets
Croft's outfit as a comical send-up of the conventional dress
of London toffs: 'In particular the top hat, unique mark of the
English gentleman of the 19th century, battered beyond recognition in its journey down the social ladder and commonly
worn by dockers and street mendicants, was thus raised by
Henry Croft to the topmost height of impudent glory.'

His example began a craze, and by 1911 each London borough had its own Pearly royalty, familiar figures around the
city, rattling tins for charity. By the time of Croft's death in
1930 he had collected £5,000 for good causes – in pennies,
farthings and ha'pennies. The horse-drawn hearse carrying
his coffin was attended by around four hundred Pearlies. The
cortège – donkey-carts, banners, a pipe band – stretched for
half a mile. A marble statue of Croft, in full Pearly get-up,
was erected over his grave at St Pancras cemetery, but frequent vandalism resulted in it being removed to the crypt of
St Martin-in-the-Fields. That church, by Trafalgar Square,
hosts a Pearly harvest festival that has been going for a lot
longer than the one at St Mary-le-Bow. Pearly culture has
experienced schisms, and there are a number of separate
groups. What unites them is a shared ethos: keep your chin
up, keep your tin up. 'Anything mean, humourless, genteel
snobbish, mercenary or unpatriotic is anathema to them,'
Binder wrote. 'They are Dickensian in spirit.'

Pearlies sew their own suits. Each is different, but certain symbols recur: the Wheel of Life, the Eye of God, hearts for love, horseshoes for luck. When a King or Queen dies, the buttons, which are expensive, are often recycled for new patterns, a sort of Pearly reincarnation, so that the waves of the Thames might become a shoal of fish or a brace of bells. The Bow bells, linked to so much London history and mythology, are especially meaningful for Pearlies. In particular, there's the notion that to be a true cockney you must be born within hearing of their sound. The bells are mentioned in the nursery rhyme 'Oranges and Lemons' – *I'm sure I don't know / Says the great bell at Bow* – and from the fourteenth century they were rung to mark both the 9 p.m. curfew and the end of the apprentices' working day.

*

Earlier, while the Pearlies mingled outside St Mary-le-Bow, enjoying a good old chin-wag with the borough mayors in their red robes and gold chains, or at least as good a chin-wag as was possible over the band playing 'Pack Up Your Troubles In Your Old Kit Bag', the man responsible for the church bells was one hundred feet above them in the tower, replacing a worn clapper with the pragmatic tenderness of a doctor examining a throat. His name is Simon Meyer and he is steeple-keeper of St Mary-le-Bow. 'This is my world,' he said, gesturing around the chamber where twelve bronze bells hung in their frame. He was making sure that they would ring properly after the Pearly service. When you are responsible for the care and maintenance of iconic church bells that, taken together, weigh around five tons, you learn to be painstaking and cautious. Meyer was, I noticed, wearing both braces and a belt.

There is a long tradition of giving names to bells, as if they were people. The bells of St Mary-le-Bow are, from lightest to heaviest: Katharine, Fabian, Christopher, Margaret, Mildred, Faith, Augustine, John, Timothy, Pancras, Cuthbert and Bow. Each is inscribed with a line from a psalm or canticle, the first letters of which spell out D WHITTINGTON – a reference to the folk tale that Dick Whittington, hearing in their chimes the prophecy that he would be thrice Lord Mayor, turned back to London from Highgate Hill.

As steeple-keeper, Simon Meyer is custodian not only of the bells themselves but of the sound they make. This is one of London's great intangibles: the light on the Thames, the view from Parliament Hill, that warm rush of air along the platform as the Tube arrives – and Bow bells.

'The sound is of international importance,' he said. 'It was broadcast across the occupied territories during the war, bringing a feeling of hope, and is still used as a time signal by the BBC World Service. It's not just the voice of London, it's almost the voice of the kingdom.'

Meyer, who is fifty-seven, is a member of the Ancient Society of College Youths. It was this ringing society that Charles Dickens observed at their practice in Southwark Cathedral in 1869, by which point they were already reasonably ancient, having been established in 1637. From the roof of St Mary-le-Bow, Meyer pointed out the tower of Southwark and the other churches where he and his fellows ring: St Paul's, St Sep's, St Michael Cornhill, St Lawrence Jewry. I couldn't see St Giles-in-the-Fields, but remembered the words of the priest there: 'Bell-ringing is the most fascinating aspect of English culture,' he had told me on the day I climbed the steeple. 'It is so intriguing and ancient and unchanged and secret. No one has any idea about it, really, but it's hidden in plain sound.'

The English style, known as change-ringing, has nothing to do with playing melodies. The bells are rung in complex and lengthy sequences with the order continually changing. These are known as methods. Part of the charm of the world of ringing is the esoteric names given to these methods. Grandsire Doubles, Stedman Cinques, Plain Bob Triples, Bristol Surprise Maximus, Yorkshire Surprise Maximus, Cambridge Surprise Maximus – all are recorded on boards hung in the ringing room of St Mary-le-Bow, commemorating celebrated peals from over the centuries.

Change-ringing does take physical effort, but it is more of an intellectual challenge, requiring great concentration, dexterity and skill. The ringer, writes Dorothy L. Sayers in *The Nine Tailors*, seeks 'mathematical completeness and mechanical perfection' and 'the solemn intoxication that comes of intricate ritual faultlessly performed'. Imagine trying to control a two-ton weight with a rope. Imagine that it is seventy feet above your head, that you cannot see it, and that it takes around a second after you pull the rope for the bell to sound. Now imagine doing that for almost four hours, as the elite ringers do, without making a mistake. This is only possible because of an important technological breakthrough in the sixteenth century: the rope was connected to a wheel and the bell could now swing through a full circle, thus allowing for greater control of timing. 'The top ringers can place bells to about 25,000ths of a second accuracy,' Simon Meyer told me. 'There are very few things in life that are as difficult as bell-ringing. People think that it's dangling on the end of a rope. Well, it's not.'

St Mary-le-Bow first rose from Cheapside around 1080. The street was an important marketplace of old London, another connection with the Pearlies. Thomas Becket was born on Cheapside, as was John Milton. After the Great Fire, the church was rebuilt by Christopher Wren. Following its destruction during the Second World War, the general foreman in charge of reconstruction broke into a sealed vault and discovered a thousand coffins stacked to the ceiling; these were opened and the dead found to be most lifelike. There was, in fact, a general air of resurrection in the centre of the city at that time. The Blitz had created a wasteland between St Mary-le-Bow and St Paul's, and this was being reclaimed by nature. Madeleine Henrey, in *The Virgin of Aldermanbury*, her delightful account of the post-war restoration of churches, describes an odd sort of London pastoral:

> On sunny days office girls in summer frocks sat talking or reading in the long grass, which was criss-crossed by paths bearing such famous names as Old Change, Friday Street, Bread Street and Watling Street. Traffic continued to run, of course, along Cheapside and Cannon Street, but everywhere between these two thoroughfares grew long grass and wild flowers. Occasionally one would come across a mason chipping stone as peacefully as if he were in the middle of a Yorkshire moor, and he would have made a very pretty subject for a seventeenth century print.

She noticed, too, Wren's broken and blackened spire laid out on the earth, each stone numbered in preparation for being raised once more into the sky. The tower had not fallen in the bombing raid of 10 May 1941, but was gutted by fire, causing the bells to smash to the ground. Judged unsafe, it was brought down to about halfway and then reconstructed with a concrete lining and much of the original stonework reinstated. A new ring of bells was cast in 1956 at the Whitechapel Bell Foundry, where Big Ben and the Liberty Bell had been made, using metal salvaged from those damaged in the air raid. 'One of the reasons we ring for the Pearly Kings and Queens,' Meyer explained, 'is that they raised a lot of money for the new bells by going round the pubs in the evenings, collecting.'

*

There they go now, the Pearlies, processing out of St Mary-le-Bow, passing beneath the lion and unicorn above the doorway as 'Oranges and Lemons' plays on the organ. There's Gwendoline Jones, the Pearly Queen of Royal Greenwich, with her button display of crown and anchor; on her left sleeve, silver thread for whiskers, is Dick Whittington's cat. And there's the Pearly King of Woolwich, a clipper at full sail crossing his broad back.

Outside, on Cheapside, the Bow bells are so loud that it is hard to hold a conversation. Still, the Pearlies are all smiles. This noise is their birthright. I am curious, though, about how long their culture can keep going. There are said to be only around forty Pearlies left in the whole of the capital, and many are elderly. The bells, those bronze giants, will endure, but what about the men and women in buttons? They, too, represent this city and it would be a shame to see them scattered.

I raise this matter, gently, with one Queen. She, regal and resolute, insists that the Pearlies are here to stay.

'It's a London fing,' she says. 'And we can't let it go.'

*

St Sepulchre's stands on the Newgate Road, a smirr of rain darkening the maple leaves that carpet the churchyard.

For all its size, the largest parish church in London feels a little overlooked. It has been upstaged for the last century or so by its neighbour across the road: the Central Criminal Court, better known as the Old Bailey. Atop the court's dome is one of the capital's icons: the bronze statue of Lady Justice, arms outstretched, never wearying, holding her sword and scales. She is not – as is often thought – blindfolded; her gaze beneath that sunburst crown is stern and steady. But even she, despite her unsurpassed view, makes no effort to look at the church. Perhaps, though, she listens. Perhaps, though, she hears.

What would Justice hear on this autumn evening if she bent her head towards the church? Maurice Duruflé's Requiem sung by a dozen choristers in white robes: *Libera me, Domine, de morte aeterna* . . .

St Sepulchre's is a place of commemoration for classical musicians; their 'spiritual home' so-called. Sir Henry Wood, the founder of the Proms, learned to play the organ here, an association depicted in a window of the side-chapel in which his ashes are interred. At one end of this Musicians' Chapel is displayed a book of remembrance. There are famous names inscribed within – Edward Elgar, Nellie Melba, Benjamin Britten – but one needn't have achieved prominence to be thus recorded. It is enough to have earned your living by music. This is a democratic space. Great composers and local violin teachers share the same paper and ink. Each year, two services of remembrance take place in the church. The first, in summer, is a thanksgiving, honouring those who have died in the previous twelve months. The other, held on an evening close to All Souls' Day, is a requiem mass for every musician named in the book. It is on this latter occasion that the Duruflé piece is being performed.

I arrive with Sylvia Junge, a pianist in her eighties, who has spent her life working in music.

'Whose relation are you?' a woman asks, kindly, as we cross the nave to the chapel.

'A friend,' Sylvia replies. 'Of Peter Maxwell Davies.'

'Oh, lovely.'

The book is open at his name. The composer Sir Peter Maxwell Davies died in 2016. Sylvia and he were close for almost fifty years. Theirs is a love story, though not a romance: he was gay, she married. It was a deep, deep friendship. They fell into conversation one day in 1970, and never stopped. 'I spoke to Max on the night before he died,' Sylvia had told me. 'He couldn't speak, but he could hear. So I was able to say goodbye.'

*Sanctus, Sanctus, Sanctus,*
*Dominus Deus Sabaoth . . .*

The song of the choir fills the air, rolls back the years. There has been a church here since the ninth century, but the present building dates from 1450. The interior was rebuilt following its gutting in the Great Fire. The church was at one time connected by tunnel to Newgate Prison, allowing the priest to visit the condemned before execution. The prison, demolished in 1902 after more than seven hundred years on the same site, lives on in literature and folk-memory. Charles Dickens does not name St Sepulchre's, but it is surely its tolling of the hours that torments Fagin in his cell as he counts down the night to the gallows: 'The boom of every iron bell came laden with the one, deep, hollow sound – Death.' In a glass case within the church, fixed to a pillar, is a small, dark handbell that was rung at midnight, outside the cell of the condemned, on the eve of their hanging – a reminder that they should spend their last night in repentance, in hope of avoiding hell.

*Pie Jesu, Domine,*
*Dona eis requiem sempiternam . . .*

The priest offers the bread and wine. Perhaps half of the twenty people gathered for the service walk up to receive it. What would Davies – known to friends as Max – have made of being remembered in this way? Although not a believer, he was fascinated by religion. He had an intense interest in good and evil, the diabolic and divine, and the art which has emerged from faith. Mass he regarded as a wonderful poem. He kept a fourteenth-century book of plainsong handy in his study on the island of Sanday. He had first visited the Orkney archipelago in the summer of 1970 – 'Beethoven in his twenties might have looked like him,' a poet later recalled – and chose to make it his home, settling first on Hoy and then on Sanday, where he was buried, on a fine spring day, to the sound of champagne corks and the chill fizz of the tide.

Salford was where he was born. Some of his earliest memories were of the Blitz. He remembered the sound of bombing, mingled with the blare of big band 78s, as he sheltered in the pantry under the stairs with a wind-up gramophone for company. He remembered a neighbour, 'the lady from two houses away,' running up the street on fire.

The narrative of Davies's career, as laid out in obituaries and personal profiles, often casts him as an uncompromising young composer who, over time, became an eminent member of the establishment – Master of the Queen's Music, the equivalent of the poet laureateship. Better though to see his whole working life as the intellectual pursuit of a personal vision, a man chasing sounds and ideas through the decades. He wanted to understand who he was. He wanted to understand what meaning, if any, life might have. He was a seeker. You could see it in those blue eyes. You could hear it in his work.

Sylvia met Max when they were both in their thirties. By the time of his death, she was seventy-eight and he eighty-one. Talk, wine, food, music, laughter – these had flowed through their life together.

Davies had chemotherapy for leukaemia in 2013; however, a year later, around the time of his eightieth birthday, the cancer returned. His oncologist told him that he would have to make monthly trips to London from Orkney for treatment. Sylvia gave up her piano teaching and gave herself over to looking after Max, keeping him company during his hospital stays for the next fifteen months. In the symphony of their friendship, here was the great final movement.

'It just felt like the right thing to do,' she had recalled when we met for a drink in the old pub next to St Sepulchre's, before the service. 'He wouldn't have gone on his own. It was such an ordeal. Some days there would be three hours of blood transfusions. He wouldn't have stuck that out. He would have gone home and given up and died. But, of course, in that time he wrote the Tenth Symphony, an opera, and an enormous number of other pieces.' She accompanied him to the joint premieres of his Tenth in London and Rome. In the winter of 2015, shortly before Christmas, he took the ferry back to Orkney for the last time.

*Lux aeterna luceat eis, Domine ...*

The last notes fade into silence. We walk out of the church together and say goodbye. It's dark and cold. Winter feels close.

A few days later, my phone pings. Sylvia has sent a picture, and a message: 'The view from Max's house on Sanday on the day of his funeral.' The photo shows a track leading through a field. The gate is open, the light gentle, and nothing but sea and sky lie beyond.

\*

A BRIGHT SUNDAY in the heart of the city. Fountains, sleepless, sparkle and froth. Bronze lions doze in the sun. In Room 30 of the National Gallery, St Francis – as painted by Francisco de Zurbarán – cradles a skull and holds his breath inside the darkness of his hood, awaiting the morning's first visitors.

At the north-east corner of Trafalgar Square, across the road from the gallery, St Martin-in-the-Fields is opening for the day. Father Richard Carter stands within the famous portico, unlocking the chain around the heavy iron gates and, with practised effort, swinging them wide. He loves this little ritual. It is a pragmatic act that goes to the core of what the place is all about. 'This is a church with an open door,' he says. 'Everyone is welcome.'

Richard is sixty-two and has been a priest at St Martin's since his forties. He has a packed day ahead. Christmas is coming and arrangements must be made for the Nativity play in the square; a donkey has been sourced, but it comes loaded with paperwork. At 10 a.m. there is the usual busy Sunday morning service within the white and gold interior, and then he will swap his clerical robes for a navy-blue apron and help cook enough food to serve the forty or so homeless people who are expected for lunch.

The International Group meets on Sunday afternoons in the building next to the church, the premises of The Connection, a homelessness charity. These are men and women, mostly men, who, to use the formal expression, have no recourse to public funds. They may be asylum seekers refused or not yet granted refugee status, migrants recently arrived, or citizens of countries outside the European Economic Area who have lost their jobs (as many have done during the pandemic) and are no longer able to support themselves.

Individual status and circumstances will vary, but immigration rules mean that they cannot access benefits and social housing, most likely are not allowed to work legally, and therefore may well find themselves destitute and on the streets. The International Group offers certain comforts to those in that situation – showers, laundry, good hot food, emergency supplies of shoes, underwear, waterproof coats, etc. 'But more than that,' Richard explains, 'we want to create a sense of community, where we know people's names and they are treated with respect. We want this to be a welcome, a sanctuary, a safe space. We want it not to be clear who is the guest and who is the host.'

The church has a long history of generosity to those in need: 'the least and the last and the lost,' as one preacher put it in 1945. St Martin, after whom the church is named, was a Roman soldier who, on a cold winter day on the road to Amiens, used his sword to cut his cloak in two and gave half to a beggar. Once, some decades ago, an envelope was popped into a post box with these words written upon it: 'God, some-where in the world.' The Royal Mail, naturally, redirected the letter to St Martin-in-the-Fields.

That distinctive portico and steeple appear from time to time, as if from swirling fog, in the recollections of London writers. In his 1860 essay 'Night Walks', Charles Dickens recalled arriving at the great steps of St Martin's as the clock was striking three one March morning. 'Suddenly, a thing that in a moment more I should have trodden on without seeing, rose up at my feet with a cry of loneliness and houselessness, struck out of it by the bell, the like of which I never heard. We then stood face to face looking at one another, frightened by one another.' It was a young man, a ragged spectre, one of the many dispossessed who, over the centuries, have haunted those steps. His teeth were chattering with cold and fear, and when Dickens laid a hand on his shoulder, intending to give him money, he fled.

Towards the end of August 1931, George Orwell had his own encounter with rough sleepers, but this time he was among them – an undercover researcher faking a cockney accent. 'I had meant to sleep in St Martin's Church,' he wrote in the diary he kept of the experience, 'but from what the others said it appeared that when you go in you are asked searching questions by some woman known as the Madonna, so I decided to stay the night in the square.' Between the cold and the police shaking sleepers awake, it was impossible to rest, and so, at about 5 a.m., the writer visited a cafe on St Martin's Lane, where down-and-outs were allowed to doze for the price of a cup of tea. 'One meets a very mixed crowd there – tramps, Covent Garden porters, early business people, prostitutes – and there are constant quarrels and fights.'

Orwell later used the church – and the 'Oranges and Lemons' rhyme in which it appears – as a symbol of the old, lost London, from a time before Ingsoc and Airstrip One. Trafalgar Square, in *Nineteen Eighty-Four*, is Victory Square, and the church has been repurposed as a propaganda museum. Yet its former name has a pastoral quality (in both senses of that word) that seems to offer, in its yearning echo of the past, some hope for the future. 'St Martin's-in-the-Fields it used to be called,' Winston Smith is told, 'though I don't recall any fields anywhere in those parts.'

St Martin's Lane, now a busy road of restaurants and theatres, was once a country path running between St Martin-in-the-Fields and St Giles-in-the-Fields – it takes about ten minutes to walk between them now, and the bells of St Martin's – *You owe me five farthings* – can be heard for much of the way. There has been a church on the site since at least the thirteenth century. In 1542, Henry VIII made St Martin's a separate parish to that of St Margaret's, Westminster, so that cart-loads of plague victims would no longer be carried past his palace on their way to burial.

The present church building dates from 1726. The development of Trafalgar Square did not begin for another hundred years, but, once built, the square became the focus of what Orwell called 'a process of gravitation that draws all roofless people to the same spot'. It is estimated that one in thirteen of all rough sleepers in England are in the borough of Westminster. St Martin's marks the spot where London's great tides – need and plenty, power and powerlessness – meet. Downing Street is nearby, and Buckingham Palace is within the parish, meaning that the monarch is a parishioner. But so, too, are many who spend their nights on the streets. About half of those sleeping rough in London are from outside the UK. The last few years have made it clear that borders – between countries, between bodies – do not count for much.

Many of those who attend the International Group have been through traumas which led them to flee their native lands and seek refuge here. It is notable that the Covid-safe protocol for entry to the building – the taking of one's temperature – requires the thermometer gun to be pointed at the wrist rather than the forehead. A gun to the head is an experience some will have had before, and care is taken not to echo that ordeal.

At half past one, the first guests are shown to tables, and there is a steady flow of arrivals for the next few hours. Father Richard thanks them for coming and says a prayer of thanksgiving for food and fellowship. Prayer at St Martin's often feels distinctively London, as if the words could be uttered here and nowhere else. Blessed are the bus drivers, the breakdancers, the workers who dig fatbergs from the sewers.

I am put to work as a waiter, taking orders and bringing food and drink. Most speak good enough English to ask for what they want, although it is often broken and heavily accented. People from forty-five countries have attended over the years. There is a blurring of the lines between who is helping and who is being helped. It sometimes happens that those who come in deprivation and distress are asked, after a few weeks, whether they would like to become volunteers. The atmosphere is fraternal, based on common experience of hardship. There is also an air of deep weariness. New arrivals are hungry and cold, eating large portions of halal curry or pasta bake or both, drinking tea or coffee with heaped spoons of sugar. Physical need suddenly met is a powerful sedative. Bellies filled, many fall asleep, scarves wrapped around faces, hats pulled low against the light. One man, face half-hidden within the darkness of his hood, sleeps sitting up at his table, breath deep and slow, an orange held gently in his right hand.

These people, who have so little, carry what they do have with them: bags and the clothes on their backs. Invisible, but in abundance, are their personal stories. It is these stories which, often, have driven them from their native countries and made them willing to endure difficult journeys to Britain and hard lives once they are here. Jacob,* a Ugandan, grew up in a war zone. 'My family was killed,' he told me. 'I saw my dad's head cut off when I was very young. My mum was raped. The soldiers came during the night.'

It is important to note that those who attend the International Group are more than their burdening stories. That is to say, their stories do not end when they get to London and walk through the doors of the church. Migration is physical, but it is also a psychological and even spiritual journey.

Jacob has come from a place of deep trauma, unable to sleep, or stay in one place because of the fears that haunt him. He now has a real sense, for the first time, of belonging and contributing to a community. He has a job and a bedsit,

---

* 'Jacob' and 'Jonathan' are pseudonyms. It was a privilege to meet them and hear these stories.

and volunteers in the kitchen at the International Group. It is a pleasure to watch him prepare food. The alchemy of cooking suggests that in his own life. The pain he experienced finds expression in the care he shows to others. The soldiers came in the night. Jacob, on a Sunday morning, stirs pots of rice with love in his heart.

It is the same with Jonathan, who plates up the food that Jacob cooks. I am no theologian, and couldn't easily define the meaning of grace, but this man surely has it. He has been coming to the International Group since 2018. Nigeria is a dangerous and miserable place to be gay, so he travelled to the UK in hope of a better life. What he found, as so many find, was a long – and ongoing – struggle with the Home Office for the right to remain. He spent ninety days in a detention centre. Back out on the streets and suicidal, he was walking past St Martin's one day when he noticed a sign: Refugees Welcome. 'I found a home here,' he says. 'You come, you have your hot meal, and you go back out into the hostile environment. But this isn't just shelter. They are so loving. I call these people my family.'

'What is it you want?' I ask Jonathan. 'What would make you happy?'

There is a long pause. It is as if the concept of happiness has become unfamiliar.

'I just want to live in a place where I feel safe and where I can practise my sexuality without interference from family and government.'

It isn't much, is it? Or shouldn't be.

St Martin's is a place where people bring their wounds. This is as true of the priest as it is the congregation. Richard Carter came to London after fifteen years in the Solomon Islands in the South Pacific, where he was a member of and chaplain to the Melanesian Brotherhood. He was there in

2003 when seven of his friends and brethren were taken hostage by a rebel group during a period of ethnic conflict – and murdered.

'That is something I'll never get over, in some ways,' he says. 'Yet it was also a time when I discovered why I'm a Christian and why I want to stand where Christ stood. I don't want to be part of the destruction and self-interest. I want to stand with those in need.'

These are the proper sentiments of a St Martin's priest. They could have been said by Dick Sheppard. A descendent of Napoleon, a friend of Charlie Chaplin, a very famous and sometimes controversial man in his day, he was priest there between 1914 and 1927. It was Sheppard who decided to keep the church open all night, hang a red lamp above the doors, and invite troops newly returned from the trenches to sleep in hallowed darkness while awaiting trains to take them home on leave. Later, during the next war, the church was used as an air-raid shelter, with almost two thousand Londoners crammed into vaults where the dead once lay. Carolyn Scott, in *Betwixt Heaven and Charing Cross*, her history of St Martin's, described one night as the bombs fell:

Barbara came, dead drunk because her husband had left her. A soldier came the day before being discharged from the army as unfit for service, and spent his last night in uniform separated from his bottle of methylated spirits, crying in the corner of the crypt. A mother snuggled her baby boy into a niche in the stone wall in the crypt, originally made to hold a picture or a statue, and it became his cot for so many nights that he went to sleep immediately. Rip Van Winkle came, with his long white hair flowing down his back, and the barmaid who never failed to put her hair in curlers. And at the far end of the main hall, a plain blue iridescent cross beamed in the dark.

According to the National Churches Trust, religious buildings have a vital role to play in the well-being and cohesion of society through their hosting of food banks, mental-health counselling, addiction support groups and so on. Based on Treasury calculations, the NCT estimates the social value of churches in the UK at £55.7 billion. That churches are used for such purposes is not merely to do with the obvious convenience of having four walls and a roof accessible to most communities. There is something about the felt seriousness and sincerity of a church, and about Christianity's regard for those who are suffering, that makes these appropriate venues for initiatives that seek to help people in pain and need. Which, at one time or another, is all of us.

The International Group finishes at about half past five. The sky is black. Trafalgar Square is cheery with the light and spice of a Christmas market. A soup kitchen has set up next to the church and a long line of homeless men and women are queueing for food. Two worlds, one shadowed, separated by a few feet of road.

*

FROM ST MAGNUS the Martyr they process: the priests and the archbishop, the churchwardens and servers, in bright embroidered copes, white mitre, white albs, gowns with faux-fur collars, all their ecclesiastical glad rags, following a golden crucifix as it is carried aloft along Lower Thames Street and into a narrow underpass of blue and white tile. Clouds of incense mask (almost) the sharp stink of urine, and then it is up and up and out on to London Bridge.

We are here for a ritual. It is a co-production, so to speak; the clergy from Southwark Cathedral have processed from the other side of the water and assembled by the eastern parapet, awaiting our arrival. A crowd has gathered too, drawn by the spectacle, by the sudden arrival of spiritual flash in the midst of the quotidian. Passing buses blush at the realisation that they have nothing on the dean of Southwark's red robes. Cormorants perched on river moorings hold out Rorschach wings to dry; they know in their hearts that they will never be as black as the biretta of Father Philip Warner, cardinal rector of St Magnus the Martyr. 'Welcome,' he says, 'to the Blessing of the Thames.'

The blessing takes place each January on the feast of Christ's baptism, the first Sunday after Epiphany. It is based upon ceremonies within the Orthodox tradition, in countries such as Greece, in which a cross is thrown upon the waters and young men dive in to fish it out. 'That's connected with ideas of fertility,' Father Philip had explained earlier. 'Whoever brings back the cross becomes the most eligible bachelor in the village and attracts all the girls.' In the London version, the cross is not retrieved from the Thames and thus the aphrodisiac aspect is not put to the test. Father Philip believes this is probably for the best. 'There are better ways of dating, I'm sure.'

Although this particular tradition has only been taking place for around twenty years, it can be regarded as an echo – or ripple – of ancient practice. People have been making offerings to, or through, the Thames for a very long time. Neolithic axe heads, Bronze Age spears and swords, Iron Age shields, Roman statuettes and coins – all have been found in the water and interpreted as votive objects intended as a sacrifice to the gods or perhaps to the fluvial spirit of the river itself.

The coming of Christianity did not end this custom. Old London Bridge, which was crowded with houses and shops, had on its eastern side a chapel dedicated to Thomas Becket. Pewter badges bearing the saint's image have been found in the river and on the foreshore, suggesting that such tokens were cast into the Thames by medieval travellers in hope of a successful pilgrimage to Canterbury – or more distant shrines – and in thanks for a safe return.

Work had begun on that first stone bridge in 1176, only six years after Becket was slain, but there had been wooden bridges here since the coming of the Romans, and probably before. This was the only bridge over the Thames in the area of the City until the completion of the Blackfriars crossing in 1769. 'It is the most frequented of all bridges,' Peter Ackroyd has written, 'the great highway of the city; if we may speak in an Aboriginal sense of a songline, or dreamline, of London then it is represented by this path across the river.' On display at St Magnus the Martyr is a four-metre-long model of London Bridge as it might have looked circa 1400, a tiny Henry V on horseback entering from the Southwark side.

Southwark Cathedral, even today, is an unmistakeable part of the riverscape, its tower visible from across the Thames, the English flag fluttering at the centre of four pinnacles. In Claes Visscher's 1616 panorama of the city, the church dominates the foreground; immediately to the east is the gateway to London Bridge, turrets bristling with traitors' heads on spikes. St Magnus the Martyr, which can also be seen on Visscher's map, stood near the northern end of the bridge until that crossing was demolished in 1831 and a new span built a short distance upstream. Once prominent, the first major building people would have seen when arriving in the city from the south, St Magnus has become hidden by generations of development; the tip of its spire is now only

just visible over the roof of Adelaide House, an art deco
office block. Yet the Thames has a way of washing together
the centuries. To the river, ancient beyond ancient, its life
paid out in tides not tithes, even our oldest churches must
seem new.

St Magnus the Martyr is named for Magnus Erlendsson,
the Earl of Orkney, who was murdered on the island of Egil-
say in the early twelfth century. Peter Maxwell Davies wrote
an opera about his martyrdom.

The church was destroyed in the Great Fire, being close
to the bakery on Pudding Lane where the disaster began, and
rebuilt under the direction of Wren. The great clock on the
side of the tower hung over the northern approach to the old
bridge. Walk beneath the clock now, into the churchyard, and
you are walking in the footsteps of Londoners and visitors to
the city who, for almost seven hundred years, passed this way
over the Thames. There is a trinity of meaning created in the
relationship between these three spaces: the holy church; the
sacred river; the earthly bridge.

T. S. Eliot wrote of this trinity in 'The Waste Land': barges
with oxblood sails move, in the poem, on water dark with oil
and tar, and London Bridge is a highway of the lost. As for
the church, Eliot noted its 'Inexplicable splendour of Ionian
white and gold'. His appreciation is likely to have been intensified by concern that it was threatened with destruction. In
June 1921, he had written for *The Dial* magazine against the
proposed demolition of nineteen City churches, St Magnus
among them: 'Probably few American visitors, and certainly
few natives, ever inspect these disconsolate fanes; but they
give to the business quarter of London a beauty which
its hideous banks and commercial houses have not quite
defaced. Some are by Christopher Wren himself, others by
his school; the least precious redeems some vulgar street . . .'

# WEN

Up on the bridge, the blessing is under way. It is a bright afternoon and some of the priests are wearing sunglasses. The Shard is a flint dagger thrust into the belly of the sky.

Father Philip – difficult to hear over the wind and traffic and church bells despite his microphone – prays for the cities, towns and communities of the Thames; for those who work on the river and whose livelihood depends upon it. 'We pray for those who have died in the waters,' he continues, 'by accident, by their own hands, or the hands of others.'

A few days ago, the body of a young man was found close to here; he had been missing since shortly before Christmas. Ninety per cent of drownings in the Thames are the result of people taking their own lives, and such incidents account for around half of the search-and-rescue missions carried out on the river. The water is cold, its grip eager. It cares nothing for a changed mind, a sudden will to live. In ten minutes the current can drag you a mile.

The river has undone so many. That same sleepless night on which he encountered the homeless man by the steps of St Martin's, Charles Dickens crossed Waterloo Bridge in a mood of fanciful woe. The Thames, he noted, 'had an awful look, the buildings on the banks were muffled in black shrouds, and the reflected lights seemed to originate deep in the water, as if the spectres of suicides were holding them to show where they went down.'

At a quarter to one, following a blast of a lifeboat siren to sound the all-clear, a bishop and archbishop lift a small wooden cross above the edge of the parapet. Mitres almost touching as they lean in to heave, they are like chess pieces, advanced from opposite sides of the board, and together they throw the cross from the bridge. It seems to hang for a moment; and then falls with an unheard splash. It belongs to the river now.

Perhaps it will drift ashore somewhere along the banks. It seems to be in the nature of the Thames to gloat for a while over the objects of its hoard and then let them go. Prehistoric skulls rolled by the tide; pearl buttons fallen from the bonnets of Pearly Queens; pins from swaddling cloths and shrouds – they fetch up on the foreshore and are found by those with an eye for such things.

In his journalistic study of the city in the 1840s, *London Labour and the London Poor*, Henry Mayhew wrote about the mudlarks, ragged children who lived by what they could find left behind by the retreating water: lumps of coal, pieces of rope and canvas, iron rivets, copper nails. He interviewed a barefoot nine-year-old – 'a quick, intelligent little fellow' – who had become a mudlark at the age of six and who, in the course of his day's work, often stepped on broken glass or long nails, but could not afford to spend much time dressing his wounds as he needed to collect material to sell or else starve. 'God was God,' said this boy, when asked by Mayhew about religion. 'He had heard he was good, but didn't know what good he was to him.'

An occupation that was created by poverty and desperation has become, in the last few decades, a hobby – a sometimes obsessive, sometimes contemplative way of exploring the city's history through objects that wash up on the shore. As the crowds on London Bridge go on their way, I spot Lara Maiklem, the best known of the new generation of mudlarks. This was her first time at the Thames blessing. 'It's nice,' she says, 'that there is a reverence for the river.'

We walk down to the foreshore, on the north bank. The bridge looks huge from here, its name engraved on a concrete pier. Jagged stumps poking from the brown water are the remnants of platforms built by the Victorians to hold back the Thames and make it easier to unload ships. Above

us, at street level, the city is noisy and busy, but down here
there is a feeling of being set apart from all that, and somehow to have stepped out of one's own time. On the last day
of January 1939, Virginia Woolf stood on much the same spot
– at low tide, as it is now – and took in a scene not so different
from today. 'People on the bridge stared,' she wrote in her
diary. 'Difficulty walking. A rat haunted, riverine place, great
chains, wooden pillars, green slime, bricks corroded, a button
hook thrown up by the tide.'

Our feet crunch through stones and bones and fragments
of broken pottery. A pair of Egyptian geese regard us with
amber eyes. 'We're right in Roman London,' Lara says. 'This
is the oldest part of the city.' She points out chunks of Roman
roof tile, and stoops to lift and pocket a tiny white cube: a
tessera, part of a mosaic. It is thought that the Romans may

have had a shrine in the middle of their London crossing, just as the Christians later did. Perhaps this tessera was on the floor of that shrine, and only now, almost two thousand years later, has returned to the light.

Lara has found a few pilgrim badges on this part of the river, including a fragment of one showing the Virgin Mary that may have come from Southwark Cathedral, and an intact diamond-shaped fifteenth-century badge bearing the mitred head of St Osmund that may well have been cast into the river by a pilgrim returning from the shrine at Salisbury. 'The time I like the most is that precious moment between spotting a find and touching it,' she says. 'As soon as you touch it, you're almost breaking a spell. It hasn't been touched for all those years, since the last person dropped it, and you know you're going to be the first person to hold it in so long.'

The Thames remains sacred. The churchgoers at their respective ends of London Bridge are not the only people to feel that. The river is so large and so old, and yet ever new, that it is able to swallow and contain all belief systems. Islamic prayer amulets, plastic statuettes of Hindu deities, African ritual objects – these and more continue to be found.

Can you understand, I ask Lara, why people of faith think of the river in this way?

'Absolutely,' she says. 'I'm not Christian, but there is something spiritual about this place. There's a definite feeling when you're down here that you're with an entity, you're with *something*. This isn't just water. It is a calming, wonderful place to be.'

Yes, though the river has other moods. There is something about the tide that can trouble the heart. Woolf, standing here, thought of refugees of the Spanish Civil War, walking from Catalonia to France, mothers carrying their babies for many miles. Perhaps it was the water, its endless forced movement, that carried her thoughts in the direction of exile.

'The abiding sense I get from the river is patience,' Lara says. 'It's such a patient place. It puts up with us.'

She gestures across the riverscape: the bridge, the water and passing boats, the buildings crowding the south bank. Somewhere out there, a wooden cross is riding the current. Lara, with her ability to plunge through the centuries, is able to see the Thames as it would have looked when a cross stood on Calvary and the Romans were still a decade from founding Londinium.

'Look what we've done to the Thames,' she says. 'This isn't how it should be. It should be a wide, spreading, shallow, meandering river. We've forced it into this fast-flowing channel. At any time it could overflow and flood us. It's so powerful. I've seen that power when the waves come in. But you can sense its patience when you sit quietly on a stone by the river and watch the sun set.

'It makes you realise how short your life is, and what a tiny blip in history we are. Most of the things I find are all that is left to say that a person had been here. The pin-maker, the potter, or the tavern-keeper who scratched his initials into a copper token. There's nothing else to say they ever lived. There's a sense of insignificance when you're down here, but a good insignificance because it makes you think "What's the point in waiting?" Live for the now, because we're not here for long.'

*

THE YOUNG MAN stood on the steps of the mortuary chapel in West Norwood cemetery: baseball cap, dark glasses, jewellery flashing in the sun. He wagged a preacher's finger at the camera, rapped over a wintry synth and sombre beat –

'Whatever you sow, just know that you will reap / The wage of sin is death, just know that hell is cheap.'

Konola is a musician in his early twenties. He is tall and slender, and has a sombre sense of purpose that makes him seem older than his years. His voice in performance – for example in that video shoot for his track 'Rest In Peace' – is gruff and stentorian. In conversation, he speaks softly but with the same authority. His stage name (he prefers to give no other) is a nod to the Congolese heritage of his family.

He works in the sub-genre of gospel drill: a faith-focused variant on drill, the astringent form of rap which originated in Chicago but has come to soundtrack life on London's housing estates. Drill has been much debated in the media and by lawmakers, the discussion tending to centre on the question of whether it documents street violence, incites it through lyrical provocations, or some mixture of both. Gospel drill, by contrast, is little known and considered, and it can be difficult to understand, at first, how this bleak and angry style could carry a Christian message. It sounds like the wilderness, like the whirlwind, like paradise lost. But perhaps, in a way, that's the point.

'The whole notion of Christianity being this fairy-tale walk in the park? That's not what it is,' Konola says, shaking his head, when we meet in a cafe in north-west London. 'I'm trying to show the youth that there's people like me, and even people with a worse past than me – ex-convicts, ex-drug dealers, murderers – who have turned to Christ and are really on it. I'm aiming for people who are in lower-income places and trying to let them know that Christianity is not what they think.'

Songs seem to spill out of him. 'It's not me, it's the holy spirit doing his thing.' They lack all sentiment. They're not happy-clappy. They're not even happy. His lyrics are full of

references to specific Bible verses: Corinthians and Revelation in 'Rest In Peace'; Deuteronomy in 'Born Again'. They
are also thick with the slick argot that can make drill incom-
prehensible to outsiders, but acts as a bonding agent for
participants in that culture. 'If I'm speaking to the mandem
who are out on the streets, I'm not going to talk to them in
the King James version,' he explains. 'I'm going to speak in
a language and with a demeanour that they can understand.'

He is from north London. 'Born and raised in Tottenham.
It's not an easy area to grow up in. I saw a lot of stuff. Fighting, stabbings, robberies. Sometimes you can't handle it, but
you have to go to school and act like everything's alright. If
you misbehave, you're deemed a problem. You have to keep
your grades up, but you can't focus cos your friend just died.
There was no help back then. Maybe things are better now;
more psychiatrists.'

'You had a friend who died?' I ask.

'I know a lot of people that have died. The first person I
knew, I was maybe eleven. He hung himself. And I still had
to go to school.'

Konola experienced bullying. This, together with other
motivations, led him to seek membership of a gang. 'I liked
what came with carrying a weapon,' – a knife, he clarifies
– 'and knowing that I could get out of situations, or create
situations if I wanted to. Yeah, it was a power trip. When
you're young, going through puberty, testosterone is through
the roof. It was bad choices.'

Bad, but not binary; not between a right and wrong way
of living. Economic necessity complicates morality, and a
gang – as Konola tells it – can begin to seem like a nurturing
community. 'If you live in Kensington and Chelsea, there's
only two sides,' he explains. 'When you live in a low-income
place, there's three, four, five sides. Are you going to be the

guy that goes all-in trying to be a good person and go to school and all of that? Or do you pick up your first pack of drugs when you're thirteen, fourteen because you live in a single-parent home and your mum's working two jobs and can hardly keep it up?'

In his early to mid teens he began to make music. His raps were secular and typical – money, sex, drugs, violence – but he already had his characteristic intensity. The difference now is that the aggression and tropes of drill have been repurposed for evangelism. Take his song 'Dojo'. It contains a word, 'cheffing', which is a term for stabbing. Konola does not use it in its usual context, but rather in relation to doing battle with sin and evil spirits. This young Londoner, who spreads his music and message through Instagram and Spotify, sees the world in a way that would be familiar to the medieval citizenry. He believes in a literal hell, in demons and the devil. He regards himself as being engaged in what he calls 'spiritual warfare'. His skills as a writer and rapper are not artistic, to his mind, so much as martial. 'God,' he says, 'wouldn't give me armour and a sword for me not to use them.'

What caused this change? How did he come to be, as he puts it, saved?

'When I was sixteen, I got stabbed in my chest. And in my side.'

It was at his school prom. He almost died. His mother, who must have sensed some coming darkness, had prayed over his prom suit that day.

He survived, but his life changed. He moved into care, and tried to kill himself. 'Twenty-plus sleeping tablets,' he raps in 'Born Again'. 'I tried to go without a sound.'

Later, while living in a hostel, he was approached by one of the workers from the care home, who offered to bring him to church. He had been raised as a Catholic, but faith seems not to have been important to him in his early life. Now, in a moment of despair, he found Christ. 'I was in such a dark place, but I saw his light.'

He recounts these events quickly, without drama or emotion, as the counter staff serve customers and the radio plays. I suppose this is how a book gets written: you drink coffee and talk for an hour and you learn a little more about life and death – and then you move on. Still, some encounters stay with you. Some lives can't be filed away.

I tell Konola that I'm sorry for his troubles, and he shrugs. 'Everyone has a story, innit?'

*

EASTER SUNDAY at the Tower. In this most English of sites, the most English of scenes: a queue to get into church. Quite the London mixture, too. Note the old gentleman in top hat, tailcoat, pinstripes, spats. He wants only a monocle for the effect to be complete, and of course he walks with a cane. Behind him is a young woman; the green streaks in her blonde hair are the exact shade of the Brompton bicycle which she cradles, folded, and stows next to the medieval font before finding a seat.

St Peter ad Vincula is one of two chapels in the Tower of London; the other, St John the Evangelist, was built for William the Conqueror. The 'ad Vincula' bit means 'in chains' – apt, given the Tower's long history as a prison and the many executed prisoners buried beneath the nave and chancel. Two of Henry VIII's queens are among that number, slaughtered on his whim and laid in shallow graves.

A small, rather boxy church, it is in the north-west corner of the Tower complex. The place of execution was just outside, and is marked these days by a memorial of granite and glass. It is believed that there may have been a church on this spot since before the Norman conquest; in other words, since before the fortress that now contains it. The present building was constructed in 1520 at the request of the queen, Catherine of Aragon, with a roof of Spanish chestnut in tribute to her homeland. The chapel is sometimes described as the parish church of the Tower, because it has always served as the place of worship for those who live and work here: the soldiers, scullions, grooms, pages, armourers, keeper of the beasts, and so on. Even the man who winds the rack needs a place to kneel in prayer. So then, so now: the chapel meets the needs of the 110 residents, including thirty-two yeoman warders – the Beefeaters, as they are known – and their families.

'The other thing to understand is that it's a royal peculiar, one of the private chapels belonging to the Queen, and everything else is an add-on,' Canon Roger Hall, the priest here, explained when we first met. 'The principal purpose of the chapel is to pray for the Queen and the members of the royal family. If nobody came on Sunday morning, I would still be saying the prayers for the monarch.'

Roger joined the British Army as a chaplain in 1987 and has served in Northern Ireland, Bosnia, Kosovo and East Timor. He was based in Edinburgh when, in 2007, he received the phone call from Buckingham Palace. The job offer felt like a vocation, a calling, and so he said yes. In any case, the position is residential and not without perks: 'I live in an amazing house built by Henry VIII. Legend has it that thirteen members of the royal family had their heads sewn back on in what is now my dining room, before being buried in the chapel.'

Today, Easter, is one of three annual state services held at St Peter's. The others are at Whitsun and Christmas. I watch

as a group of nine yeoman warders march the short distance around Tower Green to the chapel. They are accompanying the governor of the Tower, who represents the monarch. The governor wears a bircorne with a plume of swan feathers and yet, so dazzling are the men in scarlet, that he appears drab in their midst.

The Beefeaters have guarded the Tower since the days of Henry VIII. Entering the church and removing their Tudor bonnets, they sit at the ends of rows, swords resting on the floor. Their shadows, falling on flagstones, show bulldog profiles and the sharp angle of stiff ruffs. Those of us seated behind take the opportunity to study the symbolic detail of the dress uniform: the embroidered thistle, shamrock and rose, and those golden letters that have been woven through our lifetimes – E.R.

The chief yeoman warder and his deputy, the gaoler, wait at the back until the first hymn and then approach along the nave, handing their weapons – a ceremonial mace and axe – to the priest, who, mindful of the candles, places them on the altar. Spiritual and temporal power seem engaged in a kind of dance; the choreography of cross and crown.

'This has got to be the best show in town,' said Peter McGowran when we met shortly before the service. The chief yeoman warder is sixty-four and, like all Beefeaters, a former sergeant major. He was in the Royal Air Force Regiment from 1975 to 2000.

He considers St Peter ad Vincula 'our village chapel'. Two of his children were married here, and a third has a wedding planned. The Victorian historian Thomas Macaulay wrote of St Peter's that there is 'no sadder spot on earth' and felt that its use as a burial place for executed traitors meant that it had become associated with 'whatever is darkest in human nature and in human destiny . . . with all the miseries of fallen greatness and blighted fame'. McGowran does not feel this atmosphere of sorrow. The chapel means a lot to him. It is the part of the Tower in which he feels most comfortable – 'and I'm a Catholic!' – and where he spent a few happy years performing the duties of clerk, changing candles, polishing the silver. St Peter's, of course, started out as a Roman Catholic chapel, but those days were numbered when the king, who had ordered it built, tilted his fancy toward Anne Boleyn.

On 19 May 1536, a Friday, Henry's second queen climbed the few steps to the scaffold built close to St Peter's, and kneeled down to die. Her head was struck off with a single blow from a sword, a skilled French executioner having been recruited for that purpose. Less consideration seems to have been given to what to do with her once life had flown. The body was placed by ladies-in-waiting in an elm chest used for storing arrows, and carried into the chapel for burial.

On 9 November 1876, at a little after noon, the stones in front of the altar were lifted, and the earth below dug with care to a depth of two feet. The bones of a woman were found, and judged to have been buried for more than three hundred years. A surgeon, examining what remained, noted the 'intellectual forehead' of the skull, the 'short and slender neck', the delicate hands and feet. If this was indeed Anne Boleyn then the eight fragments of pelvis, much eroded, had birthed a great queen and golden age – an arrow fired into our own time and yet to land.

The decision to excavate had been prompted by a visit to the chapel by Queen Victoria, who tripped on the uneven floor as she came in. The reason the floor was uneven? So many burials at no great depth. A programme of repair and restoration involved the exhumation of all bones from the nave and their removal to the crypt, where they were placed within two large chests and bricked up behind a wall. Anne Boleyn's remains were put back in their place of honour in front of the altar, the spot marked with a marble slab bearing her coat of arms. The supposed grave of Catherine Howard is similarly marked, but her young body was doused in quicklime; if anything is left, it has never been found.

*

'We beseech thee also to save and defend all Christian kings, princes and governors; and specially thy servant Elizabeth, our Queen, that under her we may be godly and quietly governed . . .' Roger Hall leads the congregation in prayer. The little chapel is busy and the Easter service in full swing. In quieter moments, the croak of ravens carries in through the open door, but there are few such spells of hush. There is an orchestra and a choir. There is an organ built in 1699, which means it was first heard by William of Orange, and now we hear it, too. Yet this is no historical reenactment. The chaplain, in his sermon, explores familiar suffering and hope. 'The pandemic has left many depleted and drained,' he says. 'And now there are financial burdens with which people are having to deal; worried about how they are going to pay their electricity bill.' It is strange but welcome, in this church in a palace, to hear a priest talk of such things.

I had first met Roger Hall the previous spring. The Tower was closed as a consequence of the virus, and it felt eerie to walk through grounds usually crowded with tourists. No queues for the crown jewels, no children wearing expressions of happy disgust on learning that the ravens are fed biscuits soaked in blood.

Roger showed me the chapel and led me into the crypt, an area not open to the general public. He had given this tour to the Obamas, and to Hilary Mantel. 'This is the ossuary,' he said, indicating a wall of whitewashed brick. 'Behind here are something like 1,780-odd bodies.' When the floor was taken up in the nave, during the nineteenth-century works, most of the remains were found to be scattered, incomplete and impossible to identify. Among them, somewhere, was Thomas Cromwell, Henry VIII's chief adviser and the subject of the *Wolf Hall* novels. He, Cromwell, witnessed the death of Anne Boleyn and was himself executed four years later. One of the excitements of St Peter's is the thought of all the *dramatis personae* of the Tudor age – rivals, conspirators and adversaries in life – who are now part of the same heap of broken bones.

Also in the crypt is the shrine of Thomas More, which pilgrims can visit by appointment. More's skull is at St Dunstan's, Canterbury, his daughter Margaret having retrieved the head from London Bridge, but the rest of his body was buried at the Tower. He was lord chancellor of England from 1529–32. He opposed Henry's annulment and remarriage, refused to attend the coronation of Anne Boleyn, and would not swear an oath that the monarch was the head of the church in England. He was executed in the summer of 1535, having been captive for fifteen months in the same prison tower that, centuries later, would hold the deputy führer Rudolf Hess. A Catholic martyr, More was canonised in 1935. His shrine is an arched alcove, painted red, within which sits his bust between two candles. To one side is a reproduction of Hans Holbein's celebrated portrait. 'Intelligence burns through pale indoor skin, like a torch behind a paper screen,' Hilary Mantel wrote of this picture. The original, painted in 1527, hangs in the Frick Collection on Fifth Avenue, New York.

Roger laughed as he told me about his visit there.

'I stood looking at this thing for so long that I must have appeared dubious, and eventually the security guard came up to me and said, "Excuse me, sir, can I ask what you're doing?"

"I have a very close association with this picture."

"Oh yes, sir, what's that?"

"Well, actually, I'm chaplain to Her Majesty the Queen and I'm chaplain to the Tower of London and I'm guardian of Thomas More's shrine, and in fact this painting should be back in the UK and not here in the USA."

'And he looked at me and said – "Sir, you spend as long as you like in front of *our* picture."'

At the Easter service it is time for communion – body and blood, for so long the currency of the Tower – and then, as the organist plays Widor's sixth symphony, we go back outside, yeoman warders leading the way.

Rise up now, above the battlements and belfry, and look down at this scene as a raven might see it: a scarlet flow seeping from the chapel, bright and delectable in the sunlight.

\*

THE FINAL MEETING of the St Paul's Watch was arranged for 8 May 1945, which, by coincidence, turned out to be VE Day, the occasion of Germany's surrender. There had been no special events planned at the cathedral, but the crowds seemed drawn by instinct. An estimated thirty-five thousand attended services that day. The choirboys, returned from the safety of Cornwall, performed the 'Te Deum', and worshippers sang 'God Save The King'.

Among them was Eleanor Verini, principal of the Cambridge Training College for Women, who later wrote that:

> The Cathedral was packed, yet even in the west end there was the stillness of worship. It focused London's heart, just as the picture later in the day on the steps – of boiling sun beating down on a blissful cockney crowd silently swaying as it sat drinking in the brass band's joy with supreme satisfaction – seemed to focus London's smile. St Paul's belongs to the people and they know within themselves that somehow it binds them to God.

Seventy-seven years and a day later, I walk up the steps to the western entrance and join a short queue. It has been eighteen months since I was last here, and seems much longer. The cathedral, so strange and empty back then, feels busy with visitors once more. In the north transept, two workmen are fixing the doors on an inner portico; a new structure, not quite finished, it's an oval made from oak, around the inside of which is written, in golden letters, Remembering All Who Died As A Result Of The Coronavirus Pandemic. Another

group of workers, up on scaffolding in the quire, are giving
the organ case and stalls the mother of all dustings ahead
of celebrations for the Queen's platinum jubilee. National
mourning and national thanksgiving: business as usual for
St Paul's.

A priest stands beneath the dome. Loudspeakers carry her
voice through the cathedral – 'We hold the people of Ukraine
in our hearts.' The news, of late, has become magic realism: a
woman encourages a Russian soldier to fill his pockets with
seed so that sunflowers will sprout where he falls; a mother
buries her son in the garden, covering his grave with a floral
rug to keep off dogs.

Now, the priest says the Lord's Prayer, and it brings to
mind that member of the St Paul's Watch who had made it
his habit to recite those words at midnight while patrolling

the Golden Gallery. He would be dismayed, no doubt, to learn that bombs were still falling in Europe, but heartened that the bells of St Michael's – the domed monastery in Kyiv – still toll the hour. He would recognise the meaning of that sound: endurance, continuity, hope.

To climb the 528 steps to the Golden Gallery is to sense how difficult it must have been for the Watch, doing this in the blackout and carrying equipment as incendiaries fell. One ascends narrowing spiral staircases and cramped stone passageways, every now and then passing an intriguing little wooden door that leads to some other part of the labyrinth. The gallery is above the dome, but below the lantern topped by the golden cross, and it looks out over the city. From this height – 280 feet up – the capital appears at once vast and dainty. Hornby trains roll into Blackfriars. The Thames is brown, the tide low. Tourist boats plough the swell. Tiny mudlarkers stoop and gather fragments by the river-stairs leading down from the Globe.

But London exists in a perpetual present and so down there, too, Virginia Woolf walks the shore, brooding upon the fall of Barcelona. Elizabeth and Leicester glide by on a gilded barge. Thomas More, downriver, downfallen, shares a cell with Rudolf Hess.

The Golden Gallery is narrow and has a railing at somewhere between chest and shoulder height. It is possible to make a complete turn in less than a minute, plenty of time for the Lord's Prayer, but I take the circuit slowly. I want to make an inventory of the churches I have visited. Even with binoculars, it isn't easy, and not just because of the strong wind. The eye snags on clock towers, cupolas, flagpoles bearing defiant banners of yellow and blue. Persist, though; first find somewhere distinctive and near at hand; find, in fact,

St Mary-le-Bow. The dragon on the weathervane is by now an old friend. I have often looked up at her from the street. She is nine feet long from arrowhead tongue to whiplash tail. She seems, as serpents do, to taste the air. She is almost 350 years old, and appears to be swooping past a dark ridge of office blocks in the direction of the Monument to the Great Fire. That copper ball of flame would make a fine nest, or perhaps she means to pass over it on her way to Southwark Cathedral, where the St George's Cross flying from the tower matches the flags on the underside of her wings. They have a new cat at Southwark now. Hodge is no replacement for Doorkins, never that, but a worthy successor – not at all the sort to be daunted by dragons.

From Southwark Cathedral I follow the river west and there, just visible between the two huge golden pineapples that crown the towers of St Paul's, is Nelson on his column and the spire of St Martin-in-the-Fields. A little further and there is St Giles. I wonder where James Preston, the steeple-jack, is today? The last I heard he was at Stonehenge, up among the megaliths.

St Bartholomew the Less, the hospital church, is much harder to find, but I do eventually spy its odd little square tower and turret. And not far away, there's Lady Justice on top of the Old Bailey. She has her back to St Paul's and is still paying no mind to St Sepulchre's. Scales in her left hand, sword in her right, she stares out over the city as the court below works through its case-loads of murders, its banal transubstantiation of blood into ink.

The wind is getting up. Best be heading back inside. Spiral staircases twist, like DNA, between the outer and inner domes. Down and down and down within the walls until, at last, there is the cathedral floor once more. Choirboys sing evensong as the sun slants in through clear glass windows and warms the marble flesh of John Donne. London, outside, goes about its day. St Paul's, entire of itself, gathers in the living and the dead.

# LIGHT

A SONG HAD TAKEN OVER the country. A song from the old days heard anew in these dog days, these doldrums, a song alive with heatwave lightning. Midsummer, it was everywhere. On the radio, on buses, in bars: all thunder and restless desire, and that beautiful voice – Kate Bush's voice – yearning for a deal with God.

I played it on headphones as I walked the Pilgrims' Way. The sand was wet and clinging; the cellos swooped like terns. I checked my map, with its names for the land and the not-quite-land: The Snook, The Swad, The Slakes. It had been drawn in 1946, before the road causeway was built, but this older way was marked, a straight white line through a grey landscape. I followed the line on the map, I followed the lines of the song, and there, a few miles ahead, was the castle and the hill – the Holy Island of Lindisfarne growing closer with every step.

Twice a day, Lindisfarne is cut off and becomes an island. Twice a day, the sea rolls back and it can be reached by car, or on foot across the flats. The crossing times change daily and are not the same for both routes; there is a formula for working out when it is safe to take the Pilgrims' Way. The thought of getting caught by incoming water is frightening enough to prompt double- and triple-checking of the calculation. There are two refuge boxes – little more than wooden platforms on stilts – but you wouldn't want to be in a situation where you had to race the tide to the ladder and climb for your life.

A deal with God, though. I'd noticed that sort of bargaining a lot over the last year or so:

*Take the life I have left and give it to my wife so she can live
with our son . . .*

*I can't ask for a miracle that I walk again, but pray that I am
able to stand for longer . . .*

*We will say our Hail Marys in this freezing cold pool if you
will only heal us . . .*

I had taken off my boots and socks. The ground was firm
underfoot, except for those parts where it was more mud
than sand. Here and there, shallow pools had been warmed
by the sun. These were pleasant to splash through, but you
had to watch your step. A large jellyfish, beached by the tide,
was a glossy brownish-red. It looked at once like a distant
galaxy and the slopped guts of a gralloched deer.

The Pilgrims' Way is marked by a line of poles cut from
slender tree trunks, each about fifteen feet high, and driven
into the ground. A constellation of barnacles clings to their
lower parts. It is strange. You know intellectually that where
you are walking will, in a few hours, be underwater, but it is
hard to believe that it will ever happen. Perhaps that is why
people get caught out. It would feel rather like crossing a
desert were it not that there are worm-casts everywhere. A
Victorian naturalist once calculated that for every hundred
acres, lugworms throw up 4.5 million casts and displace nine
hundred tons of sand and mud. Their little mounds of spoil
seemed to mirror Lindisfarne Castle on its rock.

About two-thirds of the way over, I came to the worst of
the mud, a boggy black patch that looked at least ankle deep.
It was a wellies graveyard: the upper parts of lost boots stuck
out from the muck. There was no way round. Until now, I
hadn't met anyone else as I'd walked, but Nicola and Lesley,
sisters visiting from Devon, had stopped at the edge and were

considering how to proceed. A small black and brown face poked out from Lesley's backpack – her dog, Bruno.

'He's an elderly dachshund,' she explained. 'He wouldn't be able to walk across. Besides, he doesn't like getting his paws wet.'

I could relate. I didn't like the look of that mud. But it appeared that I was being volunteered as a pathfinder.

'You go first,' Nicola said, 'and see what's the best way through.'

It wasn't too bad. Mud oozed up between my toes – rather a nice feeling – and was soon sloshed off at the next pool of water.

When I reached the island and sat to dry my feet, Nicola and Lesley weren't far behind. Bruno, set down on dry sand, sniffed the marram grass with intense interest. Lindisfarne has a reputation as a 'thin place' – where the space between this world and the next is like a newborn's fontanelle: fragile, pulsing, not quite closed. I wonder if dogs can sense that sort of thing?

The origin of the word Lindisfarne is uncertain, but thought to be Anglo-Saxon. 'Holy Island' – a translation of *Insula Sacra* – was a title bestowed by Benedictine monks who settled in the twelfth century, building the red sandstone priory that now stands in picturesque ruin. In naming the island, they will have had in mind its history as a cradle of Christianity. King Oswald of Northumbria (he whose skull is buried with St Cuthbert at Durham Cathedral) invited Aidan, an Irish monk from the monastery at Iona, to bring his people to the faith. Aidan arrived at the royal stronghold of Bamburgh in the year 635 and chose the island within sight of Oswald's castle as the base of his mission. Here, he trained a new generation of monks and priests, and went about the country on foot, speaking English – a language he had to learn – to the ordinary people he encountered. In this new tongue, he spread the word.

Aidan, unlike Cuthbert, does not seem to have been a man whose life was full of miracles. Those few that are associated with him we know from Bede. Once, while on Inner Farne, a small island two miles off the coast, he noticed smoke carried by the wind from the mainland. Bamburgh was under attack. Penda, the pagan king of Mercia, had destroyed the surrounding villages and now piled against the walls and gates a great quantity of wood and straw, the wreckage of homes his men had pulled down. This he used as kindling, setting it on fire, hoping to make ashes of the town. Aidan stood on his island, weeping, and uttered a simple prayer: 'Lord, see what evil Penda does!' At this, the wind changed and the flames were driven back towards the Mercian army. Some burned, the rest fled.

*

The Pilgrims' Way comes ashore at a part of the island called Chare Ends. From there, it's a short walk to the village. Lindisfarne is home to around 160 people, most of whom live in a cluster of streets in the south-west corner. The walls and verges, as I arrived, were bright with ox-eye daisies, red valerian and purplish catmint.

But I didn't have time to appreciate the flowers. I was looking for a particular cottage, a particular person.

Kate Tristram is ninety-one. She can divide her life: before she came to Holy Island and after. She has lived here since 1978. 'But I mustn't call myself an islander,' she laughed. 'I must call myself what I am – a tolerated incomer.'

We sat in her front room. I was pleased to meet her at last. It was Lilian Groves, the Durham Cathedral guide, who had first mentioned her name. They've been close pals since starting on the staff at St Hild's College on the same day in 1960. They talk on the phone every evening at seven, a habit begun during lockdown, making sure that each has at least that company in a day. 'If you're going to Holy Island, you must speak to my friend,' Lilian had said. Oh, anything I wanted to know about the place, Kate would be sure to tell me. She had written a book about it. She had even gone back to university at the age of seventy in order to study Old Irish and Latin, the better to enter the mind of her beloved Aidan and the other northern saints.

Kate is a midlander. She grew up in Stourbridge. She was eight years old when the war started, fourteen when it ended. She had a brother, two years older. 'One night, we were lying in our bunks in the shelter as usual and our father got us up and said to come outside, he wanted to show us something. The sky was blood red and Dad was so upset. He said, "That's Coventry. I hope you never see a thing like that again in your life."'

Richard Holloway, I remembered, had told a very similar story about the Clydebank Blitz. Two children, either side of the border, watching cities burn; and now, at the other end of their lives, still carrying reflected fire in their eyes.

Kate went to Somerville College, Oxford, at the age of nineteen, reading history and then theology and becoming confirmed in the Church of England. Many of the young men studying theology at Oxford went on to become priests, but this route was not open to women and so Kate, although she would like to have become ordained, had no thought of it at that time. She became a teacher, like her parents, and then a lecturer.

By the time she moved to Lindisfarne from Durham she was well into her forties and felt that if she was ever going to do anything different in life then it had better be now.

She became warden of Marygate House, a retreat available to those visiting for educational, cultural and religious purposes. The island, when she first knew it, was a fishing culture, not, as it has become, dominated by tourism. 'I discovered that the best way for me to get on with people was to keep my mouth closed for a year, but listen to everything that came my way to hear.' The only trouble was following what was said. 'Northumberland has several dialects and one foreign language,' she laughed. 'That's how different the speech on Holy Island seemed.'

Six boats fish out of Lindisfarne, whereas when she first arrived there were around twenty. It was a place of fishing families going back centuries. Their customs and way of life had long attracted the curiosity of outsiders. One nineteenth-century visitor noted the unusual way in which game could be trapped for the pot. A tallow candle stump was stuck to the back of a large crab which was sent scuttling down a rabbit hole. The animals, alarmed at this visitation, would come bolting out and into a waiting net.

In 1994, Kate became a curate at St Mary the Virgin, the church next to the priory. She was among the first wave of women to enter the Anglican priesthood. 'Actually, it was all spoiled because there was so much nastiness around. There were people outside Newcastle Cathedral trying to stop us getting in so we wouldn't be ordained.' Once, as she was about to start Communion prayers, the congregation stood up and walked out, rather than take wafer and wine from her hands. She was sixty-three when she became a priest, and seventy when she retired, but is still involved in the church, preaching every third Sunday. The island community has always been supportive, and in any case attitudes are different now. Not long ago, she attended the ordination of a woman and was pleased to see everyone happy and offering congratulations. 'But it wasn't like that for me.'

She said this without bitterness. In living a life of faith on Holy Island, she is part of a long tradition. Archaeological evidence suggests that there were women present in the religious community from its early years. The priory museum has fragments of what look like small grave markers that were found around the site, mostly during conservation works. The stones date from the mid seventh to the mid eighth centuries. What makes them exciting is the names carved into them: Aedberecht, Audlac, Ethelhard. These people may have known Cuthbert, may have been among the first readers of the Lindisfarne Gospels; perhaps one of them had slaughtered the calves whose skins were used for vellum, so that Eadfrith, the artist-monk, would have a smooth surface over which to run his ink. Among the carved names, one stands out, being that of a woman: Osgyth, written in Latin and runes. It has been speculated that she may have been a nun, and perhaps a noble who helped finance the priory. She will have made a life here, adjusting to the rhythm of the prayers and tides. She gave her soul to Christ, her body to the ground, her name to the future.

Kate doesn't leave the island much these days, especially now she has stopped driving. She has problems with balance, and her days of walking the dunes are behind her. 'Still,' she says, 'I can see, I can hear, I can speak. What more should I want?'

She anticipates spending the rest of her life on Holy Island. 'I would like to die here. But I don't want a place in that churchyard. I want cremation and burial at sea.' She grew up about as far inland as you can get, and for much of her life did not think of the coast with fondness. Nothing there but a great mass of dirty water, she used to joke.

'But I don't know,' she said now, 'somehow we've made it up, and I've become friends with the sea, and I've decided to go into it as my very last act.'

*

The following morning I was up and out by three. It was the summer solstice and I wanted to see the dawn.

Holy Island welcomes 650,000 visitors a year, but I was the only one around, and found myself walking through a medieval bestiary. A curlew trilled overhead. A young rabbit cropped the grass. A hedgehog, ambling like a small bear along the west front of the priory, placed her front paws on the lowest bar of the locked gate, pushed with her back legs and heaved herself over and in.

There was a noise all through the village. A sorrowful lowing, like God blowing on the neck of a bottle. It was the hour of the seal. There were hundreds of them out there on a sandbank. I began to make them out as the sky lightened, a convocation of grey friars greeting the day with their sad and endless song.

The tide was coming in. If I was quick, I could get over to Hobthrush and back before it was cut off. The islet is a short distance off the south-west tip of Holy Island. It is often referred to as St Cuthbert's Isle as this is believed to be the place where the monk, while prior of Lindisfarne, began to try the life of a hermit. Bede says that it was where Cuthbert 'gained victory over our invisible enemy by solitary prayer and fasting' – giving him the confidence to move to Inner Farne, 'a remote battlefield farther away from his fellow men', where in 687 he died.

A party of monks had sailed to Inner Farne to be near their brother in his final suffering, and his death was announced by the agreed method: lighting two candles and climbing with them to an area of higher ground. Bede writes of a Lindisfarne monk, sitting up in a watchtower, looking out into the dark. Seeing candle-fire across the water, he had run down to the church with the news. Excavations on the high ridge known as the Heugh have, in the last few years, revealed the foundations of a tall building. Was this the watchtower from which the Holy Island brethren first learned that Cuthbert's light had been snuffed?

Kate Tristram had told me that she thinks of Aidan and Cuthbert as 'living personalities', just as alive as we are, though in a different state, and that she has every hope of one day meeting them. Whether or not one shares her belief in an afterlife, Holy Island encourages a feeling of closeness with these almost legendary figures because we can walk where they walked and see what they saw. We can stand where the watchtower stood and look over to the same islands the saints knew well. We can pick our way over seaweedy rocks to Hobthrush and, if we choose, kneel where Cuthbert knelt.

It is a scrap of land with a turret-like hump that looks, at high tide, like a submarine gliding through the water. A small medieval chapel had been dedicated to Cuthbert, but all that remains are low walls overgrown with grass. A wooden cross stands on the site of the altar, at the base of which a small heap of rocks have become a makeshift shrine. I noticed a rusting crucifix, a sun-bleached teddy, a few pieces of slate with names scratched on. Ben was one, Rob another. No Osgyth, no Audlac. Like the Angel of the North, this is where people come to remember their dead. A fine place for that, I think, keened over by curlews and seals.

Eighteen months had passed since I sat in the church at Pluscarden and listened to the monks chant the psalms. I had thought to end my journey on a note of hope, but those had been difficult months, siren-shrill, a time of anxiety, disillusionment and war. This is the deal we all strike, without signature. We are born into circumstances where, if we are lucky, we will be safe and loved, but we may not be so fortunate, or not all the time. Being alive for beauty – the cry of an owl, the song of the seal – means also being alive for the burning city, the capsized boat, the sobbing that soundtracks both.

I had found comfort in the churches I visited, though not because of their promise of a better world. Why wait for that? It was more to do with what they said about those who had built them, tried their best to maintain them, and valued these old places, in all their cobwebbed glory, as manuscripts on which is written the unfinished human story. We read about ourselves in churches, I think, as much as we read about God. We sing our own lives. We ask an unspoken question: we matter, don't we?

We've been asking that for a long time. The lives and minds of the medieval worshippers from whom we have inherited these buildings did not seem so distant, as I stood there on Hobthrush. Most of us do not live in fear of God. We no longer have a sense that the world is governed by his will. If the land floods or grows parched, if crops fail and the cost of bread rises beyond our purse, we do not regard these calamities as divine wrath. But that feeling of helplessness, of being at the mercy of forces beyond our control – political, economic, environmental – *that* is what it feels like to live now.

Those people I had encountered on my journey seemed to me strong-hearted; not saints or martyrs – ordinary men and women with a tremendous capacity for endurance and love. I had met them in and around churches, but such folk are everywhere, and it was a blessing to be reminded of that as the darkness grew ever deeper.

# LIGHT

So: the sunrise? Not dramatic. No fierce Turner master-piece in oil. It was a watercolour, a splash of pink that smeared itself along the horizon behind the Longstone lighthouse, behind Brownsman, Staple Island, Inner Farne, Bamburgh Castle and the great navigation obelisks at Guile Point. The longest day had begun.

One last look and I made my way back over the rocks. The water was rising. It was time to go home.

# Selected Sources

## DARKNESS

Cooper, Susan, *The Dark is Rising* (Chatto & Windus, 1973)

Dunn, Martin Joseph, *Always With Love* (self-published, 2021)

Golding, William, *The Spire* (Faber & Faber, 1964)

Hiley, David, *Gregorian Chant* (Cambridge University Press, 2009)

MacNeice, Louis, *Autumn Journal* (Faber & Faber, 1939)

Melville, Herman, 'Bartleby, The Scrivener: A Story of Wall Street', *Putnam's Monthly*, November and December 1852 (Penguin 60s, 1995)

*Pluscarden Benedictines* (No. 193, Lent 2021)

*The Psalms: A New Translation* (Fontana Books, 1963; translated by Joseph Gelineau)

Rankin, Ian, *A Song for the Dark Times* (Orion, 2020)

*The Rule of Benedict* (Penguin Classics, 2008; translated with an introduction and notes by Carolinne White)

*The Rule of St Benedict in English* (Liturgical Press, 1982; Timothy Fry, editor)

Weil, Simone, 'Human Personality' in *Simone Weil: An Anthology* (Virago Press, 1986; Siân Miles, editor)

*

*A Resurrection: The Story of Pluscarden Priory* (1948; photography by F. G. Ratcliff, under the direction of the Right Reverend Dom Wilfrid Upson)

*Beloved Sinners* (University of Stirling, 2014; Rajmund Bakonyi, David Kotai, Magnus Rasmusen, Ehssan Shamoradi)

*In Search of God* (2017; directed by Pawel Rokicki)

*

Lennon & McCartney, 'Lucy In The Sky With Diamonds', from *Sgt. Pepper's Lonely Hearts Club Band* (Parlophone, 1967)

Perhacs, Linda, 'Chimacum Rain', from *Parallelograms* (Kapp Records, 1970)

*Tempus per annum: Gregorian chant from the monks of Pluscarden Abbey* (Ffin Records, 2017)


STEEL

'The Anonymous History of Abbot Ceolfrith' (in *The Age of Bede*, Penguin, 2004; translated by D. H. Farmer)

Bede, *Ecclesiastical History of the English People* (Penguin, 1990; translated by Leo Sherley-Price)

Bede 'Life of St Cuthbert' (in *The Age of Bede*, Penguin, 2004; translated by J. F. Webb)

Clifton-Taylor, Alec, *English Parish Churches as Works of Art* (Country and Gardeners Book Society: Readers Union Group, 1974)

Eliot, T. S., *Journey of the Magi* (Faber & Gwyer, 1927)

Holloway, Richard, *Waiting for the Last Bus: Reflections on Life and Death* (Canongate, 2017)

Jenkins, Simon, *England's Cathedrals* (Little, Brown, 2016)

Julian, Helen, *The Lindisfarne Icon: St Cuthbert and the 21st Century Christian* (The Bible Reading Fellowship, 2004)

Mayhew-Smith, Nick and Guy Hayward, *Britain's Pilgrim Places* (Lifestyle Press Ltd, 2020)

Raine, James, *Saint Cuthbert: with an account of the state in which his remains were found upon the opening of the tomb in Durham Cathedral, in the year MDCCCXXVII* (Geo. Andrews, Durham, and J. B. Nichols, London, 1828)

Rosewell, Roger, *Saints, Shrines and Pilgrims* (Shire Library, 2017)

Sadgrove, Michael, *Durham Cathedral: The Shrine of St Cuthbert* (Jarrold Publishing, 2005)

Somerville, Christopher, *Ships of Heaven: The Private Lives of Britain's Cathedrals* (Transworld, 2019)

Stanford, Peter, *Angels: A History* (Hodder & Stoughton, 2019)

Willem, David, *St Cuthbert's Corpse: A Life After Death* (Sacristy Press, 2013)

*

*Another Six English Towns: Durham* (BBC2, 1984; written and presented by Alec Clifton-Taylor; produced by Jane Coles

*

'Fear and Trembling in Durham Cathedral'; 'Concerning the Examination of Cuthbert's Body'; 'Concerning the Exhumation of St Cuthbert' (*Medieval Death Trip: A Podcast Exploring the Wit and Weirdness of Medieval Texts*; Lane, Patrick, host)

## FIRE

Ackroyd, Peter, *London: The Biography* (Chatto & Windus, 2000)

Aubrey, John, *Aubrey's Brief Lives* (Martin Secker & Warburg Ltd, 1949)

Barton, Helen, 'St Paul's Survives' in *Londoners Remember Living Through The Blitz* (Age Exchange, 1991; Pam Schweitzer, editor)

Creighton, Charles, *A History of Epidemics in Britain, Volume II* (Cambridge University Press, 1894)

Darley, Gillian and David McKie, *Ian Nairn: Words in Place* (Five Leaves Publications, 2013)

Donne, John, *Devotions upon Emergent Occasions, Together with Death's Duel* (University of Michigan Press, 1959)

Evelyn, John, *The Diary of John Evelyn* (Oxford World's Classics, 1985)

Flanner, Janet, 'Letter From Cologne', *New Yorker*, 23 March 1945

Hannan, Archbishop Philip, *The Archbishop Wore Combat Boots: Memoir of An Extraordinary Life* (Our Sunday Visitor, 2010)

Huelin, Gordon, *Vanished Churches of the City of London* (Guildhall Library Publications, 1996)

Jardine, Lisa, *On a Grander Scale: The Outstanding Career of Sir Christopher Wren* (HarperCollins, 2002)

*The Losley Manuscripts* (John Murray, 1836; John Alfred Kempe, editor)

Mortimer, Gavin, *The Longest Night 10–11 May 1941: Voices from the London Blitz* (Weidenfeld & Nicolson, 2005)

Matthews, W. R., *St Paul's Cathedral in Wartime: 1939–1945* (Hutchinson & Co Ltd, 1947)

Matthews, W. R., *Memories and Meanings* (Hodder and Stoughton, 1969)

Nairn, Ian, *Nairn's London* (Penguin, 1966)

Neve, Christopher, *Unquiet Landscape: Places and Ideas in 20th Century British Painting* (Faber & Faber, 1990; new edition, Thames & Hudson, 2020)

Partridge, Frances, *A Pacifist's War: Diaries 1939–1945* (Hogarth Press, 1978)

Pepys, Samuel, *The Diary of Samuel Pepys: A Selection* (Penguin Classics, 2003)

Sebald, W. G., *After Nature* (Hamish Hamilton, 2002; Michael Hamburger, translator)

Sebald, W. G. 'Air War and Literature' in *On the Natural History of Destruction* (Hamish Hamilton, 2003; Anthea Bell, translator)

Sebald, W. G., *Vertigo* (Harvill Press, 1999; Michael Hulse, translator)

*St Paul's Cathedral* (Scala Arts & Heritage Ltd, 2019; Helen Cornell and Matthew Taylor, editors)

Stubbs, John, *Donne: The Reformed Soul* (Viking, 2006)

Taswell, William, *Autobiography and Anecdotes* (J. B. Nichols and Sons, 1853; George Percy Elliott, editor)

Tinniswood, Adrian, *By Permission of Heaven: The Story of the Great Fire of London* (Pimlico, 2004)

Walton, Isaak, *The Life of Dr. John Donne* (1670, read at anglicanhistory.org)

Woolf, Virginia, *A Writer's Diary* (Hogarth Press, 1953)

Woolf, Virginia, *The London Scene* (Daunt Books, 2013)

*

*Fire of London* (Ministry of Information, 1945)

## CATS

Bourne, Dorothea St. Hill, *They Also Serve* (Winchester
   Publications Limited, 1947)

Dickens, Charles, 'Ancient College Youths', *All The Year Round*, 27
   February 1869

Eliot, T. S., *Old Possum's Book of Practical Cats* (Faber & Faber, 1939)

Hughes, M. V., *The City Saints* (J. M. Dent & Sons Ltd, 1932)

Nunn, Andrew, https://southwarklivinggod.wordpress.com

*

*Southwark Cathedral Masterplan* (2018)

*

Barber, Samuel and W. H. Auden, 'The Monk and His Cat'
   from *Hermit Songs* (Recorded 1954; released on vinyl LP by
   Odyssey, 1968)

## STONE

Adcock, Fleur, 'Kilpeck' in *The Scenic Route* (Oxford University
   Press, 1974)

Arnold, Matthew, 'Dover Beach' in *New Poems* (Macmillan and
   Co, 1867)

Boase, T. S. R, *English Art 1100–1216* (Oxford University Press, 1953)

Clifton-Taylor, Alex, *The Cathedrals of England* (Thames &
   Hudson, 1967)

Erlande-Brandenburg, Alain, *The Cathedral Builders of the
   Middle Ages* (Thames & Hudson, 1995; Rosemary Stonehewer,
   translator)

Fiorato, Veronica, 'The Font at St Nicholas' Church, North
   Grimston, North Yorkshire', *Medieval Yorkshire*, No. 26
   (Yorkshire Archaeological Society, 1997)

Freitag, Barbara, *Sheela-na-gigs: Unravelling an Enigma* (Routledge,
   2004)

Gimpel, Jean, *The Cathedral Builders* (Michael Russell, 1983;
   Teresa Waugh, translator)

Jenkins, Simon, *England's Cathedrals* (Little, Brown, 2016)

Johnson, Paul, *British Cathedrals* (Weidenfeld & Nicolson, 1980)

McClain, Aleksandra and Carolyn Twomey, 'Baptism and Burial in Stone: Materializing Pastoral Care in Anglo-Norman England' in *Fragments*, Volume 7 (Michigan Publishing, 2018)

Murphy, Seamus, *Stone Mad* (Blackstaff Press, 1966)

Pevsner, Nikolaus, *The Buildings of England – Yorkshire: York & the East Riding* (Penguin, 1972)

Piper, John, *A Painter's Camera: Buildings and Landscapes in Britain 1935–1985* (Tate Gallery, 1987)

Rees, Emma L. E., *The Vagina: A Literary and Cultural History* (Bloomsbury Academic, 2013)

Ruskin, John, *The Seven Lamps of Architecture* (Smith, Elder & Co., 1849)

Thomson, Celia, *Gloucester Cathedral Guidebook* (Reef Publishing, 2019)

Thurlby, Malcolm, *The Herefordshire School of Romanesque Sculpture* (Logaston Press, 2013)

Twomey, Carolyn, 'Romanesque Baptismal Fonts in East Yorkshire Parishes: Decoration and Devotion' in *Devotional Interaction in Medieval England and its Afterlives* (Brill, 2018)

Woodcock, Alex, *King of Dust: Adventures in Forgotten Sculpture* (Little Toller Books, 2019)

Ziminski, Andrew, *The Stonemason: A History of Building Britain* (John Murray, 2020)

*

Harvey, PJ, 'Sheela-Na-Gig' from *Dry* (Too Pure, 1992)

## DUST

Banham, Reyner, 'The New Brutalism' in *The Architectural Review* (9 December 1955)

Bulmer-Thomas, Ivor, *Dilysia* (Becket Publications, 1987; previously privately circulated, 1939)

Catling, Christopher, 'Go thy Way' in *The Future of the UK's Church Buildings* (National Churches Trust, 2021)

'Fatal Fall at a Nursing Home' *The Merthyr Express*, 27 August 1938

Grindrod, John, *Concretopia* (Old Street Publishing Ltd, 2013)

Rodger, Jonny, ed., *Gillespie, Kidd & Coia: Architecture 1956–1987* (The Lighthouse, 2007)

Poole, Eve, *Church of England Mission in Revision: A Review of the Mission and Pastoral Measure 2011* (2021)

Southwell, David, *Phoenix Guide to Strange England* (Twitter, @HooklandGuide and @cultauthor)

Watters, Diane M., *St Peter's, Cardross: Birth, Death and Renewal* (Historic Environment Scotland, 2016)

Webb, Michael, 'Scottish Homage to Le Corbusier' in *Country Life* (27 July 1967)

Wenell, Karen, 'St Peter's College and the Desacralisation of Space', *Literature and Theology* (September 2007, Vol. 21, No. 3)

\*

*Gillespie, Kidd and Coia: Lessons In Architecture* (GKC Productions, 2007; Saul Metzstein, director)

\*

Interview with Bob Davey by Matthew Gudgin, BBC Radio Norwich, 2 April 2021.

*Last Word*, BBC Radio 4, 4 April 2021

## PAINT

Beechey, James and Richard Shone, 'Picasso in London, 1919: the premiere of The Three-Cornered Hat', *The Burlington Magazine* (October, 2006)

Behrend, George, *Stanley Spencer at Burghclere* (Macdonald & Co. Ltd, 1965)

Carr, J. L., *A Month in the Country* (Harvester Press Ltd, 1980)

Collis, Maurice, *Stanley Spencer: A Biography* (Harvill Press Ltd, 1962)

Dreher, Rob, 'Paul Kingsnorth's Alexandria', *The American Conservative*, 23 October 2020

Hauser, Kitty, *Stanley Spencer* (Tate Publishing, 2001)

Holloway, Richard, *Leaving Alexandria: A Memoir of Faith and Doubt* (Canongate, 2012)

Holloway, Richard, *Stories We Tell Ourselves: Making Meaning in a Meaningless Universe* (Canongate, 2020)

Kingsnorth, Paul, *Alexandria* (Faber & Faber, 2020)

Robinson, Duncan, *Stanley Spencer: Visions from a Berkshire Village* (Phaidon Press Ltd, 1979)

Robinson, Duncan, *Stanley Spencer at Burghclere* (National Trust, 1991)

Rosewell, Roger, *Medieval Wall Paintings* (Boydell Press, 2008)

Rothenstein, Elizabeth, *The Masters, 80: Stanley Spencer* (Purnell & Sons Ltd, 1967)

Rouse, E. Clive, *Medieval Wall Paintings* (Shire Publications Ltd, 2004)

Spencer, Stanley, *Letters and Writings* (Tate Publishing, 2001; Adrian Glew, editor)

Spencer, Unity, *Lucky to be an Artist* (Unicorn Press, 2015)

Thomas, R. S., 'The Absence', *Frequencies* (Macmillan, 1978)

Waller, J. G., *On a Painting Discovered in Chaldon Church, Surrey, 1870* (Mitchell and Hughes, 1885)

*

*Alison Watt: A Painter's Eye* (Skyline Productions, 2008; Thomas Riedelsheimer, director)

## BONE

Archer, Fr Michael, *St John Southworth: Priest and Martyr* (Catholic Truth Society, 2010)

Atherton, David W. and Michael P. Peyton, 'Faith and Martyrdom: The Holy Hand of Saint Edmund Arrowsmith' (2013, read at saintsandrelics.co.uk)

Bedoya, Juan G., 'La mano incorrupta y el dictador obsesionado', *El País*, 19 December 2014

Bourke, Cormac, 'The Shrine of St Patrick's Hand', *Irish Arts Review* (Vol. 4, No. 3, 1987)

Butler, John, *The Relics of Thomas Becket: A True-Life Mystery* (Pitkin Publishing, 2019)

Cahill, Thomas, *How the Irish Saved Civilization: The Untold Story of Ireland's Heroic Role from the Fall of Rome to the Rise of Medieval Europe* (Hodder and Stoughton, 1995)

Chaucer, Geoffrey, *The Canterbury Tales* (Penguin, 1951; Nevill Coghill, translator)

Eire, Carlos, *The Life of Saint Teresa of Avila* (Princeton University Press, 2019)

Flechner, Roy, *Saint Patrick Retold: The Legend and History of Ireland's Patron Saint* (Princeton University Press, 2019)

Freeman, Charles, *Holy Bones, Holy Dust: How Relics Shaped the History of Medieval Europe* (Yale University Press, 2012)

Freeman, Philip, *St Patrick of Ireland: A Biography* (Simon & Schuster, 2005)

Guy, John, *Thomas Becket: Warrior, Priest, Rebel, Victim – A 900-Year-Old Story Retold* (Viking, 2012)

Longley, Katharine M., *Saint Margaret Clitherow* (Anthony Clarke, 1986)

Longley, Katharine M., 'The "Trial" of Margaret Clitherow', *The Ampleforth Journal* (Vol. 75, Part III, 1970)

Murphy, Cornelius, *A True Account of the Life and Death of Saint Edmund Arrowsmith* (Catholic Pictorial Limited, 1960)

Mush, Father John, 'A True Report of the Life and Martyrdom of Mrs Margaret Clitherow' (1586; reproduced in *The Troubles Of Our Catholic Forefathers, Related By Themselves*, Burns and Oates, 1877; John Morris, editor)

Purdie, Albert B., *The Life of Blessed John Southworth* (Burns Oates & Washbourne Ltd, 1930)

Sackville-West, Vita, *The Eagle and the Dove: A Study in Contrasts* (Michael Joseph Ltd, 1943)

Sister Agatha, with Richard Newman, *A Nun's Story* (Metro Books, 2017)

Tadié, Solène, 'For This French Priest, Rushing Into Notre Dame's Flames Was Part of His Mission', *National Catholic Register*, 23 May 2019

Wadham, Juliana and Katharine M. Longley, 'Saint Margaret Clitherow: Her "Trial" on Trial', *The Ampleforth Journal* (Vol. 76, Part II, 1971)

Weiss, Daniel, *Art and Crusade in the Age of Saint Louis* (Cambridge University Press, 1998)

'A Yorkshire Recusant's Relation' (1586, reproduced in *The Troubles Of Our Catholic Forefathers, Related By Themselves*, Burns and Oates, 1877; John Morris, editor)

## BATS

Altringham, John D., *British Bats* (Collins New Naturalist Library, Book 93, William Collins, 2014)

Laird, Tessa, *Bat* (Reaktion Books, 2018)

Nagel, Thomas, 'What Is It Like to Be a Bat?', *The Philosophical Review* (Vol. 83, No. 4, October 1974)

Peterson, Russell, *Silently, By Night* (Longmans, Green and Co Ltd, 1964)

White, Gilbert, *The Natural History of Selborne* (B. White & Son, 1789)

## FEN

Angier, Carole, *Speak, Silence: In Search of W. G. Sebald* (Bloomsbury, 2021)

Betjeman, John, *Betjeman on Faith: An Anthology of his Religious Prose* (SPCK, 2011, Kevin J. Gardner, editor)

Betjeman, John, 'The Purpose of this Book' in *Collins Guide to English Parish Churches* (Collins, 1958)

Bevis, Trevor, *March's Very Own Saint: Wendreda the Peacemaker, and List of Saints Connected with the Fens* (Trevor Bevis BA, 2005)

Boyce, James, *Imperial Mud: The Fight for the Fens* (Icon Books Ltd, 2020)

Carracedo, Juan Manuel Castro, 'Apocalyptic Elements in Richard II's Coronation', *Proceedings of the 29th International AEDEAN Conference* (Universidad de Jaén, 2006)

*The Cawston Rood Screen Guide* (Cawston Parish Church, 2018)

Cole, Teju, 'Always Returning', *New Yorker*, 30 July 2012

*The Funeral Effigies of Westminster Abbey* (Boydell Press, 1993; Anthony Harvey and Richard Mortimer, editors)

Gilchrist, Alexander, *Life of William Blake: A New and Enlarged Edition* (Vol. 1, Macmillan and Co, 1880)

Johnson, Daisy, *Fen* (Jonathan Cape, 2016)

Lambton, Lucinda, 'Sarah Hare wax effigy, Norfolk', *The Oldie*, December 2016

Minnis, Kate, *A History of the Gardens at Stow Hall* (Stow Estate Trust, 2019)

Mortlock, D. P. and C. V. Roberts, *The Popular Guide to Norfolk Churches: No.3 West and South-West Norfolk* (Acorn Editions, 1985)

Oliver, Kathleen M., *Narrative Mourning: Death and its Relics in the Eighteenth Century British Novel* (Bucknell University Press, 2020)

*The Parish Church of St Peter, Upwell* (Upwell St Peter's Parochial Church Council; Howard Klein, editor)

Park, Julie, *The Self and It: Novel Objects and Mimetic Subjects in Eighteenth Century England* (Stanford University Press, 2009)

Philips, Seymour, *Edward II* (Yale University Press, 2012)

Pryor, Francis, *The Fens: Discovering England's Ancient Depths* (Head of Zeus Ltd, 2020)

Rimmer, Michael, *The Angel Roofs of East Anglia: Unseen Masterpieces of the Middle Ages* (Lutterworth Press, 2015)

Rosewell, Roger, *Stained Glass* (Shire Publications, 2012)

Sayers, Dorothy L., *The Nine Tailors* (Victor Gollancz Ltd, 1934)

Sebald, W. G., 'Die hölzernen Engel von East Anglia: Eine
 individuelle Bummeltour durch Norfolk und Suffolk', *Die
 Zeit*, 1974. Translated from the German by Richard Sheppard,
 as 'The carved wooden angels of East Anglia: Travelogue
 1974.' *Journal of European Studies*, 21 December 2011
Sebald, W. G., *The Emigrants* (Harvill Press, 1996, translated by
 Michael Hulse)
Sebald, W. G., *The Rings of Saturn* (Harvill Press, 1998, translated
 by Michael Hulse)
Spalding, Frances, *John Piper, Myfanwy Piper: Lives in Art* (Oxford
 University Press, 2009)
*St Agnes Church, Cawston: Guidebook* (Cawston Parish Church,
 2018)
Streeting, Jessica, *Sea-Change* (Propolis Books, 2021)
Swift, Graham, *Waterland* (William Heinemann, 1983)
Syson, Luke et al., *Life Like: Color, Sculpture and the Body* (Yale
 University Press, 2018)
Vigar, John E., *Churches of Norfolk* (Amberley Publishing, 2021)
von la Roche, Sophie, *Sophie in London: Being the Diary of Sophie
 von la Roche* (Jonathan Cape, 1933; Clare Williams, translator)
Wilson, A. N., *Betjeman* (Arrow Books, 2007)

*

*A Passion For Churches* (BBC2, 1974; written and narrated by John
 Betjeman; produced by Edward Mirzoeff)

## WELL

Benham, Patrick, *The Avalonians* (Gothic Image Publications,
 1993)
Berry, Wendell, *The World-Ending Fire: The Essential Wendell Berry*
 (Allen Lane, 2017; Paul Kingsnorth, editor)
Christian, Roy, *Well-Dressing in Derbyshire* (Derbyshire
 Countryside Ltd, 1991)
Fiennes, Celia, *Through England on a Side Saddle in the Time of
 William and Mary* (Field & Tier, Leadenhall Press, 1888)

Greenfield, Diana, 'Kingdom and Crystals' in *Fresh Expressions of Church and the Kingdom of God* (Canterbury Press, 2012)

Howard-Gordon, Frances, *Glastonbury: Maker of Myths* (Gothic Image Publications, 1982)

Hughes, T. J., *Wales's Best One Hundred Churches* (Seren; Poetry Wales Press Ltd, 2006)

Lancelyn Green, Roger, *King Arthur and His Knights of the Round Table* (Penguin Books, 1953)

Mann, Nicholas R., *The Red & White Springs: The Mysteries of Britain at Glastonbury* (Triskele Publications, 1992)

Marson, C. L., *Glastonbury: The Historic Guide to the 'English Jerusalem'* (George Gregory, 1909)

Mayhew-Smith, Nick, *The Naked Hermit* (Society for Promoting Christian Knowledge, 2019)

Naylor, Peter and Lindsey Porter, *Well Dressing* (Landmark Publishing Ltd, 2002)

Pearson, N. F.; illustrations by Roger Hall, *Stories of Special Days and Customs* (Ladybird Books Ltd, 1972)

Redwood, Ark, *The Art of Mindful Gardening: Sowing the Seeds of Meditation* (Leaping Hare Press, 2018)

Steward, Vicki, *Normal for Glastonbury* (Normal for Glastonbury Publications, 2020)

Wardle, Natasha and Paul Fletcher et al., *Chalice Well: The Story of a Living Sanctuary* (Chalice Well Press, 2009)

White, Norman, *Gerard Manley Hopkins in Wales* (Seren; Poetry Wales Press Ltd, 1998)

## WEN

Ackroyd, Peter, *Thames: Sacred River* (Chatto & Windus, 2007)

Bell, Doyne C., *Notices of the Historic Persons Buried in the Chapel of St. Peter Ad Vincula in the Tower of London. With an Account of the Discovery of the Supposed Remains of Queen Anne Boleyn* (John Murray, 1877)

Betjeman, John, *Summoned By Bells* (John Murray, 1960)

Binder, Pearl, *The Pearlies: A Social Record* (Jupiter Books, 1975)

Binder, Polly, *Pearly Kings and Queens* (Royal Pavilion, Art Gallery and Museums, Brighton, 1986)

Bird, James and G. Topham Forrest, *Proposed Demolition of Nineteen City Churches* (London County Council, Odhams Press, 1920)

Borman, Tracy et al., *The Tower of London* (Sarah Kilby and Clare Murphy eds, Historic Royal Palaces, 2020)

Brown, George Mackay, *For the Islands I Sing: An Autobiography* (John Murray, 1997)

Carter, Richard, *In Search of the Lost: The Death and Life of Seven Peacemakers of the Melanesian Brotherhood* (Canterbury Press, 2006)

Carter, Richard, *The City is My Monastery: A Contemporary Rule of Life* (Canterbury Press, 2019)

Dickens, Charles, 'Night Walks', *All The Year Round*, 21 July 1860

Dickens, Charles, *Oliver Twist* (Richard Bentley, 1838)

*Drowning Prevention Strategy* (Tidal Thames Water Safety Forum, May 2019)

Eliot, T. S., 'London Letter', *The Dial*, June 1921

Eliot, T. S., 'The Waste Land' (Boni and Liveright, 1922)

Fox, John, *Fox's Book of Martyrs: A History of the Lives, Suffering, and Triumphant Deaths of the Early Protestant Christian Martyrs* (First published, 1563. Zondervan Publishing House, 1926; William Byron Forbush, editor)

Gordon, Lyndall, *The Imperfect Life of T. S. Eliot* (Virago, 2012)

Halliday, Stephen, *Newgate: London's Prototype of Hell* (Sutton Publishing Ltd, 2006)

Harrison, John, *Bells and Bellringing* (Shire Publications Ltd, 2016)

Henrey, Mrs Robert, *The Virgin of Aldermanbury: Rebirth of the City of London* (J. M. Dent & Sons Ltd, 1958)

Hughes, M. V., *The City Saints* (J. M. Dent and Sons, 1932)

Jarman, Derek, 'Why shutting Bart's would be a crime', *Independent*, 4 May 1993

# Selected Sources

Johnson, Malcolm, *St Martin-in-the-Fields* (Phillimore & Co Ltd, 2005)

Maiklem, Lara, *Mudlarking* (Bloomsbury, 2019)

Mantel, Hilary, *Wolf Hall* (Fourth Estate, 2009)

Mantel, Hilary, *Bring Up The Bodies* (Fourth Estate, 2012)

Mantel, Hilary, 'Letter to Thomas More, Knight' from *Holbein's Sir Thomas More* (Frick Collection, 2018)

Mantel, Hilary, *The Mirror & The Light* (Fourth Estate, 2020)

Mayhew, Henry, *London Labour and the London Poor* (George Woodfall & Son, 1851)

Orwell, George, *A Clergyman's Daughter* (Victor Gollancz, 1935)

Orwell, George, *Nineteen Eighty-Four* (Martin Secker & Warburg Ltd, 1949)

Orwell, George, *The Orwell Diaries* (Harvill Secker, 2009; Peter Davison, editor)

*The Oxford Dictionary of Nursery Rhymes* (Oxford University Press, 1951; Iona and Peter Pie, editors)

Pevsner, Nikolaus, *The Buildings of England: London, Volume One: The Cities of London and Westminster* (Penguin, 1957)

Raven, Dame Kathleen, 'Waiting For The Bombs To Fall', *Nursing Standard* (Vol. 5, Issue 6, 31 October 1990)

Scott, Carolyn, *Betwixt Heaven and Charing Cross: The Story of St Martin-in-the-Fields* (Robert Hale, 1971)

Scott, Carolyn, *Dick Sheppard: A Biography* (Hodder and Stoughton, 1977)

Thornbury, Walter, *Old and New London: A Narrative of its History, its People and its Places* (Cassell, Petter, Galpin & Co, 1872)

Wells, Samuel, et al., *Finding Abundance in Scarcity: Steps to Church Transformation* (Canterbury Press, 2021)

Woolf, Virginia, *The Diary of Virginia Woolf – Volume 5 1936–41* (Chatto & Windus/The Hogarth Press, 1984)

\*

Konola, 'Rest In Peace' (Gospel Hydration, 2020)

\*

# Selected Sources

*Desert Island Discs: Sir Peter Maxwell Davies* (BBC Radio 4, 4 February 2005)

## LIGHT

Magnusson, Magnus, *Lindisfarne: The Cradle Island* (Tempus Publishing, 1984)

Moffat, Alistair, *To the Island of Tides* (Canongate, 2019)

Perry, Richard, *A Naturalist on Lindisfarne* (Lindsay Drummond Ltd, 1946)

Tristram, Kate, *The Story of Holy Island: An Illustrated History* (Canterbury Press, 2009)

*

Bush, Kate, 'Running Up That Hill' from *Hounds Of Love* (EMI, 1985)

# Acknowledgements

Written during a period when to travel and meet people was difficult and unpredictable, *Steeple Chasing* had a number of false starts and dead ends. To stay cheerful, I tried to bear in mind the words of Nikolaus Pevsner, recorded by the *Guardian* in 1960, when he was observed getting lost during a field trip in Norfolk: 'It always pays to go the wrong way.'

I was fortunate in having a collaborator with a good sense of direction and enough good cheer to keep me going on hard roads: Richard Roper, my editor at Headline. His patience and understanding was vital when the journey seemed impossible, and his enthusiasm for the work – when I was able to start sending it to him – has been fuel in my tank. Richard, thank you for the compass-reading and company.

My agent Kevin Pocklington at The North Literary Agency believed in *Steeple Chasing* from first to last. Thank you, Kevin.

A book is a joint effort, the work of many minds and hands. I'd like to thank the following people: Cathie Arrington for picture research; Edward Bettison for the beautiful cover; Jill Cole for proofreading; Penny Gardiner for copy editing; Lucy Hall, marketing manager; Patrick Insole, art director; Rosie Margesson, senior publicity manager; Feyi Oyesanya, editorial assistant; Felicity Price, at Reviewed & Cleared, for her legal advice; Caitlin Raynor, publicity director.

The ecclesiologist John Vigar read the manuscript and made a number of helpful corrections and suggestions. I'm grateful to him for his expertise and for the church-crawl around some of his favourite Norfolk churches.

A few chapters of *Steeple Chasing* had early readers who offered useful comments and much-needed encouragement. I'd like to thank, in particular, my friend Dani Garavelli for her insights, generosity and kindness. It was such a pleasure to share my writing with her.

Lindsey Ward and Joe Hodrien let me stay at their flat on my many visits to London. This saved me a great deal of money, but I also gained their company, which is always a delight. Having put up in the past with me droning on about graveyards, they now had to suffer similar about churches. They are very tolerant and hospitable, and I'm grateful to them for it.

While I was writing *Steeple Chasing*, my previous book *A Tomb With A View* was named non-fiction book of the year at Scotland's National Book Awards. That meant a lot to me, and I thank the Saltire Society and judges for the honour.

There are a number of people whose interest, support and friendship have been important to me during the writing of this book. They include Kelly Apter, Brian Donaldson, Rob Fraser, Jane Graham, Jamie Lafferty, Barry and Fiona Leathem, Damien Love, Paul McNamee, Stephen Phelan, Helen, David and Michael Ross, Alison Stroak, Graeme Virtue, and Paul and Christine Ward.

To Jenny and Jump, good companions.

To the late Hilary Mantel, with thanks for her kindness, her example, and the pleasure and thrill of her writing. '*And now no more for lack of time.*'

Finally, with all my heart, to Jo, James and Jack. I love you.

\*

Many thanks to Richard Dawson for permission to quote from his song 'Soldier', taken from the album *Peasant*. Thanks to Oscar Lawrence at Domino for his help. Virginia Astley's song 'All Shall Be Well' contains an echo of Julian of Norwich, sounding down the centuries. I am grateful to Virginia for permission to quote the song, and for all her beautiful work. Reading Virginia Woolf's 1936–41 diary was one of the melancholy pleasures of working on this book. My thanks to Isabella Depiazzi at Granta for arranging the rights to use part of Woolf's diary entry for Christmas Eve 1940; thanks, too, to Sarah Baxter at the Society of Authors.

## DARKNESS

This chapter contains elements from a story first published in *Scotland on Sunday* and subsequently in my journalism collection *Daunderlust* which was published by Sandstone Press. Thank you to the newspaper and the publisher.

The chapter contains a reference to Ian Rankin's novel *A Song for the Dark Times*. Many thanks to Ian for those words, and for his continued support.

The final two sentences contain allusions to *The Dark is Rising* by Susan Cooper. I am grateful to her for allowing me to make these references to her book, and for her kind encouragement during the writing of *Steeple Chasing*.

Many thanks to Linda Perhacs for giving her blessing to me quoting her song 'Chimacum Rain', which appears on her beautiful 1970 album *Parallelograms*. It was a privilege to speak with her, and my book is graced by having this fragment of her writing within it.

I did not know it at the time, but I was fortunate to glimpse Baxter the cat during my stay at Pluscarden as he was in the last days of the last of his nine lives. Brought into the monastic enclosure for his own protection, to keep him from fighting feral cats, his love of food proved his downfall and he fell ill after eating a piece of Stilton that he had nosed out in the calefactory. He died on 19 December 2020 at the age of seventeen, having lived at the abbey since 2005. A song composed in his honour was sung by the brothers to the melody of a hymn for the Office of the Dead. It began:

> *Felem murumque canimus,*
> *Fletu aelinum plangimus,*
> *Morso caseo morbido,*
> *Noniam claustro ambulabit.*

'We sing of a cat and mice,' runs the translation. 'In tears we bewail our dirge. Having bitten the deadly cheese, he will no longer walk the cloister.'

*Acknowledgements*

## STEEL

Thanks to: Guy Hayward, British Pilgrimage Trust; Ruth Mac-Leod, Church of Scotland; Kate Pawley, Durham Cathedral; Alison Robertson, Scottish Stained Glass Trust; Jan Rowland, St Mary and St Cuthbert, Chester-le-Street.


## FIRE

Jill Finch, Sarah Radford and Pauline Stobbs, St Paul's Cathedral.


## CATS

Maria Budgen, Borough Market; Hodge of Southwark; the market traders who shared their memories of Doorkins in her ratting days.


## DUST

Fr John Campbell, Sacred Heart, Cumbernauld; Ronnie Convery, Archdiocese of Glasgow; Stuart Cotton, The Kilmahew Education Trust; Nick Dastoor, the *Guardian*; Professor Robert Davis; Manus Deery, Historic Environment Division, Dept for Communities, Northern Ireland; Cat Doyle, Lucy Janes, Jennifer Lightbody and Susannah Waters, Glasgow School of Art Archives & Collections; Fr Thomas Doyle, Holy Trinity, Coatbridge; Sue Gattuso, Friends of St Mary's Church, Houghton-on-the-Hill; Mgr Gerard Hand, Holy Cross, Edinburgh; Fr Hugh Kelly; Mgr Philip Kerr, St Paul's, Glenrothes; Hannah McGill; Saul Metzstein; Fr Daniel Rooney; David F. Ross; David Southwell @HooklandGuide; Michael Walker; Diane M. Watters, Historic Environment Scotland.


## STONE

Revd Steven Baggs, St Michael and All Angels, Castle Frome; Sandie Conway, Gloucester Cathedral; John Harding, the Sheela

# Acknowledgements

Na Gig Project; Jude Rogers; Gill Ryan, The Wild Gees; Carolyn Twomey, St Lawrence University, Canton, New York; Revd Stephen Walker, St Nicholas, North Grimston.

## PAINT

Liz Bonsall, Chaldon History Group; Dr Sheila Brock and Revd Canon John McLuckie, Old Saint Paul's, Edinburgh; Adrian Glew, Tate; Paul Grist and Jane Jones, National Trust; Leslie Hills, Skyline Productions; Paul Kingsnorth; Hugh Lane, Sandham Memorial Chapel.

## BONE

Niamh Baker and Eiméar Cassidy, National Museums Northern Ireland; Robert Burns, Glasgow; Br David Chadwick, Prefect of the Shrine of St Margaret Clitherow; Fr Richard Duffield, York; Rose Drew, Stairwell Books; Roy Flechner; Stephen Phelan for the translation from Spanish; John Rayne-Davis; Fr John Scott, Westminster Cathedral; Dr Hannah Thomas, Special Collections Manager, Bar Convent. A version of the story of the stone and the tree first appeared in the *Sunday Post*; my thanks to Jim Wilson for the commission.

## BATS

Sarah Kerkham, St Mary, Gayton Thorpe; Diana Spencer, Bats In Churches; Rebecca Easter, Lisa Gabriel, Kate Garner and Emily Parker of Philip Parker Associates.

## FEN

Alan Brindson, Houghton-on-the-Hill; Dr Claire Daunton; Bob Dixon; Rosemary Fuller; Lucy Hare; Kate Jackson, Friends of St Clement's, Outwell; Dr Susan Jenkins and Christine

Reynolds, Westminster Abbey; Valerie Kaufmann; Zenzie Tinker. Special thanks to Daniel Weir, who first told me about Sarah Hare, and to the late Lady Rose Hare, with whom I had such an enjoyable conversation.

### WELL

Stephen Brooke-Jones and Fr Justin Karakadu, St Winefride's Well Shrine; John Constable; Revd Sister Diana Greenfield; Sol Nigrum, the White Spring, Glastonbury; Catherine Owen; Liz Pearson, St Margaret's Chapel, Glastonbury.

The section on Glastonbury contains elements from an article written for the *Guardian* in 2018; my thanks to Andy Pietrasik for the commission.

I feel I know Glastonbury much better for having read Vicki Steward's insightful and entertaining writing about the town on the Normal For Glastonbury website and in her book of that title. Vicki has been very helpful to me in my work, for which I thank her. I also recommend her *Crap Views of Glastonbury Tor* postcard book and calendar – for those who prefer the numinous to come with a side of bathos.

### WEN

Rita Castle and Andrew Morris, Friends of the Musicians' Chapel, St Sepulchre's; Siân Conway and Eugene Ling, St Martin-in-the-Fields; Signe Hoffos, Shirley Karney and Michael Young, Friends of the City Churches; Alison Knapp, League of St Bartholomew's Nurses; Dickon Love, St Magnus the Martyr; London Bird Club; Revd Tom Sander, St Giles-in-the-Fields; Chris Skaife, Tower of London; Derrick Tchie, Gospel Hydration.

### THANKS ALSO TO:

Peter Aiers and Chana James, Churches Conservation Trust; Maureen Akers and Revd Shuna Body, St Augustine's, Brookland;

# Acknowledgements

Robin Barr, Debbie Corrigan, Sarah Jane Gibbon, Yvonne Gray, Fran Hollinrake, Stuart Little, Tim Morrison and Helen Woodsford-Dean, Orkney; Andrew Bell for helping me to access academic papers relating to St Peter's Seminary and the angel roofs of East Anglia; Peter Burton, Shepherds Stream Prayer Retreat; Revd Prebendary Jeremy Crossley, St Mary Woolnoth; Nathan Crouch and Revd Dr Emma Pennington for discussions about Canterbury Cathedral; Revd Steve Daughtery and Revd Jules Middleton, Lewes; Catherine Anne Davies, The Anchoress; @DevonChurchLand, Kirsty Hartsiotis and Cameron Newham for conversations about their own visits to churches; Trevor Dietz and Fontaines DC; Benjamin Finn, St Peter's, Wickham Bishops; Revd Canon Kathryn Fleming, Coventry Cathedral; Revd Mike Gilbert, Eyam; Andrew Hitchon; Judith Hodgson and Simon Kershaw, Friends of Little Gidding; Jampa, St Melangell's Church & Centre; Sheila Jones and The Scarecrow, Day of Syn, Dymchurch; Canon Jessica Martin at Ely Cathedral, Justine Spencer in York, and Lindsey Rix in Norwich for our conversations about cathedral cats and dogs; Niko Miaoulis, Dungeness; Alex Neilson; Padre David Osborn, St Clement Danes; Gillian Porter, Hall or Nothing; Julie Rainey, RNLI; Cameron Simcock, Creative Folkestone; David Thorpe at the Chapel of St Peter-on-the-Wall, Bradwell-on-Sea, Debbie Sanders of the Othona Community, and to William Hogger – for his generosity and understanding; Nigel Taylor, for the discussion about his work with bells; Modesto Tondelli, Our Lady of Mount Carmel; Alexander Tucker; Fr Stephen Weston, St Fursey's, Sutton; Ed and Jackie Yarrow of the George Inn, Hubberholme.

# Index